Ways of Reading

Over the last two decades energetic debates have taken place concerning the nature and purpose of English Studies. Whatever view is taken of the issues contested in these debates, there is a growing need for materials that can help translate new theoretical and analytic insights into practical methods of study. *Ways of Reading* contains a series of units which introduce techniques of analysis and interpretation necessary for the critical reading of texts – literary and non-literary, verbal and visual. Each unit ends with a practical activity or exercise which demonstrates the use of the technique, and gives readers scope to extend their competence in applying it.

Across a range of genres and periods, the book moves from smaller features of texts (such as rhyme) to larger features (such as story structure); from poetry to prose; from advertisements to film; and from text to context. Fusing theory and application, *Ways of Reading* will be invaluable for students of English who wish to develop an awareness of reading as a broader process.

Martin Montgomery and Nigel Fabb are Senior Lecturer and Lecturer respectively in Literary Linguistics, and Tom Furniss is Lecturer in English Studies, all at the University of Strathclyde; Alan Durant is Professor of English at Goldsmiths' College, University of London; and Sara Mills is Lecturer in English and Drama at Loughborough University.

Ways of Reading

Advanced reading skills for
students of English literature

Martin Montgomery, Alan Durant,
Nigel Fabb, Tom Furniss and Sara Mills

London and New York

British Library Cataloguing in Publication Data
Ways of reading: advanced reading skills for
    students of English literature.
    I. Montgomery, Martin
    428.24

Library of Congress Cataloging in Publication Data
Ways of reading: advanced reading skills for students of English
    literature / Martin Montgomery ... [et al.].
        p.   cm.
    Includes bibliographical references and index.
    1. English literature—History and criticism—Theory, etc.
    2. English literature—Study and teaching. 3. Reading (Higher
    education) 4. Reading comprehension. 5. Books and reading.
    I. Montgomery, Martin.
    PR21.W39 1992
    808'.042—dc20   91-39237

ISBN 0 415 05319 6
        0 415 05320 X paperback

In memoriam
Gillian Skirrow

Contents

Acknowledgements

This book has grown out of a course, developed and taught primarily by staff of the Programme in Literary Linguistics, University of Strathclyde. The original planning team for the course also included Gillian Skirrow and Derek Attridge, and *Ways of Reading* owes much to their inspiration. The title itself derives in part from John Berger's book, *Ways of Seeing*; but there was also a course of the same name (though different in aims, scope and constituency) taught by Deirdre Burton and Tom Davis in the English Department at the University of Birmingham.

In writing this book, the authors have benefited a great deal both from the responses of students in workshops and also from the input of post-graduates who have assisted in the teaching of many of the units – Shan Wareing, Christine Christie, Lena Garry, Vassiliki Kolocotroni, Lindsay Hewitt, Luma Al Balaa and others. In addition, we would particularly like to thank Judit Friedrich and Professor Michael Toolan, who read and commented upon the complete typescript of the book. Its faults, of course, remain our own.

The following have given permission for material to be included in the book: United Distillers UK for Plate 5; Matthew Gloag & Son Ltd for Plate 6; Smith & Nephew for Plate 36; Lancôme for Plate 37; Van den Berghs for Plate 38; The Samuel Goldwyn Company for Plates 25–35 (© 1960 Woodfall Films Ltd, all rights reserved); Hodder & Stoughton Ltd, and King's College, Cambridge and the Society of Authors as the literary representatives of the E.M. Forster Estate, for extract from *A Passage to India*; Faber and Faber Ltd and Farrar, Straus & Giroux, Inc. for 'High windows' by Philip Larkin, from *High Windows*; Martin Secker and Warburg Ltd for extract from 'Valentine' by John Fuller, from *Beautiful Inventions*; Granada, part of HarperCollins Publishers and Liveright Publishing Corporation for 'swi(/across!gold's' and 'yes is a pleasant country' by e.e. cummings (reprinted from *Complete Poems, 1913–1962* by e.e. cummings, © 1923, 1925, 1931, 1935, 1938, 1939, 1940, 1944, 1945, 1946, 1947, 1948, 1949, 1950, 1951, 1952, 1953, 1954, 1955, 1956, 1957, 1958, 1959, 1960, 1961, 1962 by the Trustees for the E.E. Cummings Trust. © 1961, 1963, 1968 by Marion Morehouse Cummings); Rogers,

Coleridge & White Ltd for extract from 'On the late late massachers stillbirths and deformed children a smoother lovelier skin job' by Adrian Henri, from *Collected Poems* (Allison & Busby, 1986); Faber and Faber Ltd and New Directions Publishing Corporation for 'L'art, 1910' by Ezra Pound, from *Collected Shorter Poems* and *Personae* (© 1926 Ezra Pound), respectively; the Estate of Ernest Hemingway and Jonathan Cape for extract from 'A very short story' by Ernest Hemingway, from *The First Forty Nine Stories*; Charles Scribner's Sons, an imprint of Macmillan Publishing Company, for extract from 'A very short story' by Ernest Hemingway, from *In Our Time* (© 1925 Charles Scribner's Sons, renewal copyright 1953 Ernest Hemingway); Carcanet Press Ltd for 'Message clear' by Edwin Morgan, from *Collected Poems*; James MacGibbon for extract from 'The river god' by Stevie Smith, from *The Collected Poems of Stevie Smith*; Carol Cosman for translation of 'I am a young girl' from the Old French, from *The Penguin Book of Women Poets*; Duckworth & Co. Ltd and Viking Penguin, a division of Penguin Books USA Inc. for 'One perfect rose' by Dorothy Parker, from *The Portable Dorothy Parker* (Introduction by Brendan Gill. © 1928, renewed 1956 by Dorothy Parker); Elizabeth Barnett, literary executor, for 'I, being born a woman and distressed' and Sonnet XVI of 'Fatal interview' by Edna St Vincent Millay, from *Collected Poems* (Harper & Row. © 1923, 1931, 1951, 1958 Edna St Vincent Millay and Norma Millay Ellis); Alfred A. Knopf, Inc. for 'Harlem' by Langston Hughes, from *The Panther and the Lash* (© 1951 Langston Hughes).

Introduction

Over the last two decades significant debates have taken place concerning the nature and purpose of English Studies – debates which have often been conducted in terms of theoretical critique and analysis. Important advances have taken place in our ways of understanding the subject matter of English; but alongside such critique, and in the wake of it, there is a growing need for materials that can help translate such theoretical and analytic insights into practical methods of study, especially for students in the earlier stages of their work. *Ways of Reading* is designed to provide such materials.

One fundamental question to emerge from recent debates has concerned the problem of which texts should be studied. Any attempt to define English Studies in terms of Literature has rested upon some degree of assumed consensus about which particular works of English Literature were worth studying. But the consensus has always proved fragile, has never been durable, especially in the face of increasingly difficult questions posed around exclusions from the list or 'canon' of great works and anomalies within it. More recently, for instance, feminist critics have pointed instructively to the disproportionately small amount of writing by women included within the canon.

Moreover, defining the field of English Studies in terms of Literature has only partially been able to deflect attention away from the difficulties attendant upon the term 'English' itself. If this term is used to refer to a national literature (the Literature of England) then only a cursory glance at key figures in the field of English Literature over the last two hundred years reveals symptomatic anomalies: we find writers from Scotland (e.g. Robert Burns), Ireland (e.g. James Joyce), Poland (Joseph Conrad), the United States (Henry James), to mention only a few. Nor is it possible to claim that the term is actually intended to designate Literature written in English, since this, by rights, should then include Literature from Canada, the United States, Nigeria, Sri Lanka, India, Australia, New Zealand, amongst others. English Studies in practice is rarely able to support such an inclusive definition, and an intricate negotiation takes place between the two senses (Literature-in-English versus Literature-of-the-English) whenever an actual syllabus is drawn up.

Our perspective in *Ways of Reading*, however, is one which places less emphasis on Literature as such and greater emphasis on exploring relationships between, on the face of it, quite different types of text; and so examples in this book will be found from the fields of journalism and advertising, film and television, as well as from the field of Literature as traditionally defined. *Ways of Reading*, then, explores non-literary as well as literary texts, at the same time and in relation to each other. In this respect, our use of the term 'text' may be sometimes puzzling. For one thing, we use it not in the familiar sense of 'set text' – one of the canon of great books. Instead, we use it more abstractly to refer to the trace or record of a communicative event, an event which may be performed in words but which may equally take place in images or in a combination of words and images. And so, not only do examples discussed in this book come from everyday life as well as from Literature, some of them also include a significant visual component.

Important changes of critical emphasis follow from broadening the range of texts which we examine. Although the texts which we use for illustration and discussion tend broadly to be playful or persuasive in character, we do not focus particularly on questions of relative value, or on issues of tradition or influence. We focus instead on what might be called the rhetorical organization of texts – on how they work to create meanings in terms of identifiable techniques each of which can be described, analysed and studied. The ability to identify and recognize modes of patterning and rhetorical organization in text is part and parcel for us of ways of reading.

To this end, the book is composed in terms of discrete units, each of which aims at establishing a technique of analysis and interpretation. Indeed, while most of the units which comprise *Ways of Reading* transcend differences of author, genre or period, all should prove useful in reading texts whether they are literary or non-literary, verbal or visual. Each unit not only introduces a concept or technique relevant to critical reading; it is also designed to give crucial practice in its use, by culminating in a concrete activity. These activities at the end of each unit are thus as important as the exposition itself, providing simultaneously a test of the concept's usefulness, and also scope for the reader to extend for herself or himself, in a practical fashion, competence in its application.

Although the units are devoted to discrete topics, they may also be seen as working collectively to furnish tools for use in interpretation. As such, they provide a compendium of critical and analytic strategies to support critical reading. Critical reading, as we envisage it, examines how texts make sense, what kind of sense they make and why they make sense in one way rather than another. This is important because – we believe – the rhetoric of texts contributes to the creation and circulation of meanings in society, to the point that we understand the world and our place within it through the texts which we make and interpret – hence our concern in *Ways of Reading* to relate readings of the text to readings of the world around the reader.

The book is loosely organized into six main sections. Section 1 deals with basic techniques and problem solving, and addresses the most basic issues involved in studying text. Section 2 paints a broad picture of the dimensions along which language may vary, including attention to issues of historical change, gender and social position. The units that comprise this second section thus help us to see the range of possibilities that provide the communicative background to the particular choices we may discover in a specific text. Section 3 considers aspects of the sound patterning and grammar of texts, including ways in which texts may break with received patterns of construction. Section 4 focuses more on what might be called figures of speech – ways of making meaning indirectly by implication and allusion. Section 5 is concerned broadly with aspects of narrative – what makes a story and how stories are told. Section 6, the final section, opens out beyond the text to address questions concerning the text's relation to its author, on the one hand, and its audience, on the other.

The book, therefore, does exhibit certain kinds of progression – from smaller features of texts (e.g. rhyme) to larger features (e.g. story structure); from poetry to prose; from text to context; from practical questions to theoretical questions. But we would not wish to make too much of these kinds of progression. Although each unit may be seen as part of a line of development, it may also be seen as part of network of concepts; and, because each unit opens out upon others in different parts of the book, the reader will find cross-references from one unit to another. At the same time, because many of the units can work in a relatively self-standing fashion, it is possible to study or consult them individually without necessarily referring to other parts of the book. In sum, it can be used as a classbook; for individual study (working through it topic by topic); or for reference (by consulting the index or table of contents). In this respect we hope that *Ways of Reading* will itself be put to use productively in different ways which none the less contribute to its underlying aim: to develop an awareness of reading as a broader process, where reading the word is a part of reading the world.

A NOTE ON READINGS

At the end of each unit there are some suggestions for further reading. Titles without an accompanying asterisk are considered to be important background or follow-up reading. Core readings that are considered to be particularly useful because they are both accessible and centrally concerned with the topic of the unit have been denoted with an asterisk.

Section 1

Basic techniques and problem solving

Unit 1   Asking questions

WHAT HAPPENS WHEN WE READ?

It is common enough to say that we 'respond' to the text we are reading. In the case of a written text, we respond to its wording by identifying the meaning of individual words, and by working out the relationships between words by drawing on our implicit knowledge of grammar (see Unit 2: Using information sources).

But readers do more than simply respond passively to texts. Instead, readers approach texts *actively*, with certain expectations in mind. As we read words and sentences, we look for patterns and develop hypotheses; we establish contexts by making decisions about who we think is making an utterance, and to whom; and we draw inferences about implied meanings, filling in gaps in what is explicitly said. We also establish a relationship between the text and its **genre** (see Unit 17); or we form an idea of the text's relationship to specific places, times and other texts by attending to its explicit references and use of **allusion** (see Unit 16).

In this sense, we creatively interpret not only aspects of the text itself, but also the text's position in society and history. In doing so, we also need to reflect on the context of our own reading. Are we studying the text? Reading it for pleasure? Skimming it for information? Do we intend to try to remember it, enjoy it, write about it, etc.? Such questions suggest that an implicit *agenda* is brought to any act of reading; different situations and purposes for reading will influence the kind of questions you are likely to ask of a text. This will distinguish the way you read on a train or in bed from what you are likely to do in a seminar room (though this does not mean that one kind of reading is necessarily better than another).

AGENDAS FOR READING IN FORMAL STUDIES

But knowing that ways of reading are always goal-oriented does not in itself, however, help you to start reading any given text. All too often little help is given for this problem by the prescribed tasks and examination questions set in institutions of higher education—which are often vague and open-ended invitations for your comments and 'response'.

To engage with a text, therefore, you are likely to have to define your *own* interest in reading it, and to investigate the text through a set of questions you yourself decide to ask. Even if these questions ultimately clash with the expressed or implied directions of your course of study or with published commentary, they will nevertheless enable you not only to engage with aspects of the text which interest you, but also to identify how your own concerns relate to the different notions of reading which you find around you.

The questions you ask of a text need to be as specific as possible. It may seem that there should be one single route for investigation to follow: a search for the text's 'meaning'. But meaning is never singular in this way. Looking for the meaning or meanings of a text involves asking a number of different sorts of question – or, alternatively, blocking these different sorts of question off. Such diversity in the types of meaning which can be found in a text can function productively, however, as a catalyst to discussion and theoretical reflection. We list the main alternative kinds of meaning to illustrate this point.

The intended meaning?

One way of looking for the meaning of a text is to consider what the author meant by it. To speculate about authorial intention, such as Shakespeare's intention in writing *Hamlet*, involves trying to work from what the text actually says into an imagined set of social circumstances possibly very different from your own. In effect, you try to reconstruct the likely meanings or effects that any given sentence, image or reference might have, since these may well be the ones the author anticipated; in doing this, you make the imaginative leap of trying to gauge an author's beliefs, emotions, knowledge and attitudes, as well as guessing what the author 'had in mind' at the time of writing.

But in looking for a meaning of this sort, there are evident difficulties. A persona, or invented voice, might have been deliberately adopted, separating what the text says from the writer's own feelings; and in drama or novels, characters speak as constructs created by the author, not necessarily as mouthpieces for the author's personal voice to come through. In any case, there is no infallible way of verifying an intention, which is why the critics W.K. Wimsatt and M.C. Beardsley (1946) dismissed the quest to discover what the author 'had in mind' as an 'intentional fallacy', or unwarranted shift from what the words of the text appear to mean to what we imagine the author meant by using them. Language can in any case escape our intentions, producing not only meanings which were not anticipated, but also slippages or failures of meaning which can be carefully exposed to undermine any seemingly intended meaning (see Unit 24: Authorship and intention).

The text's own meaning?

In this view of looking for meaning (which some critics have called 'objective' interpretation), features of the text itself are taken to be primarily responsible for guiding interpretation. How the text you are reading is organized (what words and structures it uses, how images and ideas are patterned) directs you towards a specific meaning. In this framework, what is important is to focus on details of the language and layout – examining choices of expression and the use of stylistic devices (such as figurative language, irony, paradox), or contrasting the ways the text is presented with other, alternative, ways it *might* have been presented (which would have produced different meanings).

If pursued in isolation, however, this search for a meaning which should be predictable simply from the organization of the text runs into difficulties. The fact that texts are interpreted very differently in different historical periods, and by differing social groups or readerships, challenges the idea of such an 'objective' meaning determined by the text alone, and suggests that the social circumstances in which a text is produced and interpreted, and the expectations readers bring to it, crucially affect what it is taken to mean.

An individual meaning?

In this view, the meaning of the text is whatever your personal response is: what the text means to you as you read it. Texts are suggestive, and connect with individual experiences, memories and associations for words and images. What is to be valued, therefore, in this approach is sensitivity in response and direct personal engagement with the text, recreating the text in a new form in the reader's own experience.

But Wimsatt and Beardsley (1949) argued that this sort of reading involves an 'affective fallacy', or overattention to response at the expense of what the words of the text actually say. Concern with personal resonances of the text can displace attention from its structures and rhetorical organization; and it is possible that many of the memories or associations triggered by texts will either be stock responses or idiosyncratic reactions which go off at purely personal tangents.

The general properties of meaning?

In this view, meaning is seen as primarily something produced by processes involved in reading. Instead of investigating in detail what a given text means, emphasis is accordingly placed on *how* texts come to mean anything. Interest lies in the conventions and social institutions of reading, and in theories of reading. Particular readings are valuable as evidence of general reading processes, and any given meaning is only as interesting as the processes through which it was arrived at.

Reading individual texts in this way, however, can become simply an illustration of more general reading processes: reading any text would be equally useful or interesting. But although reading clearly does involve general processes (making inferences, applying idiomatic conventions, etc.), reading a given text also needs to attend to its particular use of language and form and to draw on the specific background knowledge it takes for granted. In addition, readers will bring different expectations and ideologies to bear upon different texts. Thus readings cannot be analysed completely in terms of general codes; our interest in reading texts is hardly reducible to *how* interpretation happens in the mind of a reader. An adequate analysis of reading would also need to take into account the ways our attitudes, values and social priorities affect particular acts of reading.

Shared social meanings?

In this view, what a text means is what it has meant to different readerships in the past, together with the different meanings it will have for different groups of readers today. Readers of texts form diverse groups, and the shared meanings of these groups change over time, and between places. Understanding the meaning of a text therefore involves not only accounting for individual personal responses, but also placing them within the social and historical patterns of reception of that text.

In advertising and market research, groups of readers are classified on the basis of variables such as class, age, gender and income (as As, Bs, ABs, C1s, C2s, etc.). In literary criticism, readers are often distinguished on the basis of their imagined relative taste (elite and mass audiences, for example). But readerships can also be identified on the basis of other considerations, including the function reading a given text serves (for study, as a marker of social accomplishment, as distraction from pain or work, as relaxation, etc.).

Critical social meanings?

What might be called critical social meanings are formed where personal responses and social meanings meet. As an individual reader, you are always also a specific social subject, with an age, gender, ethnicity, class and educational background. So it is possible to locate your personal responses within larger social frameworks of the reception of texts. In doing so, you can ask questions from a critical or polemic position – as an engaged rather than a detached reader. You can examine not only a culture's established imagery (how particular topics such as race, sexuality, work or money are conventionally represented), but also how such images fit in with or diverge from your own sense of how such things might or should be represented.

HOW TO GET STARTED IN WAYS OF READING

These different senses of the 'meaning' of a text are not completely separable from one another. Rather, they form a network of overlapping but distinct viewpoints from which any search for meaning in a text can be seen. Historically, different senses of a text's meanings have been emphasized in different schools of criticism and theories, and embedded in different kinds of reading technique. Listing the main directions of analysis can be useful, if only to forestall a tendency to identify one kind of meaning or approach and assume that this exhausts the interpretative possibilities with regard to a given text.

In practical terms, however, it is often necessary to find ways to get going on a text, especially if it seems to resist the ways of reading we are used to using. As catalysts to reading in any (or any combination) of the directions outlined above, therefore, the following list of more specific questions is offered as an initial checklist. Each of the questions should lead into speculations that finally have to be assessed on the basis of the insights and judgements they make possible about the text you are reading.

Textual questions
Is the piece of text you are looking at the whole of the text?
Does the text exist in only one version, or many different versions?
If in many versions, are there likely to be significant differences between
   them (e.g. as regards layout, typeface)?
Has the text been cut, edited or expurgated?
Has the text been annotated? If so, who provided the annotations, and do
   the annotations direct you towards a particular way of looking at the
   text?

Contextual questions
Was the originator of the text (author or producer) male or female? Professional or amateur? Native speaker of English or non-native speaker?
How old was s/he when the text was produced?
Who was the text originally aimed at? Are you part of that expected or
   anticipated readership or audience?
When, where and in what circumstances was the text written or produced?
(See Unit 5: Language and place; Unit 6: Language and context: register;
   Unit 7: Language and gender; Unit 23: Positioning the reader or spectator; Unit 24: Authorship and intention: Unit 25: Judgement and value.)

Questions of voice
Who is supposed to be speaking the words of the text?
From whose point of view is the text (poem, film, etc.) being told?
Who is the text being spoken to?
(See Unit 19: Point of view; Unit 20: Narration in film and prose fiction; Unit
   21: Speech and writing; Unit 23: Positioning the reader or spectator.)

Referential questions:

Does the text contain quotations?

Does the text refer to particular social attitudes, facts or suppositions about the world, or to particular interests or geographical knowledge?

Does the text contain specific references to other literary, media, historical, mythological or religious texts, figures or events? If so, do you know what these references refer to?

Would it be helpful to understand the precise meanings of the references or allusions, or merely their general origin and flavour?

(See Unit 5: Language and place; Unit 6: Language and context: register; Unit 16: Intertextuality and allusion.)

Language questions:

Is the text in its original language, or a translation?

Is it likely that all the words in the text mean what you think they mean? (Many words have changed their meanings, and may mean something different now than they have meant in the past.)

What sort of vocabulary do the words of the text generally come from (Latinate or Germanic; elevated or colloquial; technical or non-technical, etc.)?

Were all the words and structures current at the time the text was written, or is it possible that some (e.g. 'thou') are archaisms?

Are the sentences generally of the same length and complexity? If not, is the inequality patterned or distributed in any way that might be significant?

Is a very 'literary' language being used?

(See Unit 4: Language and time; Unit 6: Language and context: register; Unit 11: Parallelism and repetition; Unit 12: Deviation.)

Symbolic questions:

Do names used in the text refer to unique, particular individuals, or are they representative, standing for general characters or character types?

Is it appropriate to look for symbolic meanings of the places (mountains, sea), weather or events (marriage, travel) in the text?

Is the text concerned to relate a specific set of events, or does it function allegorically, representing one set of concerns in the form of a story about another?

Is the text's title a key to its meaning?

(See Unit 13: Metaphor; Unit 16: Intertextuality and allusion.)

Questions of convention:

Should the way you regard the text be guided by conventions about the sort of text it is (e.g. satire, pantomime, sitcom)?

How realistic do you expect the text to be? Is it appropriate to ask such a question of the sort of text you are reading or viewing?

(See Unit 17: Genre; Unit 22: Realism.)

Questions of representation:

Is the text typical in terms of how it represents its selected themes, or is it significantly different from other treatments of similar concerns?

Does the text create images of race, women, industry, money and other socially central themes? If so, are these images problematic: and if so, why?

(See Unit 7: Language and gender; Unit 8: Language and society.)

CONCLUSIONS

As you ask questions of these different sorts, your attention is likely to be drawn to details of the text, which should then stimulate fresh directions for enquiry. Also, your answers to the questions – even provisional or negative answers – are likely to be accompanied by informal kinds of reason or explanation, based on intuitions you have about the text's language, or about how it relates to other texts you are familiar with. (This is especially likely to be the case with questions which begin with 'why?') Patterns of intuition and justification form miniature critical arguments, which can be written down and linked together into larger interpretative or critical responses. (This is the kind of procedure you are asked to follow in many of the activities in this book.)

Generally, what asking these sorts of question shows is that you may already have a wide range of intuitions about any text you are looking at. Not having specific answers to questions (or information relating to them) becomes less of a problem when the reasons for being interested in the particular question have been identified. It is often the case that being aware of what specific answers might or might not contribute to an interpretation enables you to produce an accurate and insightful reading of a text through a process which is both efficient and pleasurable.

ACTIVITY

1 Make a list of questions you feel it would be useful to ask about the following poem. Also list the specific pieces of information you feel it would be helpful to know in order to discuss the text or comment on it. Then arrange the questions and kinds of information in your lists under the various different headings presented in the unit (i.e. 'Textual questions', 'Contextual questions', etc.). Don't worry about *answers* to the questions, or even about where such answers might be found. Focus instead on what *kinds* of questions might be worth pursuing.

Tranquerah Road

1
Poor relative, yet well-connected,
same line, same age as Heeren Street

(more or less, who knows?),
the long road comes and goes –
dream, nightmare, retrospect –
through my former house,
self-conscious, nondescript.

2
There was a remnant of a Portuguese settlement,
Kampong Serani, near the market,
where Max Gomes lived, my classmate.

At the end of the road, near *Limbongan*,
the Tranquerah English School,
our *alma mater*, heart of oak.

By a backlane the Methodist Girls' School,
where my sister studied
See me, mother,
Can you see me?
The Lord's Prayer, Psalm 23.

The Japanese came,
and we sang the *Kimigayo*,
learnt some *Nihon Seishin*.

Till their *Greater East Asia Co-Prosperity Sphere*
collapsed, and we had to change
our tune again – God Save the King.
Meliora hic sequamur.

The King died when I was in school,
and then, of course, God Save the Queen.

While *Merdeka* inspired –
for who are so free
as the sons of the brave? –
and so *Negara-ku*
at mammoth rallies
I salute them all
who made it possible.
for better, for worse.

3
A sudden trill,
mosquito whine
like enemy aeroplane
in a blanket stillness,
the heave and fall of snoring sea,
swish and rustle of coconut,

kapok, tamarind, fern-potted.
where *pontianak* perch
by the midnight road.

Wind lifts its haunches off the sea,
shakes dripping mane,
then gallops muffle-hoofed,
a flash of whiteness in sparse bamboo
in a Malay cemetery.

Yet I shall fear no evil
for Thou art with me
through the wind is a horse
is a *jinn* raving free
Thy rod and Thy staff
they comfort me
and fear is only in the mind
as Mother said
why want to be afraid
just say *Omitohood Omitohood Omitohood*
Amen.

2 When you have completed your list, consult the information about the poem given on page 249, drawn from notes provided to accompany the poem in the author's *Selected Poems*. Consider how far these pieces of information answer the questions you have asked (or indirectly imply answers to them). What difference does it make to a reading of the poem whether you have access to such information? Do all texts rely to some extent on background information in the same way that this poem appears to?

3 Now examine those of your questions which remain unanswered by the information provided on page 249. Some of these may require other pieces of concrete information than those which the notes provide. How many of your questions involve the word 'why?' Is there a difference between questions asking 'why?' and other kinds of question? If so, how would you describe the difference?

READING

Belsey (1980) *Critical Practice*, pp. 1–36.
*Durant and Fabb (1990) *Literary Studies in Action*, pp. 66–78.
Eagleton (1983) *Literary Theory*, pp. 1–16.
Fiske and Hartley (1978) *Reading Television*, pp. 13–20.
Hackman and Marshall (1978) *Re-reading Literature*, pp. 3–17.
W.K. Wimsatt and M.C. Beardsley (1946) 'The intentional fallacy', in Lodge (ed.)
    (1972) *Twentieth Century Criticism*, pp. 334–44.
——— (1949) 'The affective fallacy', in Lodge (ed.) (1972) *Twentieth Century Criticism*,
    pp. 345–58.

Unit 2   Using information sources

SOME EXAMPLES OF THE USE OF INFORMATION SOURCES

Information sources include footnotes to a poem, a dictionary of symbols in the library, the *Encyclopedia Britannica*, and the Modern Language Association bibliography on computer-readable compact disc. Many of the information sources cited here can be found in the reference section of your library. Information sources have many uses in literary study, and this chapter illustrates some of them. We begin by looking at some sample problems.

1 An old English folk poem begins 'A frog he would a wooing go'. One question you might ask about this is: why a frog? A useful type of reference book if you are concerned with the meanings of objects is a dictionary of symbols. For example, if you look up 'frog' in de Vries' *Dictionary of Symbols and Images*, you are given the following meanings:

> a frog is amphibious and therefore often ambivalent in meaning; its natural enemy is the serpent; it has a number of favourable meanings – it symbolises fertility and lasciviousness, creation, the highest form of evolution (hence princes turn into frogs), wisdom, and poetic inspiration; it also has unfavourable meanings – in religious terms it is considered unclean, and it is said to have a powerful voice but no strength.

This dictionary also tells us that 'Frogs are great wooers: there are several songs about frogs who go "a-wooing" a mouse; perhaps a spinning song as the mouse itself is referred to as "spinning" several times.' So we have our answer: frogs are symbols of fertility and lasciviousness, hence wooers. The other meanings do not seem to be relevant here (e.g. creation, wisdom, uncleanness). The next question we could ask is: why does he woo a mouse? To begin to answer this, we could return to the dictionary of symbols.

In general, dictionaries of symbols are useful in opening up meanings in a text. These meanings are not necessarily coherent with each other, and they may be drawn from different sources. Symbol dictionaries are most useful if the symbol appears in a text which is part of a particular interpretative tradition (e.g. many medieval texts use a consistent system of symbolism). Otherwise, a symbol dictionary gives hints as to possible interpretations, which you need to use at your discretion. It is often worth using a dictionary of symbolism to investigate the symbolic implications of things such as body parts, animals and plants, planets and stars, weather, geographical phenomena, etc.

2 A sonnet by Christina Rossetti (1881) begins with the following lines:

'I, if I perish, perish' – Esther spake:
And bride of life or death she made her fair.

In order to understand the poem, the reader needs to know that Esther is a historical character and to realize who she is. Some editions of the poem will explain this in a footnote, but if there is no footnote, what do you do? Many information sources are useful for finding out about names. A classical dictionary lists all the names from Greek and Roman mythology; a Bible concordance lists all the names from the Bible; and many names are also listed in general reference works like Brewer's *Dictionary of Phrase and Fable*. You need to guess which reference source will be useful. As it happens, Brewer's has nothing about Esther, but the Bible concordance does (i.e. it is a name from the Bible). If you look up 'Esther' in a Bible concordance you see all the lines listed which include this name, with references to the parts of the Bible where the lines are found; in fact they all occur in the Book of Esther, and you could look at this part of the Bible in order to find out about the character. You might also notice that one line listed in the concordance under 'Esther' is 'and Esther spake yet again', which is echoed in Rossetti's poem in the words 'Esther spake'. So you have found a biblical **allusion** (see Unit 16) in the language as well as finding out who the character is.

3 Shakespeare's play *The Tempest*, written in 1611–12, has among its themes those of sea travel, bad weather, the wrecking of ships (and loss of travellers) and the discovery of strange things in distant places. If you want to place these themes in their historical context, you could use an annals, which is a list of events, organized by date. For example, if you look up 1611 in *The Teach Yourself Encyclopedia of Dates and Events*, you find that in this year the Dutch began trading with Japan, the British explorer Hudson was lost in Hudson Bay in North America and there were publications of a scientific explanation of the rainbow, a book of maps of Britain and an auto-biographical travel book by Thomas Coryate. These facts may or may not be significant; the point is that it is very easy to get at them using this information source (you would have to decide whether to investigate any which seem to be particularly relevant).

Thus, by using a range of information sources, it is possible to find answers to some of the questions which a text poses.

ADAPTING AN INFORMATION SOURCE TO YOUR OWN NEEDS: THE OXFORD ENGLISH DICTIONARY

The Oxford English Dictionary (*OED*) is a list of English words which, in certain respects, is very complete (it is most complete for the dialect known as Southern Standard English); for each word, a number of meanings (all those the word has had in its history) are distinguished, and quotations are given showing the word in use, including the earliest known use. Dictionaries are usually used as guides to the current usage (meaning, spelling or pronunciation) of difficult words, but the *OED* can be adapted to many other uses. We can illustrate this by looking at the first stanza of Percy Bysshe Shelley's 'To a skylark' (1820):

Hail to thee, blithe spirit!
Bird thou never wert,
That from heaven, or near it,
Pourest thy full heart
In profuse strains of unpremeditated art.

If you look up 'blithe' in the *OED* you will find two appropriate meanings:

Meaning 2: exhibiting gladness.... In ballads frequently coupled with 'gay'. Rare in modern English prose or speech; the last quotation with this meaning is 1807.
Meaning 3: Of men, their heart, spirit etc.: joyous.... Rare in English prose or colloquial use since 16th century but frequent in poetry.

This dictionary entry acts as more than just a definition of the word; it tells us a number of interesting things relating to the poem. First, the word is used primarily in poetry – though in Shelley's poem it might have seemed a little old-fashioned (since 1807 is the date of the last citation for meaning 2). Second, the word is typically used in ballads; a significant fact when we consider that Romantic poets like Shelley were influenced by folk poetry of this kind. Third, it is explicitly associated with the word 'spirit' in the entry under meaning 3; the only quotation given which supports this association is in fact one from 1871, but nevertheless there may have been a traditional co-occurrence of these two words which Shelley drew upon.

We could do the same with most of the words in this stanza; we might, for example, wonder how 'hail' was generally used (what does it tell us about the spirit?), what meanings 'spirit' had, how necessarily religious the word 'heaven' was at this time, what the significance of combining 'unpremeditated' with 'art' was, and so on. It often happens that we may have one reason for looking a word up, but will find something unexpected in the process (e.g. with 'blithe' I expected the term to have been old-fashioned, but I did not expect the link with ballads or with 'spirit').

The *OED*, like other dictionaries, can also be used as a 'brainstorming' aid when starting out on a research project. For example, if you were interested in the notion of 'spirit' in Romantic poetry, it would be a good and easy start to look up 'spirit' in the *OED* to see who used the word, what its history up to that time had been, how religious or otherwise its meanings were and so on. By doing this you are adapting the *OED* to a new goal; you are using it as an admittedly partial guide to culture, as embodied in language use.

Other information sources can also be adapted in a similar way. A concordance, for example, can be used as a specialized dictionary of quotations (all from the same author), or an indication of the words which an author tends to combine together (a Shelley concordance would tell us instantly whether Shelley uses 'blithe spirit' elsewhere), or an indication of the meaning which a particular word has for an author. Often you need to interpret the facts which the information source presents to you, and use them as a hint for further research.

INFORMATION SOURCES AND COMPUTERS

Information can be stored in a 'hard' copy, such as a book, where it is laid out in a fixed order to be used in particular ways. But increasingly, information is also available in a 'soft' form, such as on a computer disc (or a compact disc – also known as CD or CD-ROM), with the advantage that it is not pre-organized and is flexible enough for you to select the organization of the data which you need.

The advantage of using computers to access information rather than reference books can be shown by comparing a Shakespeare concordance (i.e. a book) with Shakespeare's complete works on CD. Both the concordance and the CD contain the same information (basically, all the lines from Shakespeare's works), but the concordance organizes it in a fixed way – as a list of almost all the words from the plays, each word then having a list under it of all the lines which use that word. Using a concordance, you can find a quotation (if you know one word from the quotation), you can get a guide to where Shakespeare uses a specific word in his plays, and what sorts of meanings the word has for him. The CD containing all the plays can also be thought of as a list of all the lines, and by using appropriate software you can use it as a concordance. The advantage of the CD, however, is that you can do more complicated things just as easily – for example, you can restrict the type of searches that you ask the computer to do for you: to find all the uses of a word in the tragedies, or, assuming that the software is sophisticated enough, you could find all the uses of a word in speeches by women, and so on. As another example, many Shakespeare concordances will not include words like 'and' as key words, but you might be interested in how often and in what patterns Shakespeare uses 'and'. Because the CD has not been pre-organized in the way that the concordance has, you could search for this word as easily as any other.

With computer-searched information, you decide for yourself how to organize the information; with a book the information is already organized for you. In many cases, it will not make a lot of difference; it may be more convenient to use the book. But for more complicated or bigger tasks, a computer is useful, since information on a computer can be moved around easily, and you can copy the relevant part of the information source onto your own computer disc or print it out.

THE PARTISAN NATURE OF INFORMATION SOURCES

It is not possible to find an entirely neutral information source, because information sources are always produced in certain contexts, for certain purposes and certain users, and may carry within them very partisan and politicized positions. This makes information sources in a sense unreliable, but it also makes them useful in a new way because they are themselves historical documents which can be examined. In Samuel Johnson's dictionary (1755), the choice of words to include, the definitions of words, and the choice of quotations to illustrate them carry value judgements which may be used as a guide to issues in the language and society of the period. The same applies to all dictionaries and other information sources – all are to some extent partisan, though few make this explicit. One information source which does make its partisan nature explicit is Kramarae and Treichler's *A Feminist Dictionary* (1985), where quotations are used as the major form of information about words, and are selected to question the conventional meanings of words as well as to inform about them.

INFORMATION AS A HINDRANCE RATHER THAN A HELP?

Information sources are resources to be drawn upon, and can help us in solving problems raised by texts. But there are some cases in which information sources can restrict us. Consider, for example, the poem by John Donne cited in the activity in Unit 11: Parallelism and repetition. This poem contains a line which says 'All, all may use'; the poem is about relations between men and women, and one edition of the poem provides a footnote which suggests that the line means 'All men may use all women' in order to clarify what might otherwise seem an ambiguity (it could perhaps have meant 'All women may use all men' or 'All people may use all people'). The footnote here is an information source, but there is a problem in that it may be removing from the poem part of its meaning and effect (it may be that the confusion of gender is part of the poem's meaning – an effect which is potentially destroyed by the footnote).

Some critics might argue that the use of information sources to direct the reader is illegitimate in all cases, because it interferes with the flow and immediacy of the reading process, and denies the reader the right to interpret a text in any way in which s/he sees fit. Part of the problem with such a view comes from the fact that many texts are read in a context very different – geographically, socially or historically – from that in which they were written, and information which the author originally could assume the reader to know may now not be common knowledge. Christina Rossetti would have been able to assume that her readers would recognize that Esther was a biblical figure and might even have expected them to spot the allusion; but this is now not likely to be true for many readers of the poem. The necessity and role of information sources thus depends on who you are as a reader, as well as on your goals in working on literary texts.

ACTIVITY

Practice in using information sources generally means working in the library; however, it is possible to prepare speculatively for such work. This activity (which can be done without information resources) focuses on preparation.

Read the following poem by Charlotte Smith (1749–1806):

> Queen of the silver bow! – by thy pale beam,
> Alone and pensive, I delight to stray,
> And watch thy shadow trembling in the stream,
> Or mask the floating clouds that cross thy way.
> And while I gaze, thy mild and placid light
> Sheds a soft calm upon my troubled breast;
> And oft I think – fair planet of the night,
> That in thy orb, the wretched may have rest:
> The sufferers of the earth perhaps may go,
> Released by death – to thy benignant sphere,
> And the sad children of despair and woe
> Forget in thee, their cup of sorrow here.
> Oh! that I soon may reach thy world serene,
> Poor wearied pilgrim – in this toiling scene!

> (from *Elegaic Sonnets*, 1784)

Listed below is a selection of reference books, which may be of use in thinking about various aspects of this poem.

1 *Dictionary of Symbols and Images,* by A. de Vries. Select two words in the poem which would be worth looking up in this dictionary, and explain briefly in each case why you think this might be worth doing.
2 *The Oxford English Dictionary.* Each word in this dictionary is given a definition or definitions, and illustrative uses from a range of authors, all dated, including the first known use. Select two words in the poem which would be worth looking up in this dictionary and explain why you think this might be worth doing.
3 *The Collins Dictionary of Quotations,* ed. D. Fraser. Like most dictionaries of quotations, this is organized around key words. Select two words in the poem which would be worth looking up in this dictionary, and explain why you think this might be worth doing.

4   *Dictionary of British Women Writers*, ed. J. Todd. Suggest what you might possibly find in a short biographical entry about Charlotte Smith which would be useful in thinking about the poem.

5   *The Modern Language Association International Bibliography of Books and Articles on the Modern Languages and Literatures.* This is a comprehensive list of critical, descriptive and theoretical publications organized under author and under general topic (you will find it in book and CD form in some libraries). One obvious place to look would be under 'Charlotte Smith', to see what work has been done on this author. But you could also search for critical discussions of particular topics; suggest one topic which might be worth looking up references for in order to extend your understanding of the poem.

6   An annals, such as *The Teach Yourself Encyclopedia of Dates and Events.* List some aspects of the poem which might be illuminated by looking up the dates 1774–84 (i.e. the ten years up to the publication of the poem).

This activity has asked you to speculate about the possible directions you might take, using information sources to investigate this poem. Ideally, you should now to go the library and try out some of your hunches.

READING

Baker (1989) *A Research Guide for Undergraduate Students (English and American Literature).*
*Durant and Fabb (1990) *Literary Studies in Action*, Ch. 4.
Thompson (1971) *English Studies: a Guide For Librarians*, pp. 49–74.
Todd and Loder (1990) *Finding Facts Fast.*
Williams (1976) *Keywords*, Introduction, pp. 11–26.

Unit 3   Analysing units of structure

When we read, see or hear a text, our understanding is guided by a sense of the elements which make up the text (its constituent parts) and how they fit together. This intuitive judgement provides a basis for larger interpretative hunches and critical reactions. So we could say that texts have a sort of 'mechanics'; they are constructed or built for a purpose and with anticipated meanings. In many cases the arrangement of textual components involves interesting regularities in the creation of meanings and significance. Because of this, it is worth finding out about the **units of structure** from which texts can be built.

As an example, consider the twelve-bar blues. This is made up (with some variation) of the following units (among others): three lines, with the second a repeat of the first, and with each line harmonically accompanied by particular chords in a given sequence of bars (thus lines, chords and bars are important units of structure for the twelve-bar blues). This is a verse from a twelve-bar blues song in the key of C:

chords:	C	/ F	/ C	/ C7
line 1:	Early one mornin',	/ on my way to the penal	/ farm	
bars:	[1]	/ [2]	/ [3]	/ [4]

chords:	F	/ F	/ C	/ C7
line 2:	Early one mornin',	/ on my way to the penal	/ farm	
bars:	[5]	/ [6]	/ [7]	/ [8]

chords:	G7	/ F7	/ C	/ G7
line 3:	Baby, all locked up	/ and ain't doin' nothin'	/ wrong.	
bars:	[9]	/ [10]	/ [11]	/ [12]

(Francis Blockwall, written *c* 1910–20)

Thus without the notion of units of structure (lines, chords, bars) it is impossible to describe the structure of the blues.

'FORM' AND 'STRUCTURE'

Units of structure are also called **formal elements** or **formal properties**. The terms 'structure' and 'form' are being used here to describe the arrangement of elements in a text, but it should be noted that these terms are used in various different ways in the discussion of aesthetic objects and texts.

'Form' as coherence and unity

A different sense of 'form', which has a long history in philosophy since Plato, involves the idea of form as an underlying essence or ideal of something which exists beyond its physical manifestation. 'Form' in this sense is something inherent and beyond analysis. The poet Samuel Taylor Coleridge (1772–1834) developed the term 'organic form' to capture the idea that aesthetic form occurs or grows of itself, naturally, rather than being a human or social construct. In New Criticism (an American literary theory at its height from the 1930s to the 1960s), the idea of organic form in literature takes on an added dimension: poetic 'form' is said to involve a complex balancing of potentially conflicting elements (hence New Criticism's stress on irony, paradox and ambiguity). What unites this sense of form with the Platonic sense is that in both cases formal elements are seen as in some sense inseparable from the text. By contrast, when we refer to formal elements in this unit we assume that it is possible to extract and examine individual formal elements.

'Structure'

We use the term 'structure' here to refer to the 'insides' of a text, the network of underlying relations which can be discovered by analysis. But it is worth remembering that there is another use of the term 'structure' which refers to the text itself (just as a house or a bridge can be called a structure).

GRAMMARS OF LANGUAGE

The descriptive grammar of a language is a theory of how words can be thought of as different kinds of unit, and how those units fit together into larger units (called phrases) and how these larger units combine into sentences. The grammar of English (like all other human languages) appears to be quite complicated, and parts of it are not well understood; but it is possible, by looking at the most basic elements of the system – words and the different parts of speech which they can be grouped into – to begin to see the scope and power of grammatical description.

If we were to build up a grammatical description of our own, we might begin with a basic rule which says that a sentence is made up of a sequence of units called 'words'. This seems adequate for the following sentence:

(1) Someone lived in a pretty little town

But if we re-order these words, our basic grammatical rule turns out to be only partly reliable:

(2) Someone pretty lived in a little town
(3) Someone lived a in pretty little town

We can recognize that sentence (2) is an acceptable sentence, while sentence (3) is not. But our theory of units, as it stands, cannot explain why (3) is not an acceptable sentence. In order to understand why changing the order of words gives these different results, we need to distinguish between different kinds of words on the basis of their different functions in sentences. In other words, we need to divide the basic unit 'word' into a number of subunits, such as 'noun', 'verb', 'adjective', 'article' and so on. These different subunits or types of words are called **parts of speech**.

Using available distinctions between parts of speech, we could analyse our original sentence as follows:

(4) someone lived in   a   pretty   little   town
     (noun)   (verb) (preposition) (article) (adjective) (adjective) (noun)

In sentence (3) above, the problem seems to lie in the sequence *a in pretty*; using the analysis of parts of speech, this sequence takes the form: article–preposition–adjective. Since this sequence does not make sense in the above example, we might make a provisional descriptive rule which says that *a preposition does not come between an article and an adjective*. But rules are useful only if they apply in most cases, and so we would have to try out our rule using other words in the article–preposition–adjective positions. The sequence *the of happy*, for example, also turns out to be a combination which is never found in a normal-sounding English sentence. In fact, this is a general grammatical rule in English, and so we can safely predict that prepositions never appear in between an article and an adjective.

Not all grammatical rules are as straightforward and as general as this one, but the process of discovering them would be the same. By analysing sequences, formulating provisional rules, testing them out with different combinations of words and modifying the rules where necessary, we could build up our own descriptive grammar of English and learn important things about the structure and possibilities of the language in the process.

The system of units called 'parts of speech' has been studied since classical times. Some fairly generally accepted names for different parts of speech, together with examples, are set out in the following chart (note that this list of parts of speech is not exhaustive).

Name of unit	*Examples*
verb	go, went, seemed, give, have, be, am, eat, broken
noun	thing, book, theory, beauty, universe, destruction
adjective	happy, destructive, beautiful, seeming, broken
adverb	fast, quickly, seemingly, probably, unfortunately
preposition	in, on, beside, up, after, towards, at, underneath
article	the, a
demonstrative	this, that, those, these
modal	should, could, need, must, might, can, shall, would
degree word	how, very, rather, quite
quantifier	some, every, all

LITERARY APPLICATIONS OF GRAMMATICAL DESCRIPTION

Analysing a text into its constituent elements becomes useful when it illuminates how the writing of any given text is working. Like an action replay, descriptive analysis can examine in slow motion and close detail a process which in composition or spontaneous reading occurs without conscious attention.

Descriptive analysis

The most basic usefulness of the analysis of units of structure in literary texts is simply that it enables us to describe how a text works. Take the first stanza of William Blake's 'London' (1794), for example:

I wander thro' each charter'd street,
Near where the charter'd Thames does flow,
And mark in every face I meet
Marks of weakness, marks of woe.

This could be analysed and described in terms of a range of different units – stanza, sentence, line, phrase, word, parts of speech, etc. An account of the poem might want to describe and discuss the repetition of the word 'mark' in the third and fourth lines of the first stanza; but it would be more accurate and useful to note that 'mark' in line 3 is being used as a verb meaning 'to see' or 'to notice', while in line 4 it is used (in the plural) as a noun. The analysis would not stop here, of course, but might go on to ask why these 'marks' are being linked through the verbal echo with the speaker's act of seeing ('marking') them. The point here is simply that such a discussion is facilitated by the analysis and description of units of structure.

Deviation

A grammar of a language is the set of rules for combining units (parts of speech) into sequences. But it is always possible to break these rules in order to achieve certain effects (see Unit 12: Deviation). Rule-breaking texts can be analysed by looking at what rules have been broken and considering what the individual effects are of each transgression. Consider for example the first line of a poem by e e cummings (1940):

anyone lived in a pretty how town

This line seems odd, but we can explain its oddity by showing which gram-matical rules it deviates from. The sequence 'a pretty how town' is odd because 'how' is a degree word (see above chart) which appears here in a place where we would usually expect an adjective (e.g. nice, awful, etc.). In fact, the sequence article–adjective–degree word–noun is not a possible one in English (another example would be *the stone very houses*).

The other obvious problem in this line is 'anyone'. 'Anyone' is an indefi-nite pronoun, and might potentially fit into the place it appears in – the pronouns 'it' or 'someone', for example, would be perfectly acceptable before the verb 'lived'. But users of English will instinctively realize that 'anyone' does not make sense in the actual sequence of words that cummings has used.

At this point, either the reader might abandon the poem as nonsensical or s/he might try other ways of reading it. For example, it might help to try re-arranging the words in order to 'make sense' of them:

how anyone lived in a pretty town

In this new sequence, 'anyone' does make sense in the position preceding the verb 'lived', and we seem to have the beginnings of an interpretation which would go something like 'how anyone lived in a pretty town like that is a mystery to me'. But if we try to match this interpretation with the rest of the poem we find that it does not seem to work and so probably needs to be abandoned. But there is another way we can use the analysis of units of structure in order to deal with this grammatical problem. If we look at the other use of 'anyone' in the poem, we discover a consistent pattern:

anyone's any was all to her (line 16)
one day anyone died i guess (line 25)

Although neither of these makes grammatical sense, we can see that 'anyone' consistently appears in a position in sequences where we would normally expect to find expressions which refer to particular entities in a definite way (e.g. proper names; noun phrases, such as *the woman*; or pronouns, such as *he* or *she*):

one day (he/she/the man/the woman/Bill/Alice) died i guess

In fact, a close reading of the poem in this way suggests that 'anyone' was a man who lived in a pretty town and married a woman referred to as 'no-one' and that they were eventually buried side by side. Thus, we can make sense of the poem as working by grammatical substitution: indefinite pronouns are being used as if they were definite pronouns referring to particular people. The next step in this way of reading the poem would be to ask why it is written like this and what effects it has. The paraphrase given above suggests that if we substituted definite nouns in the place of 'anyone' and 'no-one', the poem would seem quite banal. The effect of using 'anyone' and 'no-one' is to make the poem ambiguous and poignant: on the one hand, it seems to give these figures and their experience a more general significance (they stand for every man and every woman), but on the other they are anonymous and emptied of individual significance (they are both anyone and no-one).

Parallelism

By identifying units we can make visible the structure of certain kinds of **parallelism** (see Unit 11) – for example, the repetition of grammatical structures.

Descriptions of style

By analysing large stretches of text (or a large number of texts), it is possible to identify characteristic linguistic choices made by individual writers. A writer may show a predisposition towards adverbs, complex sentences or relative clauses, etc. On the basis of detailed analysis of recurrent structures, it is possible for editors to ascribe a text of unknown origin to a particular author, especially with the help of computer analysis of a large number of texts. Or it is possible to begin to describe exactly why the styles of different authors feel different, irrespective of what is being written about (e.g. the perceptible differences between the writing of Ernest Hemingway and Virginia Woolf could be accounted for in grammatical terms).

EXTENDING THE NOTION OF GRAMMAR

If we think of a grammatical sequence as a set of slots which can be filled by different items, it is possible to extend the notion of grammar to other things than language – such as the possible combinations of clothes. It is possible to divide the body into zones, each of which can be thought of as a 'slot' within the clothing system: head, upper torso, legs, feet, etc. Each of these areas can be covered with an item of clothing, chosen from a set of available possibilities. These individual items of clothing are the 'fillers' of the slots (e.g. for the feet: boots, shoes, sandals, nothing at all). By examining combinations of items selected, specific styles can be described on the basis of consistency between selections. Deviations from conventional clothing 'statements' can also be described (e.g. the wearing of wellington boots and a headscarf with a suit).

Or consider a narrative film. The film as a whole will have a number of slots or units of structure: its credit sequence (and possibly pre-credit sequence); the main body of the narrative (including subunits such as establishing shots, dialogue, car-chase sequences, etc.); and end credits. Each of these can be handled in different ways by a director through selecting different options (car chases can end in the death of the person chased, loss of the person being followed, etc.) to fill slots and subslots. An overall style is produced by manipulating the possibilities within each paradigm; and, by the same token, styles can be analysed by attending to how they use the grammar of films.

The study of the units of structure (or slots and fillers) of a wide range of cultural texts, institutions and ideas (from the fashion system to literature) forms a central part of **structuralism**, a theoretical movement which developed in the late 1950s and which has been very influential in literary studies (see Culler 1976). The grammar of narrative, for example, which allows us to describe the range of possible slots and fillers for any narrative, has received particular attention (see Unit 18: Narrative, and Unit 20: Narration in film and prose fiction).

POSSIBILITIES FOR ANALYSIS

Reasons for analysing form or structure range from the need to understand how a form comes to have a particular meaning, to the desire to create new forms on the basis of old forms. In many areas of analysis, little work has been done in terms of naming units and working out their possible combinations; and it is often the case that when you analyse a text, you can invent your own units and your own rules of combination, if these can be justified in terms of the new ideas they make possible. There are only the beginnings of a grammar of pop songs, for example; in creating such a grammar, we might think of units called intro, verse, chorus, bridge or middle 8, fade, coupled with other musical levels (riffs, drum fills, hook), and so on. A more precise vocabulary for describing how such songs are organized would be interesting and useful; actually developing one would depend on the same general procedures of analysis that have long been used in descriptions of English grammar.

ACTIVITY

This activity uses a summary of Charles Dickens' *Oliver Twist* (1837). The fifteen sentences of the summary have been jumbled up into the sequence which appears below. Each of the sentences describes an event in the novel (so the unit of structure here is the sentence and/or the event). In addition, sentence 1 in the jumbled sequence has itself been jumbled up.

The activity involves two tasks: to re-arrange the first jumbled sentence into an order which makes grammatical and narrative sense; and then to re-arrange the sentences/events into an order which makes narrative sense. The most important part of the activity, however, is that you should *justify* the decisions you make in your re-ordering. (The original ordering is given on page 249.)

Part I

Try to construct a possible sentence out of the jumbled words of sentence 1 below; use all the words and do not use any word twice. Keep a record of *how* you are able to do this on a more principled basis than simple guess-work (e.g. which words, or parts of speech, can follow which others; which words are usually found together as fixed idioms, etc.).

1   escape and tries Nancy's cry to following hue the death Sikes

Part II

(a) Now work out a plausible sequence for the fifteen jumbled events listed below. Again, keep a list of the kinds of evidence – especially particular words or expressions, or possible and impossible sequences of events – that you use to help you decide in favour of one particular order rather than another. (It may help if you photocopy the page and cut the copy with scissors into fifteen strips, with one event on each, so that you can physically re-order the events.)

(b) Now re-arrange the fifteen events into a new order, which tells the story in a different way. In doing this, think only of what happens, not the particular wording of the events as they appear in the account of them you have been given. You can refer to a single event more than once – for example, you might want to insert other events into the description of a particular event in order to create a 'flashback'.

(c) How does the version you created in (b) differ from the version you created in (a) in terms of genre, point of view, suspense, thematic interest, chronology, effect.

1   [write in your re-arranged version of sentence 1 here]
2   Keen to take advantage of these offers, the gang of thieves kidnap Oliver from Mr Brownlow.
3   The thieves try to convert Oliver into a thief.
4   Nancy discovers that Monks knows about Oliver's true parentage; having developed redeeming traits, she informs Rose of the danger Oliver is in.
5   With Sikes dead, the rest of the gang are captured; Fagin is executed.
6   Oliver accompanies Sikes on a burglary, but receives a gunshot wound.

7   Nancy's efforts are discovered by the gang, and she is brutally murdered by Bill Sikes.
8   Oliver runs away and is looked after by a benevolent Mr Brownlow.
9   The thieves become especially interested in Oliver, because they receive offers concerning him from a sinister person named Monks.
10 Found and threatened with exposure, Monks confesses that he is Oliver's half-brother, and has pursued his ruin in order to acquire the whole of his father's property.
11 Oliver falls into the hands of a gang of thieves, including Bill Sikes, Nancy and the Artful Dodger, and headed by a rogue called Fagin.
12 Suffering pain from the gunshot wound, Oliver is captured by Mrs Maylie and her protégée, Rose, who brings him up for a time.
13 Monks emigrates and dies in prison; Oliver rejoins Mr Brownlow and is adopted by him.
14 He accidentally hangs himself in the process.
15 Oliver Twist, a pauper of unknown parentage, runs away to London.

READING

Aitchison (1972) *Teach Yourself Linguistics.*
Carter (ed.) (1982) *Language and Literature.*
Culler (1975) *Structuralist Poetics*, Ch. 1.
Leech and Short (1981) *Style in Fiction*, Ch. 1.
Leech and Svartvik (1975) *A Communicative Grammar of English.*
Quirk and Greenbaum (1973) *A University Grammar of English.*

Section 2

Dimensions of language variation

Unit 4   Language and time

All languages change over the course of time. When a language changes in different ways in different places dialects emerge, and these dialects may themselves become languages in their own right. The fact of language change is relevant to the study of texts in several ways. A text may be a force for language change or it may attempt to retard a change. A text may become difficult because of language change; it may have meanings, for example those carried by the use of **archaism**, which rely on an understanding of what the state of the language was at any given time.

THEORIES OF LANGUAGE CHANGE

There are various different accounts of why and how language changes over time.

Formalist theories: change as an anonymous process

Many linguists have described language change as being caused by, and working according to, structural pressures which are internal to the language itself. For example, between 1500 and 1700 many of the vowel sounds of southern British English changed into other vowel sounds in a process called the Great Vowel Shift. The modern English word *make*, for example, was pronounced in the sixteenth century with a different vowel, a little like the one you get in the modern English *mack* if you stretch the vowel out. The tongue is further from the roof of your mouth in *mack* than it is in *make*, so we can say that the vowel was 'raised' from its sixteenth-century pronunciation to its modern pronunciation (strictly speaking, we mean that the tongue is raised). Many linguists, from nineteenth-century philologists up to contemporary generative linguists, have investigated how these changes relate to each other and to the larger structures of the language: for example, one might classify vowels into 'high', 'mid' and 'low' on the basis of the height of the tongue when it makes them, and say that in the above example a low vowel became a mid vowel. What interests linguists is that this change seems to have 'pushed' the old mid vowel to become a modern high vowel (modern *meat* changed from a sixteenth-century word sounding like *mate*), and the older high vowel to have become a modern low vowel (modern *ride* was once pronounced like *reed*), so that there is a system of interrelated changes which can be understood relative to each other. These linguists give a **formalist** account of these changes (i.e. an explanation in terms of the form or units of structure of the language).

A functionalist account: change as a politically motivated process

There is another view of language change and how to study and explain it which suggests that changes in language result from social activity, in particular from political struggle. Dick Leith (1983) accounts for the Great Vowel Shift by suggesting that the migration of workers into London produced a clash of dialects which induced Londoners to distinguish their speech from the immigrants by changing their vowel system. This particular functionalist account therefore claims that language change is *socially motivated*, rather than being solely motivated by the formal system of the language itself. A functionalist way of looking at language therefore analyses language change from the perspective of the social values carried by certain usages at specific points in time.

It is possible to combine functionalist and formalist accounts; for example, the Great Vowel Shift may have been triggered and supported in general terms by a struggle for linguistic identity, but the details of the shift – for example, which vowels changed and how they changed – might best be explained in formalist terms.

Political, economic and social change can result in words being pronounced in new ways and given new meanings, and can lead to new words being invented. And it should be remembered that rarely, if ever, do words have one single fixed meaning or pronunciation. According to some Marxist accounts of language, the pronunciation and meaning of words can be a 'site of struggle' when two or more social groups or interests have a political stake in enforcing one meaning of a word or phrase (see Unit 8: Language and society). For example, a local-government tax currently imposed in Britain is called *the community charge* by the Conservative government which introduced it and *the poll tax* by those opposed to it. The latter term is both used and resisted because it has political implications in English history. The *OED* tells us that *poll* used to mean 'head' (the current usage associated with voting comes from the poll as a counting of heads); one reason for reviving the archaism *poll tax* is because it is levied on all 'heads' – that is, on everyone of a voting age. But the term *poll tax* is also a specific allusion to the Peasants' Revolt of 1381, which, *Brewer's Dictionary of Phrase and Fable* notes, was 'immediately occasioned by an unpopular poll-tax at a time when there was a growing spirit of social revolt' in England. Thus the revival of the term *poll tax* is a politically motivated gesture which seems to make an analogy between 1381 and the current situation. (Ironically enough, the *OED* informs us that an archaic meaning of poll was 'to plunder by ... excessive taxation; to pillage, rob, fleece'.) The success of the opposition to the new tax can be judged in part by how widely and by whom the alternative name 'poll tax' is used.

CHANGE AND LINGUISTIC MEDIA

The main linguistic media – the mediums in which verbal language is used – are **speech** and **writing** (see Unit 21), together with various other technologically enabled forms (language can be broadcast, recorded, telephoned, etc.).

Writing

Before the seventeenth century, written texts varied enormously in terms of spelling and punctuation. This arose partly from the lack of a central standardization of spelling, partly from the variability and rapid changes of pronunciation and partly from typesetting practices like the symbolic use of capital letters to indicate importance and the insertion of letters to fill out a line. From the seventeenth century onwards, however, printed texts begin to look more like modern English texts because standards were instituted which still hold. One of the results of this is that while spellings have stabilized, pronunciations have continued to change, so that spellings which once corresponded to pronunciation no longer do so.

Speech

It has only recently become possible to record speech as sound; our evidence for how English was spoken in the past is generally in the form of (a) the reports of contemporary linguists; (b) transcripts of speech, as in trial transcripts; (c) representations of speech in literature and drama; (d) indirect evidence from sound patterns in literature (e.g. rhymes); (e) indirect evidence from informal writing such as diaries and letters.

Speech seems to change more rapidly than writing, partly because it is not codified in the same way, and it is open to much wider cultural variation. Youth subcultures generate a large number of new terms to mark membership of groups, and more importantly to mark non-membership. Such subculture words filter into mainstream spoken English or into the written standard only very occasionally. Consider, for example, the word *wicked* as meaning something exceptionally good which appeared in mainstream pop music via Black subculture groups several years ago; only a few years later, the term no longer appears in the mainstream, except parodically. In the 1960s' subcultures, one of the key distinctions was that between 'heads' (those who took drugs and shared a set of radical beliefs about the world) and 'straights' (those who did neither of these). Today, these terms seem impossibly archaic.

Twentieth-century technologies and linguistic change

New technologies have brought new ways of using English. This is most obvious with specialized languages like those used for short-wave radio or for telegrams. But it is also true of linguistic practices developed for talking on the telephone or for being a radio disc jockey. So-called 'BBC English' was a pronunciation standard developed for radio and television.

SOME TYPES OF LANGUAGE CHANGE

Sound

We have seen that many of the English vowel sounds (particularly long vowels) changed as a result of the Great Vowel Shift. But the relics of older pronunciations are still preserved in the spellings of English words which were codified before the Shift was completed. For example, the spelling of the word *knight* reflects a very different pronunciation from the current one; if we go back 500 years we have evidence that the *k* was pronounced, that the vowel was pronounced more like the vowel in *nit*, and that the *gh* was pronounced like the *ch* of *Bach*.

The arrangement and interrelationships of words (syntax)

In the early form of English known as Anglo-Saxon or Old English (spoken in much of Britain, in various dialects, from about AD 400 into the early Middle Ages), word order was fairly flexible. Some aspects of this flexibility survived into the modern English of the seventeenth century – such as allowing particular parts of sentences (such as the verb or an object) to be moved to the front of sentences. But the fact that this flexibility seems to have survived only in literary texts (it is difficult to find examples of this in non-literary documentary evidence such as letters and diaries) provides one example of the way that literature uses archaism as a literary technique. Vestiges of this can be found in Wordsworth a century later. The first stanza of 'The last of the flock' (1798) is given an archaic feel by repeatedly placing before the verb elements (italicized in the extract) which would normally follow it:

> *In distant countries* I have been,
> And yet I have not often seen
> A healthy man, a man full grown,
> Weep in the public roads alone.
> But *such a one*, on English ground,
> And in the broad high-way, I met;
> *Along the broad high-way* he came,
> His cheeks *with tears* were wet.

In the first line, for example, a more usual sequence in modern English would be:

I	have been	in distant countries
(subject)	(verb)	(complement)

This can also be thought of as a literary **deviation** (see Unit 12) from more usual syntactical sequences.

Pronouns

The history of the distinction between the second-person pronouns 'thou' and 'you' is a revealing example of how language change relates to social change. The *OED* tells us that early forms of 'thou' (plus 'thee', 'thine' and 'thy') and 'you' (plus 'ye', 'your' and 'yours') were both used in ordinary speech in Old English, where the distinction was primarily a grammatical one. In Middle English 'you' began to be used as a mark of respect when addressing a superior and (later) an equal, while 'thou' was retained for addressing an intimate or inferior. This distinction between 'thou' and 'you' was related to the rigid stratification of society in the Middle Ages. It allowed an aristocratic speaker to distinguish between an equal (referred to as 'you') and someone inferior in social standing (referred to as 'thou'), or to signal intimacy. The lower orders, on the other hand, were required to address aristocrats as 'you' as a mark of deference. In the fifteenth century, the rising merchant classes began using 'thou' to the lower orders. Increasing social mobility and competition between this merchant class and the aristocracy meant that by Shakespeare's time there was widespread confusion about who should use the term 'thou' to whom. The seventeenth-century radical Quaker movement seized on the confusion about 'thou' and 'you' by using 'thou' for everyone, as a political act of levelling. The distinction eventually collapsed, and only 'you' survived. 'Thou' only appears now in archaizing registers, including those of poetry and religion, where it functions, curiously enough, as a marker of respect rather than of inferiority. The King James Authorized Version of the Bible (1611) perhaps influenced this change in the function of 'thou' by having biblical characters address God as 'thou'.

A second distinction between 'thou' and 'you' was one of **register** (see Unit 6), since 'thou' was a familiar form of address, whereas 'you' was more formal. Shakespeare's texts often seem to mix 'you' and 'thou' indiscriminately, but the distinction is important in the following exchange between Hamlet and his mother:

Queen: Hamlet, thou hast thy father much offended.
Hamlet: Mother, you have my father much offended.
Queen: Come, come, you answer with an idle tongue.
Hamlet: Go, go, you question with a wicked tongue.

(*Hamlet* (c. 1600), III, 4, 10–14)

The queen's initial use of 'thou' to Hamlet and his 'you' in return are quite standard choices for parent-to-offspring and offspring-to-parent respectively. It is the queen's follow-up 'you' which is significant: annoyed by Hamlet's caustic rejoinder, she switches icily to a distancing 'you'.

Lexis or vocabulary (words and their meanings)

The vocabulary of a language can change through the introduction of new terms on the model of older forms (e.g. *personal stereo* describes a new machine by using a combination of already existing words), or through adopting foreign-language forms, such as *plaza* or *piazza*. Vocabulary changes often result from pressures from social change or because of new technological inventions. The vocabulary of computers has been very productive in introducing new terms into mainstream usage (e.g. *interface, to access,* etc.).

ARCHAISM

A linguistic **archaism** is a particular pronunciation, word or way of combining words, which is no longer in current usage but which once was. Certain registers are characterized in part by their use of archaism, particularly registers associated with institutions, such as the Church or the legal system.

The Bible exists in a number of different English translations. Until recently, the King James' Authorized Version (1611) was the most widely used translation. Some Christian groups and churches have now adopted more recent translations such as the New English Bible (1961), partly because it seems more 'up to date' and accessible. A measure of the difference between them can be seen by comparing the language of equivalent passages (I Corinthians: 15, 53):

King James' Version:	For this corruptible must put on incorruption, and this mortall must put on immortalitie.
New English Bible:	This perishable being must be clothed with the imperishable, and what is mortal must be clothed with immortality.

Though the new version is easier to understand, the old version is still preferred by some Christians, in part because its archaic language seems more mysterious and appropriate to religious experience.

English legal texts are also characterized by archaism. If we take the English Copyright (Amendment) Act 1983 as an example, we find archaisms like 'be it enacted', 'shall have effect' and 'cinematograph film'. The extensive use of archaism in legal texts arises partly from the fact that the law was the last institution to leave off using the French and Latin of the

Norman occupation (French was still used in the law into the eighteenth century). (For a more extended discussion of the legal register, see Unit 6: Language and content: register.)

There is a long tradition of poetic texts using archaism. Edmund Spenser, writing in the late sixteenth century, developed a vocabulary for poems like *The Faerie Queene* by copying archaic words from Chaucer (writing 200 years earlier). Spenser's language was itself imitated by later writers – especially by Romantic poets such as Keats in the early nineteenth century. Because of this, most attempts to define a poetic register would probably include some archaism as a component feature. Here, for example, is a line from Walter Scott's 'The song of the Reim-kennar' (1822): 'Enough of woe hast thou wrought on the ocean.' Archaisms here include the syntax (word order) and words such as 'thou' and 'wrought'. A more recent poem which exploits archaism is W.H. Auden's 'The wanderer' (1930), which is explicitly modelled on an Anglo-Saxon poem of the same name and uses Anglo-Saxon word-formation patterns, such as 'place-keepers' or 'stone-haunting', and alliterative patterns common in Anglo-Saxon poetry: '*D*oom is *d*ark and *d*eeper than any sea-*d*ingle' (see Unit 9: Rhyme and sound patterning). In using such archaisms, the poem may seem to explore meanings and values which give the impression of transcending time and place.

It should be added, though, that there is a problem with the identification of archaism, since 'archaisms' are often not archaic in the register in which they are used. For example, *thee* or *thou* is not an archaic form in a certain type of poetic register; it is archaic only in relation to our contemporary day-to-day speech. Thus the use of an archaism can be interpreted as either conforming to a register or looking back to the past (or both). One of the questions you should ask, therefore, in reading a text which uses archaisms is whether they are archaic relative to our current usage, or whether they would have been archaisms in literature at the time the text was written.

FEMINIST CHANGES TO LANGUAGE

Recent writers on the relation between language and political and social power, such as Michel Foucault (1981), stress the fact that language is both an instrument of social constraint and a means of resisting that constraint.

This is most clearly seen in recent feminist theory, where language is identified as one of the means through which patriarchal values are both maintained and resisted (for a fuller discussion of this, see Unit 7: Language and gender). Feminists such as Dale Spender (1980) draw our attention to the fact that there are many elements in language which are sexist and which offend women. Jane Mills' *Womanwords* (1989) is a dictionary which demonstrates the way that words associated with women often have a revealing history of meanings. For example, the word *glamour* once meant 'magical strength', but when the word began to be used for women it took on sexual and trivializing connotations, as in *glamour girl*. It would be hard to identify a particular individual or group responsible for such changes; rather, we interpret them as occasioned by the ideological and discursive structures which make up patriarchy (i.e. the economic, social and political pressures whereby women are treated as if inferior).

To counter this verbal discrimination against women, feminists have attempted to reform the language in a variety of ways. For example, offensive or discriminatory terms can be replaced by more neutral terms: *chairperson* can be used instead of *chairman*; *humankind* instead of *mankind*; *staff* instead of *manpower*; and so on. A different strategy adopted by feminists is to modify existing words (e.g. *wimmin*) or to coin new words (such as *herstory*) in order to mark the separation of their work and themselves from patriarchy. Mary Daly (1978) argues that old derogatory words should be used in new positive ways: for example, she uses the words *crone*, *dyke* and *virago* to refer to strong women. In Daly's work especially, this process is quite playful and shows little respect for conventional etymology.

However, as Deborah Cameron (1986) has noted, although it is possible to make changes in language on a small scale, getting the changes adopted more generally is not so easy. This is partly because the changes have to go through what she calls 'the gatekeepers of language' – i.e. institutions such as the media, education, the government, lexicographers and so on – which tend to be resistant to the type of changes feminists wish to introduce.

The more general point which emerges from this is that, for the most part, changes in language occur outside the conscious control of particular individuals or groups. Even when 'the gatekeepers of language' attempt to resist or introduce change there is no guarantee that they will be successful: British history furnishes many examples of failed attempts to reform the language according to some arbitrarily imposed standard.

ACTIVITY

This activity uses two poems (Lord Byron's 'If that high world' of 1814 and Philip Larkin's 'High windows' of 1974) in order to make some provisional observations about differences in language and poetic conventions between 1814 and 1974.

1 On the evidence of Byron's poem (printed below), list the language-related conventions which appear to have held for poetry around 1814 (e.g. use of archaism, choice of words, order of words, metre, rhyme, visual layout of the lines, etc.).
2 On the evidence of Larkin's poem (printed below), list language-related conventions which appear to have held for poetry in 1974.
3 Using the evidence you have gathered, make a list of the changes in poetic language between the two poems and a list of what does not seem to have changed.
4 Prevailing conventions constrain what we say, but they also enable us

to say things in particular ways. Compare the two sets of conventions, and try to classify them for each poet into limiting and enabling conventions; in each case justify your decision (e.g. if you think Byron's use of rhyme is enabling while Larkin's use of rhyme is limiting, explain why).

If that high world

I

If that high world, which lies beyond
Our own, surviving Love endears;
If there the cherished heart be fond,
The eye the same, except in tears –
How welcome those untrodden spheres!
How sweet this very hour to die!
To soar from earth and find all fears
Lost in thy light – Eternity!

II

It must be so: 'tis not for self
That we so tremble on the brink;
And striving to o'erleap the gulf,
Yet cling to Being's severing link.
Oh! in that future let us think
To hold, each heart, the heart that shares;
With them the immortal waters to drink,
And soul in soul, grow deathless theirs!

(Lord Byron, 1814)

High windows

When I see a couple of kids
And guess he's fucking her and she's
Taking pills or wearing a diaphragm,
I know this is paradise

Everyone old has dreamed of all their lives –
Bonds and gestures pushed to one side
Like an outdated combine harvester,
And everyone young going down the long slide

To happiness, endlessly. I wonder if
Anyone looked at me, forty years back,
And thought, *That'll be the life;*
No God anymore, or sweating in the dark

About hell and that, or having to hide
What you think of the priest. He
And his lot will all go down the long slide
Like free bloody birds. And immediately

Rather than words comes the thought of high windows:
The sun-comprehending glass,
And beyond it, the deep blue air, that shows
Nothing, and is nowhere, and is endless.

(Philip Larkin, 1974)

READING

Barber (1976) *Early Modern English.*
Cameron (1985) *Feminism and Linguistic Theory*, pp. 79–90.
Daly (1978) *Gynecology.*
Foucault (1981) *The History of Sexuality*, vol. 1.
Jeffers and Lehiste (1979) *Principles and Methods for Historical Linguistics.*
Leech (1969) *Linguistic Guide to English Poetry*, pp. 1–19.
Leith (1983) *A Social History of English*, pp. 32–57.
Mills (1989) *Womanwords.*
Spender (1980) *Man Made Language*, pp. 28–36.

Unit 5   Language and place

Texts can create a sense of place in two main ways. They can simply *describe* places – for instance, in travel writing. In novels the effect of such description is what we think of as 'setting'. In many cases, such as the description of Egdon Heath at the beginning of Thomas Hardy's *The Return of the Native* (1878), or Emily Brontë's Yorkshire Moors in *Wuthering Heights* (1847), place provides both a geographical background and a symbolic dimension to the narrative. Alternatively, place can be represented in texts through the particular ways in which characters (and sometimes narrators or poetic personae), are made to speak. This latter way of representing place is possible because of connections we typically make, as readers or listeners, between distinctive properties of voices (in terms of accent and dialect) and the places with which they are associated.

Creating a sense of place in texts through incorporating regional mannerisms of speech can be more problematic than the description of place. The textual representation of different kinds of regional voice calls on our ability to recognize differences of grammar, vocabulary and pronunciation, and asks us to make associations between these differences and the way speakers are supposed to speak in different places. The representation of dialect or accent thus draws on conventional images and connotations for the varieties of language we encounter. Such images are often stereotypical; they not only allow the association of voices with places, but can also trade on received ideas that some regional voices have more authority than others, or are more naive, or more strange, etc.

To investigate how we read this 'imagery' of different voices in texts, we need to examine how variation in language correlates with place. Then we can explore how such variation is manipulated in literary, non-literary and media texts as a significant resource or technique.

LANGUAGE VARIATION AND VARIETIES

The many languages of the world are related to each other in families (Indo-European, Dravidian, etc.). The family structure of languages involves overlapping and historically connected varieties, which in many cases have loaned each other words, sounds and structures. Even within what is called a single language, there is typically variation from region to region, as well as between classes, ethnic groups and genders.

Dialect and accent

Variation within a language can involve differences in the sound system, when speakers from a particular region (or social group) consistently pronounce words in different ways from other groups. Examples of this type of variation are the words, *rather, farmer* and *such*, which are all pronounced differently in different parts of Britain; *tomato, vase* and *dynasty* differ between British and US English; *nothing, hotel* and *west* all differ between British and Indian English.

Alongside differences in pronunciation, however, there can also be consistent differences in other aspects of the language. Different words are used in different places to refer to equivalent things or ideas. The word *throat*, for example, varies with *gullet, throttle, thropple* and *quilter* in different parts of Britain. A *faucet* is what US English speakers call a 'tap'; *pants* are 'trousers'; *suspenders* can be equivalent to 'braces'. A *cot* in India is an adult's 'bed', not, as in British English, a child's bed. *Outwith* in Scotland means the same as *outside* or *beyond* in England. Dialect maps of such variation can be drawn to show the distribution of different words representing the same meanings.

Differences also occur in grammar: Scottish English *the potatoes need peeled* matches Southern English English *the potatoes need to be peeled*; Yorkshire *thou knowest* parallels Southern English English *you know*; American English *they did it Monday* parallels British English *they did it on Monday*; British English *I didn't like it either* matches Indian English *I didn't like it also*.

When variations according to place are found exclusively in pronunciation we speak of different **accents**; when variations according to region take place simultaneously at the level of sound, vocabulary and grammar we speak of different **dialects**. It is possible, therefore, to speak of a Yorkshire accent if we are referring only to pronunciation, or a Yorkshire dialect if we are referring to all the ways language in Yorkshire varies in relation to other regions. Similarly, we can speak of a 'west of Scotland' accent or dialect, and of a 'south-east of England' accent or dialect.

The issue is complicated, however, by the fact that language also varies according to class (and, to a lesser degree, subculture and profession). In fact, because these variations affect vocabulary and grammar as well as pronunciation, it is possible to speak of class dialects and social dialects as well as accents (see Unit 8: Language and society). The relation between regional dialects and social dialects is variable: sometimes they reinforce one another, sometimes one will override the other. For example, the language of the upper classes in Scotland is likely to have more in common with that of the equivalent social group in England than with that of working-class speakers in Scotland.

Attitudes towards variation

What makes issues of accent and dialect important, both in social interaction and as regards ways of reading, is that attitudes to different varieties are not equivalent. Such attitudes are often based on stereotypical contrasts, such as that between rural and industrial, and rely on our being able to 'place' a language variety accordingly (when this is not possible, and judgement is made simply on the basis of the sound itself, such stereotypical views tend to evaporate). Conventional attitudes towards different language varieties also rely on the notion of a 'standard' pronunciation or grammar which is given more prestige than those which are thought to stray from it and thus become 'non-standard'.

One of the problems with stereotypical views about accent and dialect is that they tend to be insensitive towards actual variations: do all working-class people sound the same? Or all Americans? Or all Scots? Or all Nigerians? Or all English people? The further from a person's own experience someone else's variety is, the less precise intuitions about it – and about the contrasts it enters into with other varieties – are likely to be.

Variety switching: the repertoire available to individual speakers

Although it is clear that language varies according to the regional and social identity of the user, this does not mean that there is always strict consistency in the variety which an individual speaker or writer uses. In different situations, or when talking about different topics, a speaker will automatically modify her or his own language. Speakers shift – in response to subtle changes in situation and relationship – between different areas of the linguistic repertoire available to them. Variations which arise according to *situation of use* rather than according to the *identity of the user*, are known as **registers** (see Unit 6). Speakers who are able to use more than one dialect are able to manipulate them as if they were registers, changing between them at will to achieve specific effects in any given situation (e.g. of appropriacy or marked inappropriacy). This type of shifting is especially common between a regional and a 'standard' variety (for an example of this, see the discussion of *Lady Chatterly's Lover* in Unit 8: Language and society).

VARIATIONS AND VARIETIES OF ENGLISH

Unevenness in attitudes towards varieties of English is partly a consequence of the history of the language. Virtually all languages involve hierarchies between regional varieties, but the detail is different in each case. Variation is created by, and later remains left over from, historical, social and political changes in the society. As we saw in Language and time (Unit 4), the linguistic and social dimensions of language variation are deeply entangled.

History: British Isles

Throughout their history, the British Isles have been host to many different languages, including Gaelic, Welsh, Anglo-Saxon, Latin, Norman French, Punjabi, Chinese, etc. The number of languages in regular use has been reduced at different times by military conquest, by legal and educational suppression and by the emerging prestige of one language or variety as compared with others. During the sixteenth and seventeenth centuries, English spelling was regularized and aspects of the grammar were codified, bringing the question of language standardization itself openly into critical debate. The complexity of the relations between varieties of English in modern times bears the marks of this history, even though present users of the language are generally familiar only with contrasts between current varieties, not the history which brought them into being or determined their status.

History: the English-speaking world

In the English-speaking world beyond Britain, variation within Indian English, American English, Nigerian English and Jamaican English – to take only a few instances – correlates not only with regional differences (and, in cases of bilingualism, with the first languages of the speakers), it also relates to social and educational inequalities between metropolitan and outlying regions, and between industrialized urban classes and rural classes. In many of these societies, the role of English results from an imperial history which imposed English; but processes of decolonization have led to changes in language which give new prestige to regional varieties, so producing standard varieties (such as American English, Indian English) which are nevertheless divergent from British English.

Received pronunciation

As regards accent, the major phase of standardization in British English comes much later than it does in the case of spelling, grammar or punctuation. It is only during the nineteenth century – mainly through the influence of English public-school education and the role of the army-officer corps – that one accent emerges as a non-regional prestige form: 'Received Pronunciation'. This accent, which is itself undergoing changes (and has taken on increasingly negative connotations in the context of the changing social and class structures of the society) is most closely connected with the dialect of English spoken in south-east England ('Educated Southern British English'). In this respect, standardization in speech has followed the pattern established by earlier standardization of the written system (influenced as that was by the location of the royal court and political, legal and commercial institutions).

LANGUAGE VARIETY IN LITERARY TEXTS

Historically, the language in which literary texts might be written in Britain has been a problematic question. Apart from the question of Welsh and Gaelic, it is useful to remember that, before the sixteenth century, Latin and French were serious competitors to English; and in the sixteenth century itself, English was not always thought good enough for literary work (though writing did take place in it). During the period of the late Elizabethans and early Jacobeans, this attitude changed (partly in celebration of existing writing in English, partly because of attitudes towards Latin during the Reformation). Only a century later, English was widely believed to have an especially eminent literature. Many of the arguments about which language to write in, in many parts of the world today, have analogues in the circumstances of English in Britain during the later medieval and early Renaissance period.

Dialect representation

In the history of literary writing in English, there have been clear but shifting constraints on which variety or varieties might be used and how. A criterion of decorum was often appealed to as a standard of appropriate style in a **genre** (see Unit 17), so excluding a wide range of voices from serious literary writing. Within such constraints, dialect speakers were often represented as comic characters (or vice versa), and jokes made at their expense.

An additional problem with the representation of regional voices in written texts is that accent and dialect are primarily features of speech rather than writing. Rather than reproducing the way people actually speak, the representation of speech in writing draws on a set of conventions which produce the *illusion* of speech (see Unit 21: Speech and writing). The representation of dialect speech in writing draws on a further set of conventions, such as non-standard spellings, which are meant to signal that a character's speech is different from that of other characters in the text.

The difference in the way 'standard' and 'non-standard' voices are represented in texts tends to set up a hierarchy of voices. In the nineteenth-century novel, for example, the narrator and the central characters will usually use 'standard' English, while regional or working-class characters will speak with an accent or in a dialect. This raises the question of whether the non-standard speech is used in order to reproduce the way such people actually spoke in the place where the novel is set, or whether it is used simply to give an aura of authenticity or to establish a difference of class or moral authority (see Unit 8: Language and society).

In the novels of Thomas Hardy, for example, the construction of a sense of place is central. Hardy's novels are set in 'Wessex' – his fictional name for the south-west of England – and are peopled with rural characters who speak in west-country dialect. Within this setting, Hardy typically explores the fate and fortunes of middle-class characters whose speech is more standard than that of the rural characters. *The Mayor of Casterbridge* (1886) centres on the rise and fall of Michael Henchard (from destitute rural worker, to mayor, and back to destitution). In the following scene, Henchard chastises one of the workers on his farm for being late in the mornings:

> Then Henchard ... declared with an oath that this was the last time; that if he were behind once more, by God, he would come and drag him out o' bed.
>
> 'There is sommit wrong in my make, your worshipful!' said Abel, '... I never enjoy my bed at all, for no sooner do I lie down that I be asleep, and afore I be awake I be up. I've fretted my gizzard green about it, maister, but what can I do? ...'
>
> 'I don't want to hear it!' roared Henchard. 'To-morrow the waggons must start at four, and if you're not here, stand clear. I'll mortify thy flesh for thee!'

The worker's dialect is rendered here through non-standard spelling ('maister'), non-standard grammar ('no sooner do I lie down that I be asleep'), and dialect phrases ('I've fretted my gizzard'). But of more interest here is that Henchard, in his anger, 'lapses' into dialect (and/or biblical language) in a way that reminds us of his origins (*thee* and *thy* remain in use in dialects long after their disappearance from standard English). The narrative voice reinforces this by introducing Henchard's first comments in standard English using **indirect speech** ('Henchard declared with an oath that this was the last time') and then switching into **free indirect speech** in order to let Henchard's own, non-standard speech come through: 'by God, he would come and drag him out o' bed' (for a discussion of 'indirect' and 'free indirect speech' see Unit 21: Speech and writing).

Modernist polyphony

In modernist writing, a wider range of voices is sometimes presented. Often this takes the form of variety switching (as in James Joyce's *Ulysses* (1922) or juxtaposition (as in T.S. Eliot's *The Waste Land* (1922)). But the question arises of whether these texts introduce representation (or mimicry) of regional and class voices as a new kind of polyphony (in which each voice is equal), or simply as a range of voices to be finally subordinated to, or refined or distilled into, an authoritative standard voice of the narrator (for a discussion of this issue in *Ulysses*, see Unit 6: Language and context: register, and Unit 15: Juxtaposition).

What seems significant in experimental writing of this sort is that regional varieties are often used as much to create a contrast between standard and non-standard as for their own qualities. Only in forms of dialect writing linked to an expressed sense of regional identity (as in much contemporary Scottish writing) does dialect function less in terms of contrast with the established standard than in order to affirm a distinct regional idiom.

Dialect and accent in media

Film and television have inherited, and helped maintain, the legacy of associating character stereotypes with particular accents or dialects. The simple fact of mass exposure in media, however, can alter the standing of entire dialects and accents. Soundtracks of Hollywood films in the 1930s, for instance, were sometimes thought incomprehensible in Britain – a fact hardly believable now. US radio announcers imitated *British* accents until around 1930, before the conventions of what has come to be called 'network standard' were established. It is only more recently, most obviously in contemporary pop music, that the direction of transatlantic influence has been reversed (though many pop songs are sung in a 'mid-Atlantic' voice). As regards British dialects and accents, exposure in radio and television to regional and class varieties is still increasing, largely as a consequence of reduced use of – and changing public attitudes towards – Received Pronunciation (the 'BBC accent'). This has no doubt already had a significant effect on accent connotations and stereotypes. Despite this trend, however, news broadcasting is almost invariably presented by speakers who approximate to Received Pronunciation – even on regional television.

Accents, dialects and the future

Given the increasing pervasiveness of media, some critics argue that distinctions created by accent are likely to be minimized – and may even disappear – following increased exposure to a wide range of class and regional voices in radio and television. It seems more likely, however, that while accents may *alter* in relative prestige and connotation, taking on new and different meanings as a result of changes in the images of self and class to which people aspire, contrasts between accents will retain functional importance of one kind or another. The network of attitudes towards accent and dialect in societies at large will almost certainly continue to be reflected, – as well as challenged in some kinds of dramatic work, comedy and satire – in media programming.

WRITING IN ENGLISH

In many postcolonial societies whose current use of English is a legacy of British imperialism, the idea of using English at all in creative writing is contentious. Some writers, such as the Kenyan novelist and dramatist Ngugi wa Thiong'o, argue that using the former colonial language reinforces the power of emerging neocolonial elites at the expense of developing a self-confident and emancipated local or national literature. Building local reader-ships, in this view, is thought more valuable than representing African social experience to a predominantly non-African audience spread around the English-using world. Other writers have argued, on the other hand, that the linking function of a language like English enables different communities (including different African communities) to become more aware of each other. In this view, using English opens up new possibilities for redefining the relations between African communities in a way which would be impossible if they remained separated by walls of linguistic incomprehensibility.

Traditions of writing in English which use and affirm a value for dialect voices – as in much writing in India, Anglophone Africa, the Philippines, the West Indies and many other places – engage in different ways with these complex issues. New notions of self-expression are defined, and new techniques for representing places and ways of life are devised. In some cases, arguments for using dialect are formulated in terms of an idea of authenticity, or aspiration to present an accurate or true representation of the writer's own identity. In other cases, dialect is viewed more as a kind of anti-language, or mode of expression deliberately adopted to mark it off from other, dominant traditions of writing that are implicitly being rejected. In both cases, texts using such varieties – like any text – are viewed differently when they are read by readers in different places.

In Britain, dialect writing – and writing which mixes across the range of varieties which make up the linguistic experience of virtually all members of the population – challenges established ideas that it is only standard forms of the language which are appropriate to serious creative work. The regional, class and ethnic diversity of the British population ensures that there are many quite different experiences of place, and changing and unpredictable connections between voice, region and sense of identity. Reading off a sense of place from a represented accent or dialect rarely involves a simple act of locating the writer. Instead, it involves engaging with a set of relationships between the variety represented, conventional attitudes towards that variety, the reader's own attitudes and variety and the way the variety is used to either reinforce or disrupt conventional treatments of the subject matter it represents.

ACTIVITY

It is possible to argue that although dialects are *associated with* place (among other things), they do not actually *represent* place. After all, people move from place to place, and take their dialect with them; so even though a dialect may evoke a place for a listener or reader, it is more a characteristic of the speaker or writer than of the fixed place itself. You are asked to explore this issue in this activity.

The following two passages are from poems representing aspects of

Indian life. One describes in detail a scene or 'setting'; the other focuses on how language may represent – and also misrepresent – 'Indianness'.

Passage 1

> The painted streets alive with hum of noon,
> The traders cross-legged 'mid their spice and grain,
> The buyers with their money in the cloth,
> The war of words to cheapen this or that,
> The shout to clear the road, the huge stone wheels,
> The strong slow oxen at their rustling loads,
> The singing bearers with the palanquins,
> The broad-necked hamals sweating in the sun,
> The housewives bearing water from the well
> With balanced chatties, and athwart their hips
> The black-eyed babies; the fly-swarmed sweetmeat shops,
> The weaver at his loom, the cotton-bow
> Twanging, the millstones grinding meal, the dogs
> Prowling for orts, the skilful armourer
> With tong and hammer linking shirts of mail,
> The blacksmith with a mattock and a spear
> Reddening together in his coals, the school
> Where round their Guru, in a grave half-moon,
> The Sakya children sang the mantras through,
> And learned the greater and the lesser gods.
>
> (from *The Light of Asia*, by Sir Edwin Arnold (1832–1904))

Passage 2

> I am Indian, very brown, born in
> Malabar, I speak three languages, write in
> Two, dream in one. Don't write in English, they said,
> English is not your mother-tongue. Why not leave
> Me alone, critics, friends, visiting cousins,
> Everyone of You? Why not let me speak in
> Any language I like? The language I speak
> Becomes mine, its distortions, its queernesses
> All mine, mine alone. It is half English, half
> Indian, funny perhaps, but it is honest,
> It is as human as I am human, don't
> You see? It voices my joys, my longings, my
> Hopes, and it is as useful to me as cawing
> Is to crows, or roaring to the lions, it
> Is human speech, the speech of the mind that is
> Here and not there . . .
>
> (from *An Introduction*, by Kamala Das, *Collected Poems* vol. 1 1984)

1 For each passage, make a list of words and/or grammatical constructions which are not part of your own dialect. In the case of individual words outside your own dialect, do you know what they mean or refer to? Are such words associated with any particular place or way of life? Which passage contains more of this type of locally specific vocabulary (i.e. which of your lists contains more words that are not part of your own dialect)?

2 Do the two passages give equal attention to difficulties about using language as a resource for establishing either a sense of place or a sense of belonging to a place? If not, which focuses on this issue more? In the light of your answers to 1, does this answer in 2 surprise you? If so, why? If not, why not?

3 How important is it in representing experience or life in a place to consider the particular variety of the language used in the description (e.g. in terms of the relative social prestige and authority of the variety, or in terms of how appropriate it is to the place being described)?

4 Sir Edwin Arnold was a nineteenth-century British orientalist scholar and Kamala Das is a twentieth-century Indian writer. How might their different origins (geographical, historical) affect their relationship to India? Are these differences revealed in the differences between the poems?

READING

Kachru (1982) *The Other Tongue: English across Cultures.*
Leith (1983) *A Social History of English.*
McCrum, Cran and McNeil (1986) *The Story of English.*
Montgomery (1986) *Introduction to Language and Society*, pp. 61–92.
Strang (1970) *A History of English.*
Thiong'o (1986) *Decolonising the Mind.*

Unit 6   Language and context: register

The term 'register' is used by linguists to describe the fact that the kind of language we use is affected by the context in which we use it, to such an extent that certain kinds of language usage become conventionally associated with particular situations. Our tacit knowledge of such conventions of usage enables us to judge whether what someone says or writes is 'appropriate' to its context. This is highlighted by our reactions when a text deviates from its appropriate register – as happens towards the end of the following announcement by a British Rail guard:

> May I have your attention please, ladies and gentlemen. The train is now approaching Lancaster. Passengers for the Liverpool boat train should alight here and cross to platform one. Delays are being experienced on this train and passengers intending to use this service should consult the notice board on platform one *to find out what the score is.*

The comic effect of this arises basically through a sudden (and presumably unintentional) switch of register (in the last italicized phrase). For the most part the announcement is typical of the formal language we have come to associate with British Rail announcements, though we may feel that it is a little too 'high-flown' for what is, after all, only information about trains and platforms. The unintended humour arises when the announcer **juxtaposes** (see Unit 15) the formal opening of the announcement with the much less formal conclusion ('to find out what the score is') and thereby comically undercuts what has gone before.

The most obvious way in which a text 'registers' the effect of its context is in the selection of vocabulary. Our experience of language in context allows us to recognize that vocabulary items such as 'alight' and 'consult' are characteristic of the professional idiom which British Rail has selected for communicating to the public, and we are equally sensitive to the fact that 'to find out what the score is' does not belong to that idiom. But differences in register involve differences in grammar as well as in vocabulary. For example, in the phrase 'Delays are being experienced', the use of the impersonal passive construction contributes as much as the vocabulary choice to the formality of the British Rail register.

Each of us experiences a wide variety of contexts or language situations every day and from moment to moment: speaking in a tutorial, talking on the phone to a bank manager, chatting to friends in a coffee bar, writing a letter. In response to these contexts, each of us switches from one register to another without effort and we are able to recognize when others do the same. By the same token, as we have seen in the British Rail example, we are all sensitive to **deviation** (see Unit 12) in register.

CONTEXTS WHICH AFFECT REGISTER

It is possible to isolate three different aspects of any context or situation which will affect the register of a text:

1   the mode or medium of communication (e.g. whether the language is spoken or written);
2   the social relationships of participants in the situation (which determines the tone);
3   the purpose for which, or the field in which, the language is being employed.

The mode (or medium)

The register of a text is partly constituted by the mode (i.e. the medium or the channel) which is adopted for communication. The most obvious distinction here is between **speech** and **writing** (see Unit 21). Speech is usually made up on the spot and interpreted as it is heard. Writing, on the other hand, may involve long periods of composition and revision and the resultant text may be read and reread at leisure in circumstances quite remote – both in time and place – from that in which it was written. Written texts, therefore, tend to be more formal than spoken texts, which, by contrast, tend to be looser and more provisional in their structure and to feel less formal. In public settings, of course, spoken texts may be carefully prepared in advance and may take on the formal characteristics of the written mode. The British Rail announcement begins in this fashion before slipping into something much closer to everyday speech.

Tone

A second aspect of the context which affects register relates to the social roles which are prescribed for, or adopted by, participants in the communication situation. Differences in the text will result from whether the relationships between participants are informal or formal, familiar or polite, personal or impersonal. Thus, the **tone** of the text can indicate the attitude or position adopted by the writer or speaker towards the reader or listener (see Unit 23: Positioning the reader or spectator). In the British Rail announcement, for example, 'ladies and gentlemen' constitutes a marker of social distance signalling politeness; the intricate syntax, together with words such as 'attention', 'approaching' and 'alight', signals formality; and the passive voice (avoiding reference to human agency – as in 'delays are being experienced') are all features of the impersonal register. The suggestion that passengers should 'find out what the score is', on the other hand, assumes a much more informal and familiar relation between speaker and addressee – one which seems to clash with the context which has been previously set up.

Field, role, or purpose

A third aspect of the context which affects register is the role of the communication – the purpose it is used for, the function it performs or the field in which it participates. Language can be used for a variety of different purposes (to convey information, to express feelings, to cajole, to seduce, to pray, to produce aesthetic effects, to intimidate, etc.), each of which will leave its mark on what is said and the way it is said. In addition, a wide range of human activities have developed their own characteristic registers because they employ 'field-specific' vocabularies. The legal profession, the scientific community, the culinary arts, religious institutions, academic disciplines, advertising, football commentary (and the list could be extended almost indefinitely) all employ terms which are particular to themselves, the use of which thereby invokes particular situations.

THE SOCIAL DISTRIBUTION OF REGISTERS

It is important to remember that each of us is able to control the appropriate register for a wide variety of contexts and has, in addition, a passive familiarity with a range of others (e.g. of advertising, of income-tax returns, of legal documents) which we are rarely called upon to use actively (see Leech 1969). But the range of registers we feel comfortable with (both actively and passively) will be affected by a number of factors, including our age, social background, education, gender, race and work status. Register positions, or can be used to position, the participants of a dialogue differently according to who those participants are. Thus the conventional distinction between register and dialect as that between *language according to use* and *language according to user* (see Unit 5: Language and place) seems to break down when considering how the relative social roles in any communication situation govern, or are governed by, the register adopted. The registers we become familiar with and learn how to manipulate in higher education, for example, might well be alienating to those who have not had access to them. (In fact, one of the purposes of any degree course is to familiarize the student with the special register of the discipline being studied. In the study of literature, students are generally required to write essays in a formal and impersonal register which includes the use of a specialized critical vocabulary and excludes words and phrases which they might be accustomed to using in other contexts.)

Although linguistic usages usually change with time (see Unit 4: Language and time), some historical periods, societies or professions try to preserve the 'purity' of particular registers and maintain rigorous hierarchical distinctions between registers. In the late twentieth century it is possible to see how institutions such as the Church and the law have been relatively successful in maintaining their field-specific registers virtually unchanged across the centuries. Consider, for example, the following extract from a legal notice printed in the *Glasgow Herald*:

> Notice is Hereby Given, That ... the sheriff at Campbelltown, by Interlocutor dated 30th December, 1986, ordered all parties desirous to lodge Answers in the hands of the Sheriff Clerk at Castlehill, Campbelltown within 8 days after intimation, advertisement or service, and in the meantime, until the prayer of the Petition had been granted or refused, nominated Alistair White to be Provisional Liquidator of the said Company on his finding caution before extract.

From this example, we can see that the legal register is relatively opaque to the non-specialist. It is possible to offer different reasons why this should be so: one response might be to say that the legal profession maintains its register in order to intimidate the general public and so forces us to employ lawyers and solicitors to represent us in legal matters; another response might argue that such intricate and highly specific language is necessary in order to prevent potentially costly or crucial ambiguities (see the discussion of archaism in the legal register in Unit 4: Language and time).

Leaving these questions aside, however, a brief analysis of some of the features of the legal register that are displayed in this text can serve as a model for the way we might analyse any register:

Vocabulary: The most obvious feature of this text is its field-specific vocabulary, indicated by phrases such as 'Provisional Liquidator' and 'finding caution before extract'. There are also archaisms ('desirous'), and highly Latinate vocabulary ('Interlocutor', 'intimation', 'petition', 'nominated', 'provisional', 'caution', 'extract').

Grammar: Grammatical construction makes an equal contribution to this register (and to its opacity): remarkably, the complete notice is made up of a single complex sentence with an array of subordinate clauses whose interrelations with each other are acutely difficult to follow.

Typography (the appearance of the printing): Archaic typography is also a feature of this register, since it makes extensive use of capitalization for words which are no longer capitalized in modern English.

Institutions which seek to preserve their particular registers in this way and to isolate them from the linguistic changes taking place in the society surrounding them may be said to employ 'conservative' registers. Compared with these, areas such as advertising, journalism, pop music and television have more 'open' or 'liberal' registers which change frequently and continually borrow from each other and from the 'conservative' registers which surround them.

LITERATURE AND REGISTER

Looking at the history of literature, it seems that literature has sometimes maintained a conservative register and sometimes a liberal one. Interestingly, the shifts between liberal and conservative registers seem to parallel shifts in society and in the place literature has in society (roughly indicated by whether poets think poetry is a way of preserving the language or of rejuvenating it). In the eighteenth century, for example – an age dominated by reason, politeness and rigid social distinctions – literature was governed, for the most part, by notions of decorum; its language is educated, polite, upper middle class. Its assumptions about what kind of language is appropriate to literature are best summed up by Alexander Pope in 1711: 'Expression is the dress of thought, and still / Appears more decent, as more suitable' (*An Essay on Criticism*, II, 318–19). But at the end of the eighteenth century, when ideas of democracy and revolution began to challenge the stabilities of the neoclassical period, there was a parallel revolution in the register thought appropriate to literature. In the 'Preface to *Lyrical Ballads*' (1800), Wordsworth explains that *Lyrical Ballads* 'was published as an experiment ... to ascertain, how far ... a selection of the real language of men in a state of vivid sensation' might be a suitable language for poetry, and he indicates that the language 'of low and rustic life' – suitably adopted and 'purified' – was chosen because 'such men ... convey their feelings and notions in simple and unelaborated expressions'. Romanticism can therefore be seen as a movement which attempts to change the register considered appropriate to poetry and so participates in a struggle over literature's role in society (raising questions such as whether it should be the preserve of an elite or be as widely available and accessible as possible).

In the twentieth century literature has become particularly open to other registers. James Joyce's *Ulysses* (1922) epitomizes this openness; its pages often seem like a rag-bag of odds and ends taken from a huge variety of different and usually incongruous registers. But although, as we might expect, this mixing of registers is often used for comic effect, it also seems to have more far-reaching implications. In the following paragraph, for example, one of the central characters of the novel, Leopold Bloom, has invited the other main male character, Stephen Dedalus, back to his house for tea after a bizarre night on the town; it is late, and Bloom has to move carefully in order not to wake his wife sleeping upstairs. The places where the register changes we have numbered and marked with an oblique stroke:

[1] What did Bloom do?/

[2] He . . . drew two spoonseat deal chairs to the hearthstone, one for Stephen with its back to the area window, the other for himself when necessary,/ [3] knelt on one knee, composed in the grate a pyre/ [4] of crosslaid resintipped sticks and various coloured papers and irregular polygons/ [5] of best Abram coal at twenty one shillings a ton from the yard of Messrs Flower and M'Donald of 14 D'Olier street,/ [6] kindled it at three projecting points of paper with one ignited lucifer match,/ [7] thereby releasing the potential energy contained in the fuel by allowing its carbon and hydrogen elements to enter into free union with the oxygen of the air./

[8] Of what similar apparitions did Stephen think?

In order to identify the various registers here, we need to imagine the context in which each one would *usually* occur. Tentative names for these registers are given in Table 6.1, together with the textual features which provide evidence for such decisions.

According to the above analysis, this short passage contains six different registers. Part of its comedy depends upon our sensitivity to a number of clashes between language and context – for example, the incongruity of describing the act of lighting a fire in a terraced house in Dublin in the early part of the twentieth century in various registers (the religious, the technical, the scientific) which seem too 'elevated' or too precise for this humble action. But note that each of these registers would be appropriate for describing the lighting of a fire *in a different context* (e.g. in a religious

Table 6.1 Identifying registers in an extract from *Ulysses*

Portion of text	Provisional name	Usual context	Textual evidence (vocabulary, grammar, etc.)
1	catechism	Christian teaching	question and answer
2	descriptive prose	realist novel	use of simple past tense ('He . . . drew')
3	religious	description of ceremony	'knelt', 'pyre'
4	technical description	report	'irregular polygons'
5	language of commerce	advertisement	'best Abram coal'
6	technical description	as 4	'ignited lucifer match'
7	scientific description	textbook or journal	'potential energy' 'carbon and hydrogen'
8	catechism	as 1	as 1

ceremony or in a scientific experiment). A second context to be considered is that of the novel genre itself: in a realist novel (see Unit 22: Realism) we would expect the scene to be narrated in register 2 rather than in registers 3–6. Furthermore, we do not expect a novel to be narrated in a series of questions and answers (as this whole chapter is) – this procedure is, in fact, more appropriate to religious instruction by catechism in the Christian church.

The mixing of registers in this passage not only produces comic effects but raises a series of unsettling speculations. The description of this commonplace action in the religious register seems to invite us to recall the spiritual significance of fire, while the scientific register forces us to remember that fire is a process of chemical transformation. Thus we could argue that these incongruous registers **defamiliarize** a process which has become so familiar that we hardly think about it any more. Conversely, it could be argued that the 'conservative' registers of the Church and science are being undermined in so far as they are shown to employ 'pretentious' terminology to describe the most commonplace of events (the interweaving of the commercial register perhaps adds to this by undercutting the religious and technical registers which precede it). The passage is unsettling, however, in that it gives us no clues about which of these readings is 'correct'. Hence it becomes impossible to decide whether the 'elevated' registers are meant to have more authority than the 'low' register of commerce or vice versa. This is partly because the text seems to abdicate the authority which realist texts usually maintain through a clearly defined narrative voice. The register of descriptive prose (2) is simply one register among others in this passage, without any special authority. And although the narrative is presented through a technique reminiscent of the Christian catechism, the mixing of registers undercuts the potential authority of both question and answer. By undermining or rejecting the register thought appropriate for narrating novels, *Ulysses* can be interpreted either as attempting to rejuvenate the novel genre, or as rejecting the genre's claims to be a special or elevated discourse (see the discussion of Flann O'Brien in Unit 14: Irony).

Ulysses and T.S. Eliot's *The Waste Land* (both published in 1922) are two of the best examples of the way twentieth-century literature exploits the range of potential effects of register mixing. But we should be wary of suggesting that playing with or exploiting the possibilities generated by register is peculiar to twentieth-century literature. In fact, it could be argued that the recycling and mixing of registers is central to the literary process and its effects in general. One simple but revealing example of this is that parody is a genre which depends upon the notion that certain kinds of language are conventionally associated with particular genres and themes (see Unit 17: Genre). Alexander Pope, who was cited above as arguing that poetic language should be 'suitable', can also exploit the possibilities set up by this notion in order to produce comic irony; in *The Rape of the Lock* (1712/14), the humorous effect depends precisely upon the reader's familiarity with the register used in epic poetry and consequent ability to recognize the mismatch between Pope's use of this 'high' register and the 'low' subject matter of the poem (for a brief analysis of this, see Unit 16: Intertextuality and allusion). In just the same way, a novel such as *Ulysses* depends upon the notion of appropriateness built into the fact of register in order to achieve its effect – whether this be to challenge established ideas about literature, or make a joke, or both.

We might summarize this discussion by making a number of general observations about the way literature draws upon the possibilities opened up by register:

1   Literature seems continually to renew or change its register by borrowing from other registers or by recycling the registers of previous literature.
2   Through unusual juxtaposition, parody, irony and so on, it can draw attention to the notion of register by foregrounding the features of particular registers.
3   In this way, literature can show how arbitrary and often absurd certain registers can be.
4   By being so open to the registers which surround it, literature seems to challenge the strict distinctions maintained by conservative registers and seems ultimately to question the idea that literature itself is a privileged or special discourse.

ACTIVITY

Read the following poem several times:

One perfect rose
A single flow'r he sent me, since we met.
   All tenderly his messenger he chose;
Deep-hearted, pure, with scented dew still wet –
   One perfect rose.

I knew the language of the floweret;
   'My fragile leaves', it said, 'his heart enclose'.
Love long has taken for his amulet
   One perfect rose.

Why is it no one ever sent me yet
   One perfect limousine, do you suppose?
Ah no, it's always just my luck to get
   One perfect rose.

(Dorothy Parker, 1926)

1 Mark any changes of register in the poem, showing where each register begins and ends.

2 Do you think the poem makes any **allusions** to other poems (see Unit 16)?

3 Think of a name for each register which describes its *usual* context.

4 For each register identify as many features of the language as you can (e.g. spelling, vocabulary, grammar) which make it characteristic of the register you have identified.

5 Using this evidence, try to identify the tone of the poem (e.g. the attitude of the speaker towards the rose or the man who sent it).

6 What is the effect or purpose of employing or juxtaposing these registers in this poem?

READING

*Gregory and Carroll (1978) *Language and Situation.*
Halliday (1978) *Language as Social Semiotic.*
Halliday, McIntosh and Strevins (1964) *The Linguistic Sciences and Language Teaching.*
*Leech (1969) *Linguistic Guide to English Poetry,* pp. 9–12, 49–51.
Montgomery (1986) *An Introduction to Language and Society,* Ch. 6.

Unit 7   Language and gender

That language plays an important role in shaping the social scene and constructing social identities can be seen particularly in the area of gender – the socially constructed differences of behaviour and belief considered appropriate to the two sexes. For many of us, most of the time, language seems just a neutral tool for expressing ideas and conveying information. In the domain of gender, however, as in other important areas of social life, careful analysis can reveal that language operates sometimes to disguise distinctions, sometimes to reinforce them and sometimes actively to produce them.

MALE AS THE NORM

English, for instance, has a curious way of handling reference to human beings in general: it treats them as if they were all male. This happens partly through the operation of the noun *man*, when it is used generically to stand for the species, but also through the use of *he* as a generic pronoun (generic means general rather than specific – the generic *he* is therefore supposed to include females as well as males). But, as Rosalind Coward and Maria Black (1990) have pointed out, if generic *man* is genuinely inclusive then both of the following sentences should sound equally odd:

(1)   Man's vital interests are food, shelter and access to females.
(2)   Man, unlike other mammals, has difficulties in giving birth.

In practice, however, sentences like (1) are more likely to be produced and accepted unreflectingly than sentences like (2). Even when operating generically, therefore, words such as *he* and *man* carry their masculine connotations with them. This tendency also operates at more restricted levels of reference, when generic *he* is not intended to refer to the human species as a whole but to some non-gender-specific group within it; for example, in the following:

(3)   When the police officer has completed his investigation, he files a report.

(4) The modern reader may at first feel baffled by the overpunctuation, as it will feel to him that there are too many commas.

The conventions of usage of the generic pronoun say that we should understand the use of *he* and *his* in (3) as referring to all police officers (that is, including female officers). Similarly, in (4) the conventions of usage suggest that both male and female readers are being included in the reference. However, research has revealed that readers of sentences containing generic pronouns often do not read them as having general reference, but in fact read them as referring strictly to males. Kidd (1971), for instance, has demonstrated that when students are asked to visualize the referent of a generic pronoun, they almost invariably draw a male referent, even when the intended referent seems at first sight to be general.

A similar process may be seen at work in the following caption from an advertisement for Lufthansa: 'What does today's business traveller expect of his airline?' Most people would read 'his' as having generic reference here, since it follows a generic noun 'business traveller'. But the picture which accompanies this advertisement makes it clear that the reference is only to males, since it shows a plane full of male business travellers relaxing on board an aeroplane, the only female on board being the steward who is serving them drinks. Thus, so-called generic nouns and pronouns are quite commonly not truly generic in practice; apparently non-gender-specific, they often turn out to be referring actually to males. As a consequence of this, feminists such as Spender (1979) have argued that general categories of persons, and indeed of the human species, are often constructed through the language in male terms. This process serves to make women less visible in social and cultural activity; the use, for instance, of the generic *he* in (3), or in the advertisement, serves to erase the fact that there are women who work as police officers, or who travel on business.

In some ways generic nouns (such as *business travellers*) which masquerade as non-gender-specific terms are more insidious than the generic pronoun, *he*. This is partly because there are so many of them, and partly because – unlike *he* – they do not give any explicit signals that they might be excluding women. Because of this they become powerful ways of carving up social reality in implicitly masculine ways without announcing that they are doing so. Cameron (1985), for instance, shows that even expressions such as *astronaut, firefighter, lecturer, shop assistant, scientist* and so on, disguise a tendency to refer only to men – despite their apparently neutral generic potential. Cameron cites two newspaper reports:

(5) The lack of vitality is aggravated by the fact that there are so few able-bodied young adults about. They have all gone off to work or look for work, leaving behind the old, the disabled, the women and the children.
(*The Sunday Times*)

(6) A coloured South African who was subjected to racial abuse by his

neighbours went berserk with a machete and killed his next-door neighbour's wife, Birmingham Crown Court heard yesterday.

(*Guardian*)

In example (5), the generic expression is 'able-bodied young adults', yet it is
clear from the rest of the sentence that what is really meant is 'able-bodied
young men', since women are subsequently excluded from its reference.
In example (6) the generic expression is 'next-door neighbour', since
this word ostensibly means both male and female neighbours, and yet
it is clear that when it is used to refer to women it needs to be modified to
form 'neighbour's wife'. Thus, *neighbour*, rather than being a generic in this
context, is in fact only referring to male neighbours. In the following headline from *The Observer*, 'Top people told: Take a mistress', it is significant
that a generic is used ('top people'), only to reveal that in fact it refers solely
to males, since 'mistresses' are not normally 'taken' by women.

Thus generic nouns, like generic pronouns, can be ambiguous – for
example, in the following sentence:

(7) The more education an individual attains the better his occupation is
   likely to be.

It is unclear here whether the 'individual' is supposed to be a man or
whether this is indeed a generic use (this is not cleared up by 'his' – which
may also be generic). Because the reference of generic nouns and pronouns
is ambiguous and because they serve to make women seem invisible, feminists such as Dale Spender (1979) and Casey Miller and Kate Swift (1979)
have objected to their use. Since the 1970s, some writers have begun to
avoid using generic *he* entirely, since it can alienate readers and listeners.
The *he* can be avoided by using the passivized form – as in the following:

(8) When a police officer has finished an investigation, a report should be
   filed.

Or the *he* can be avoided by using the plural *they*:

(9) When police officers have finished their investigation, they should file a
   report.

In these sentences, it is clear that the reference is truly generic. But it is also
possible to signal more positively that there may be female as well as male
police officers:

(10) When the police officer has finished the investigation, he or she should
   file a report.

FEMALE AS DOWNGRADED OR DEROGATED

There are a range of words which are used solely for males or females and
are therefore **gender-specific**. So, for example, the word *poetess* is only used

for women, and the word *courtier* is usually only used for men. Analysis reveals that there are significant patterns in the use of gender-specific language, in that pairs of gender-specific nouns are not symmetrical; instead, they tend to downgrade (or derogate) women by treating them as if they were only sexual objects rather than full human beings. This emerges in the following sets of pairs: *master/mistress, courtier/courtesan, host/hostess, king/queen*. Most of the terms on the male side have positive connotations, whereas the female equivalents often have negative sexual connotations. There is a further asymmetry in the way that women are often referred to as *girls*. In the following advertisement from the *Guardian, girl* is used as if it were the female equivalent of *man*, whereas *girl* in fact refers to female children rather than adults:

> EFL TEACHERS: required first week in February. Girl with driving licence for Italy; Man with experience and girl with degree in German for Germany. Tel: 071 . . .

This usage is also common in sports commentaries, where adult women athletes are often described as *girls* (or as *ladies*).

Jane Mills (1989) has noted that there are many more words to refer to women in sexual terms than there are for men. For example, even the words *laundress* and *nun* have been used at some stage to refer to a woman who is suspected of being a prostitute. In a similar way, insult terms for women are greater in number than insult words for men, and they tend to be concerned with women's sexuality. Women's marital status is also signalled by the use of the terms *Mrs* and *Miss*, for which there are no current male equivalents (*Mr* does not indicate whether a man is married or single). To resist this the term *Ms* was introduced and has become much more general in recent years, despite a great deal of opposition, although it is still largely restricted to younger women. Analysis also reveals a covert asymmetry in the way that women are referred to in tabloid newspapers, where they are frequently identified by their marital or family status (wife, mother, grandmother) rather than by their profession. This is clear in a headline from the *Daily Star*: 'MAD GUNMAN HUNT AS WIFE IS SHOT'. It is also quite common in tabloid newspapers for women to be described in terms of their physical appearance (hair colour, body shape and so on) whereas men are usually described with reference to their jobs and age.

THE POTENTIAL FOR REFORM

Some feminists, such as Dale Spender (1979), see such asymmetries in language as demeaning to women and urge that language should be reformed accordingly; others, such as Deborah Cameron (1985), argue that sexism is so deep-rooted within the language that it is impossible to change it by reforming individual language items. (See also Unit 4: Language and time.)

WOMEN'S SPEECH

Much early feminist research in sociolinguistics was concerned with investigating whether women speak differently from men. Robin Lakoff (1975), for example, claimed that women choose different words than men do (e.g. *pretty* and *cute*) and different sentence structures (e.g. tag questions: *This is hard to understand, isn't it?*). She characterizes women's language as being prone to hesitation, and as being repetitive and disjointed. This sociolinguistic work has now been questioned, since it is clear that women are not a unified grouping: there are many hierarchies within the grouping 'women', such as difference of class, race, economic power, education and so on, with the consequence that women speak in very different ways. The speech patterns of the Queen or of former Prime Minister, Margaret Thatcher, bear greater similarities to the speech of males in similar positions of power than they do, say, to working-class women's speech.

However, there are certain elements of speech which we can classify as stereotypically 'feminine': that is, those elements which signify lack of confidence or assertiveness. These may be drawn on by both women and men in certain situations, particularly within the public sphere. O'Barr and Atkins (1982) have shown that within a courtroom setting both men and women from low-income groups are likely to adopt what they term 'powerless speech'; that is speech which bears a strong resemblance to Lakoff's definition of women's speech; hesitant, repetitive, disjointed and so on. Thus it is probable that when discussing 'women's speech', theorists have been describing 'powerless speech' (see also Unit 8: Language and society).

THE FEMALE SENTENCE: A WOMAN'S WRITING?

Work on female speech has been echoed by work on women's writing, as many theorists claim that women's writing is qualitatively different from men's writing. For example, Virginia Woolf (1979) proposed that Dorothy Richardson's work had developed a new structure, which Woolf termed 'a woman's sentence'. Woolf did not describe in detail what this 'psychological sentence of the feminine gender' consisted of, but if we compare the two extracts below by Anita Brookner and Malcolm Lowry, it seems quite easy to argue that Brookner is using a 'feminine' style whilst Lowry is using a 'masculine' style:

> From the window all that could be seen was a receding area of grey. It was to be supposed that beyond the grey garden, which seemed to sprout nothing but the stiffish leaves of some unfamiliar plant, lay the vast grey lake, spreading like an anaesthetic towards the invisible further shore, and beyond that, in imagination only, yet verified by the brochure, the peak of the Dent d'Oche, on which snow might already be slightly and silently falling.

> (Anita Brookner, *Hotel du Lac* (1984))

Two mountain chains traverse the republic roughly from north to south, forming between them a number of valleys and plateaux. Overlooking one of these valleys, which is dominated by two volcanoes, lies, six thousand feet above sea-level, the town of Quauhnahuac. It is situated well south of the Tropic of Cancer, to be exact on the nineteenth parallel, in about the same latitude as the Revillagigedo Islands to the west in the Pacific, or very much farther west, the southernmost tip of Hawaii – and as the port of Tzucox to the east on the S. Atlantic seaboard of Yucatan near the border of British Honduras, or very much farther east, the town of Juggernaut, in India, on the Bay of Bengal.

(Malcolm Lowry, *Under the Volcano* (1967))

The Brookner passage describes the landscape from a particular point of view, that is, as seen from a character's perspective rather than from an omniscient narrator's standpoint. The personalized account consists of descriptions of colours and the effect these colours have on the character. There seems to be a certain vagueness about the description; instead of facts, this account is concerned with what 'was supposed to be', what 'seemed' and what 'might be' happening. This modification or tentativeness is conventionally said to characterize a feminine style. In contrast, the Lowry passage seems far more distanced and at the same time precise; the information emanates not from an identifiable character but from a seemingly objective, omniscient narrator. In fact, the style used is reminiscent of the **register** (see Unit 6) of guidebooks or of geographical descriptions.

For many readers, these two passages may seem to characterize a feminine and masculine style respectively: one a personalized style, describing in detail relationships and the actions of characters; and the other more concerned with factual descriptions of the world. However, it is clear that these distinctions, although fairly easy to make, are based on stereotypical notions of gender difference (women are supposed to be vague, interested in colours and concerned with relationships, whereas men are supposed to be interested in facts and are precise). Not all male writers write like Lowry, and not all women writers write as Brookner does here. Iris Murdoch, for example, often writes in a manner more akin to Lowry's writing, and frequently uses a male narrator. And it should be noted that much of the imprecision of the Brookner passage arises from the fact that she is focusing on the impressions of a character who is unfamiliar with the landscape (the character has a 'brochure' of the area).

Thus, the idea that there is a masculine style and a feminine style appears to be based more on stereotypical notions of sexual difference than on any inevitable textual difference in the way men and women write. Although the way a person uses language (in writing as in speech) will be influenced by conventional stereotypes about gender, and although readers often apply those same stereotypes when reading literature, it is important to remember that these stereotypes are neither natural nor inevitable. If women do sometimes use language differently, this is related to the way language itself derogates women and encourages them to adopt 'powerless' speech. At the same time, however, women writers (like their male counterparts) may adopt different linguistic styles for particular artistic and political ends. Feminist critics and writers often employ language in ways which challenge the gender biases embedded in language and resist the derogation and disempowering of women. On the other hand, early twentieth-century writers such as Woolf, Richardson and Rosamond Lehmann, can be seen as adopting a 'feminine' style precisely in order to subvert or question the assumptions of 'masculine' objectivity.

ACTIVITY

1 Read the text below from the 'Heartsearch' column of the *New Statesman* (May 1987), and underline the words that reveal or hint at the sex of the writer.
2 Put a circle round all uses of generic nouns (e.g. terms like *scientist* which seems to refer to all scientists, regardless of whether they are male or female).
3 Are there any differences between the way that male and female writers use generic nouns in these advertisements?
4 What other linguistic differences are there which relate either to the sex of the writer or the sex of the person being sought?

CAMBRIDGE GRADUATE: vaguely academic; likes films, opera, Europe, old things. Lithe, fit, 6', sporty. Still attractive despite thinning hair.

INCURABLE ROMANTIC, charming, uncomplicated, attractive woman, not slim, not young, feminine, wide interests seeks personable caring, retired male, sixty plus, middle brow for commitment.

GOOD-LOOKING German writer, early 30s, wishes to indulge in voyeuristic fantasy with young couple or single FORUM minded female.

LADY, ATTRACTIVE, intelligent, independent mind and means, seeks similar man 40–50. Devon Cornwall only.

Rich 1948 Claret with firm strong body sensuous flavour and adventurous bouquet, handsomely bottled, seeks younger crisp and frisky Chablis, equally well-packaged, for mulled fun, including weekends and holidays abroad with a view to durable casting. Photo appreciated.

SENSITIVE HIPPY, 24, seeks sincere and caring female for loving relationship.

READING

Cameron (1985) *Feminism and Linguistic Theory.*
—— (ed.) (1990) *The Feminist Critique of Language.*
Cameron and Coates (1989) *Women in their Speech Communities.*
Coward, Rosalind and M. Black, 'Linguistic, social and sexual relations – a review of Dale Spender's *Man Made Language*', in Cameron (ed.) (1990) *The Feminist Critique of Language,* pp. 111–33.
Daly (1978) *Gynecology.*
Kidd (1971) 'A study of the images produced through the use of the male pronoun as generic', in *Moments in Contemporary Rhetoric and Communication* 1: 25–30.
*Lakoff, R. (1975) *Language and Woman's Place.*
Miller and Swift (1979) *Words and Women.*
Mills, J. (1989) *Womanwords.*
O'Barr and Atkins (1982) 'Women's speech or powerless speech', in McConnell-Ginet (ed.) *Women and Language in Literature and Society.*
*Spender (1979) *Man Made Language.*
Woolf (1979) *Women and Writing;* also in Cameron (ed.) (1990) *The Feminist Critique of Language,* pp. 70–3.

Unit 8   Language and society

The myriad social exchanges that go to make up society largely depend on language. It is difficult to become a fully integrated member of a society or a group without taking on and developing a competence in its language. Indeed, the acquisition of language in childhood is intimately bound up with becoming a social being, for in learning to communicate through words the child takes on the concepts, values and modes of relationship of the society into which it is born. The child is assigned and begins to construct for itself its own sense of identity through language. Thus language is crucial to the creation and maintenance both of social relationships and social identities. Because of this, the way we use language (our accent, our vocabulary, etc.) carries with it important signals about the social order and our own place within it.

LANGUAGE AND SOCIAL REALITY

Language as a set of shared social conventions

Linguistic signs (spoken or written words, the gestures which make up the sign language of the deaf, etc.) have meanings only by virtue of a communal agreement among the users of a language. There is no intrinsic reason why the idea of 'tree' should be represented (in English) by the letters *t, r, e, e* (or the sounds /t/, /r/, /iː/). This is shown by the fact that other languages choose quite different sounds and letters to represent the same idea. The relationship, therefore, between the **signifier** (the sounds or letters) and what is **signified** (ideas, concepts) seems wholly arbitrary. Because of this, words only become meaningful through convention. Language works because its users implicitly agree to adhere to the conventions that underpin every aspect of its organization and which pre-exist the individual's entry into the system. In so far as the system of signs belongs not to the individual but to the community it is social rather than individual in its origins. The users of a particular language are thus parties to an implicit agreement to a set of socially held conventions. By virtue of this agreement they are also party to the way their language assigns significance and social values to the world they live in.

Language as a site of social struggle

These conventions, however, though basic to the way in which language works, are not shared equally or uniformly throughout society. What we find instead is that ways of speaking and using the language vary according to social differences and operate differently in different social domains. The adoption of particular habits of speaking leads to distinct ways of seeing and representing the world. We can detect this at the level of vocabulary in pairings such as *heart attack* versus *cardiac arrest*. These are not straightforward synonyms for each other, nor is the second simply a euphemistic version of the first. Instead, *cardiac arrest* is likely to be used by a particular social grouping (doctors, etc.) and involves a different way of seeing the phenomenon from that shared by the majority of people. In discussing the effects of war, the phrase *collateral damage* has quite different implications and effects from *civilian casualties*. Selection of one term rather than another often entails choosing particular modes of conceptualizing the reality in question. Adopting a phrase such as *collateral damage* makes it more likely that one will also select phrases such as *surgical strikes* with *80 per cent success rate* because they all serve to represent war from a particular perspective. In adopting the linguistic currency of military strategists and tacticians, it is difficult to avoid adopting their frames of reference and priorities. Vocabularies such as these thus entail particular ways of looking at the world and particular ways of defining reality which have social and political consequences. Particular linguistic choices, then, can often involve adopting certain positions regarding contentious issues and rejecting others. For this reason language becomes an arena and a means of social struggle – for instance, in the case of **language and gender** (see Unit 7).

Language as a record of social history

A term such as *family* (which became important in political debates in Britain in the 1980s) has, in fact, a long and complex history of change (see Williams 1976). It first entered English from Latin in the late fourteenth century, at which time it tended to refer to a household (incorporating not only blood-relations but also servants living together under one roof). It was then extended to include the notion of house formed by descent from a common ancestor. The specialization of the term to refer to a small kin-group living in a single house is a fairly late development in the history of the word in English (it happened between the seventeenth and nineteenth centuries), and is related – Williams claims – to the growing importance of the family as an economic unit in developing capitalism. Thus the term *family* has meant significantly different things in the 600 years since it entered the English language. Even now it means different things to different social groupings in contemporary society. A single-parent family is different from the extended family common in the Asian community in

Britain, and both are different from the two-parent–two-child family presented in television advertisements as the 'happy norm'. The word *family*, therefore, is not only inextricably bound up with the ideological struggles of the past but can become a stake in present struggles. (For further discussion of this see Unit 4: Language and time.)

One of the reasons why linguistic signs change their meanings through history is because they reflect both the transformations of social structures and the fact that society is not a single entity but differentiated along lines of class, race and gender. The use of the term *the family* in recent political debate emphasizes the sense of a self-contained economic unit living in its own home independently of state and social support (the 'nuclear family') – a sense which tends to exclude single parents, unmarried parents and so on. The fact that such a definition does not accord with the way the majority of people live in Britain in the late twentieth century goes some way to demonstrating the ideological work to which language can be recruited in an attempt to promote or legitimate particular versions of reality. It seems as if language cannot escape becoming the site of social and political contestation. It gives us categories for organizing experience and understanding the world which may seem neutral and unbiased but are inevitably partial and particular.

THE SOCIAL IMPLICATIONS FOR SYNTAX

The way language organizes experience for us is not restricted to the meanings of individual words. Significant orderings of experience are also carried out by the way in which we put the words together into sentences. Not only vocabulary but also grammatical construction help to represent social realities in determinate ways. One important kind of grammatical construction is that which linguists call **transitivity**. Transitivity is a way of describing the relationship between participants and processes in the construction of clauses – basically, 'who (or what) does what to whom (or what)'. Transitivity relations and the roles of participants depend upon the kind of process encoded by the main verb in a clause. For English, four fundamental types of process may be distinguished (but for more complete and complex treatments see Fawcett 1980, and Halliday 1985):

1 *Material action processes* (realized by verbs such as *break, wipe, dig, unbolt*) involve roles such as an **agent** (someone or something to perform the action) and the **affected** (someone or something on the receiving end of the action):

(1)   John | broke | the lock
         AGENT | PROCESS | AFFECTED

The agent in a clause is not always the grammatical 'subject' of the verb (i.e. the phrase which precedes the verb). In the **passive** form, the subject is the affected:

(2) The lock | was broken | by John
    AFFECTED | PROCESS | AGENT
    subject | verb

The passive focuses attention on the affected (rather than upon the agent). It also allows the agent to be omitted:

(3) The lock | was broken
    AFFECTED | PROCESS

2 *Mental processes* (realized by verbs such as *know, feel, think, believe*) involve roles such as the **senser** (the one who performs the act of 'knowing', 'thinking' or 'feeling') and the **phenomenon** (that which is known or thought about by the senser):

(4) James | considered | the problem
    SENSER | PROCESS | PHENOMENON

    Mary | understood | the message
    SENSER | PROCESS | PHENOMENON

    The message | amazed | me
    PHENOMENON | PROCESS | SENSER

3 *Verbal processes* are processes of saying (signalled by terms such as *suggest, promise, enquire, tell, inform,* etc.). Typical participant roles are **sayer**, **message** and **recipient**:

(5) I | said | it was time to leave
    SAYER | PROCESS | MESSAGE

    I | told | him | it was time to leave
    SAYER | PROCESS | RECIPIENT | MESSAGE

4 *Relational processes* in their simplest form involve some entity which is identified by reference to one of its attributes. The process may be realized by verbs such as *become, seem, be, have* and typical roles are **carrier** and **attribute**:

(6) The sky | is | blue
    CARRIER | PROCESS | ATTRIBUTE

Other important roles in relational processes are those of **possessor** and **possessed**:

(7) He | had | no money
    POSSESSOR | PROCESS | POSSESSED

Any event or relationship in the 'real world' is filtered through and given linguistic shape by means of one or other of the types of process outlined above. Transitivity relations, therefore, go to the heart of the linguistic construction and mediation of experience. The patterning of transitivity choices in a text can reveal its predispositions to construct experience along certain lines rather than others. The analysis of transitivity, therefore, becomes a useful way of exploring the ideological dimension of texts.

In the coverage of the 1983 miners' strike, for instance, the action of picketing was constructed in quite different linguistic ways by different newspapers, depending on their political perspective. The *Daily Mail*, which generally supported the government position, described events on the picket line in sentences such as the following:

> 41 policemen had been treated in hospital;
> police horses and their riders were stoned;
> five policehorses were also injured;
> pickets demolished a wall;
> pickets bombarded the police.

Using the categories of transitivity given above, we find that in material-action processes 'the police' figure in the accounts mainly in the role of the affected (of usually violent actions). Where 'picketing miners' appear in action clauses it is usually as agents, mostly of (violent) actions performed against the police.

In contrast to the *Daily Mail*, a newspaper such as the *Morning Star*, whose support for the miners was unwavering throughout the strike, described events on the picket line in sentences such as:

> police attacked isolated groups of miners;
> several miners were hit with truncheons;
> one miner was pounced upon by other policemen;
> the miners massed around the entrance;
> 3000 pickets yesterday gathered outside Cortonwood Colliery.

Here, police become agents of (violent) actions by which the miners are affected. And whilst the miners are sometimes presented as agents, it usually involves processes of non-violent movement (as in 'the miners massed around the entrance').

This brief analysis shows that the actual events of the picketing are constructed in quite different ways through the transitivity choices adopted in the respective newspapers. The choices in the *Daily Mail* present the industrial dispute as one in which the police are defenders of civil order in the face of a threat from the miners. The choices in the *Morning Star*, by contrast, present the dispute in terms of the solidarity of the miners in the face of state provocation. These different ideological viewpoints are not simply reflected in the language; they are produced and constructed through these different patterns of grammatical organization.

The concept of transitivity is not only useful for understanding ways in which social realities are constructed in the language of the media. It also provides a way of examining the fictional construction of reality. A study of the transitivity choices in Sylvia Plath's *The Bell Jar* (see Burton 1982) shows how the first-person narrator's own language choices typically present her as an affected entity rather than as the agent of actions that affect others. This is particularly apparent as she moves into mental crisis and begins to lose control of her life. Burton's point here is that the structures of language themselves – the character's habitual patterns of linguistic choice – contribute to her crisis precisely because they are disenabling rather than empowering. The social and political implications of this analysis are significant, since it suggests that members of marginalized social groups will potentially adopt linguistic choices which both reflect and reinforce their disempowerment (see the discussion of 'powerless speech' in Unit 7: Language and gender).

LANGUAGE AND SOCIAL STRUCTURE IN THE NOVEL

The novel is a literary genre which is more overtly 'social' than poetry (or even drama). This is partly to do with its form (by definition, it includes a range of different voices rather than the single consciousness often present in poetry), partly to do with the themes it was used to treat in the nineteenth century (typically, the tensions between different classes) and partly to do with its origins (as a means of representing the rising middle classes in the eighteenth century).

The nineteenth-century 'realist' novel in Britain often dramatizes the (usually fraught) relations between three classes – the upper, the middle and the working class. These distinctions and struggles are typically registered through a sociology of language as well as in themes, characters and plots. Dickens' *Great Expectations* (1860–1), for example, explores these issues through having a character (the narrator Pip) cross the boundaries of social class. Pip is brought up in a working-class household by his sister and her husband Joe Gargery, a blacksmith with whom he develops strong ties in the first third of the novel. Through the support of a mysterious benefactor, however, Pip becomes a 'gentleman', takes rooms in London and begins to regard his humble past as an embarrassment. Thus, when he receives word that Joe intends to visit him in London, Pip anticipates meeting his old friend 'with considerable disturbance, some mortification, and a keen sense of incongruity':

> As the time approached I should have liked to run away, but ... presently I heard Joe on the staircase. I knew it was Joe, by his clumsy manner of coming up-stairs – his state boots being always too big for him – and by the time it took him to read the names on the other floors in the course of his ascent. When at last he stopped outside our door, I could hear his finger tracing over the painted letters of my name.... Finally he gave a faint single rap, and Pepper ... announced 'Mr Gargery!' I thought he never would have done wiping his feet ... but at last he came in.

'Joe, how are you, Joe?'
'Pip, how AIR you, Pip?'

. . .

'I am glad to see you, Joe. Give me your hat.'

But Joe . . . wouldn't hear of parting with that piece of property, and persisted in standing talking over it in a most uncomfortable way.

'Which you have that growed,' said Joe, 'and that swelled, and that gentle-folked'; Joe considered a little before he discovered this word; 'as to be sure you are a honour to your king and country.'

'And you, Joe, look wonderfully well.'

(Chapter 27)

Dickens uses a number of devices here to indicate the social distance which has arisen between these characters. Apart from registering Joe's uneasiness through the way he wipes his feet and holds his hat – not to mention Pip's equally revealing attention to these details – the social difference between Pip and Joe is indicated by their different relations to language. Joe's difficulty with the written language is foregrounded through Pip's acute consciousness of his ponderous attempts to read the names on the doors. But more to the point here is the way Joe speaks. While Pip conceals his unease behind the **register** (see Unit 6) of polite affability, Joe precisely reveals his sense of awkwardness in echoing Pip. In attempting to imitate his young friend's speech, Joe 'hypercorrects' (see Montgomery 1986) his own accent by revealingly overdoing the 'proper' pronunciation of 'are' (as 'AIR'). Joe quickly 'forgets himself' by 'lapsing' into his normal accent in what we may take as a flood of genuine feeling and admiration. Pip, by contrast, continues in a polite register which signals his inability to respond to his old friend and maintains the social stratification through language which this passage dramatizes.

In the twentieth-century novel, such sociolinguistic stratifications are often challenged or undermined. D.H. Lawrence's fiction typically attempts to reverse the kind of hierarchy set up in the Dickens passage above. This can be seen in several places in *Lady Chatterly's Lover* (1928), including the following exchange between Lady Chatterly and her lover (who is a gamekeeper on her estate):

'Tha mun come one naight ter th'cottage, afore tha goos; sholl ter?' he asked, lifting his eyebrows as he looked at her, his hands dangling between his knees.

'Sholl ter?' she echoed, teasing.

He smiled.

'Ay, sholl ter?' he repeated.

'Ay!' she said, imitating the dialect sound.

. . .

''Appen a' Sunday,' she said.

''Appen a' Sunday! Ay!'

He laughed at her quickly.

'Nay, tha canna,' he protested.

'Why canna I?' she said.

He laughed. Her attempts at the dialect were so ludicrous, somehow.

(Chapter 12)

On one level, this presents a tender scene between the two lovers in which the social difference in their ways of speaking becomes material for a lovers' game. At the same time, however, the social significance of this difference cannot be overlooked. At several points in the novel Mellors, the game-keeper, uses the fact that he can move at will between one way of speaking and the other as a weapon in a class war against the upper-class family which employs him. Lady Chatterly's attempt to imitate the dialect of a 'lower' social class (which reverses the situation in *Great Expectations* examined above) can be read as a bid to escape from the restrictions of her own class. This is reinforced by the fact that the gamekeeper's dialect is treated throughout the novel as if it were the authentic language of desire in contrast to the coldly mental, sexless language of the upper classes. In this way, Lady Chatterly's imitation of this language – which is an amusing failure in Mellors' eyes – indicates her inability (in the novel's terms) fully to achieve sexual and linguistic authenticity precisely because of her social class. For Lawrence, then, language and sex become part of a larger struggle between different classes. (For a fuller discussion of accent and dialect, see Unit 5: Language and place.)

ACTIVITY

1 Read the following passage from Elizabeth Gaskell's *North and South* (1854–5). The central character, Margaret Hale, has recently moved from the south of England to Manchester (one of the main centres of industrial development in the nineteenth century) and is discussing an impending strike at a local mill with a poverty-stricken leader of the union, Nicholas Higgins (*to clem* is a dialect term for 'to starve'):

'Why do you strike?' asked Margaret. 'Striking is leaving off work till you get your own rate of wages, is it not? You must not wonder at my ignorance; where I come from I never heard of a strike.'

. . .

'Why yo' see, there's five or six masters who have set themselves again paying the wages they've been paying these two years past, and flourishing upon, and getting richer upon. And now they come to us, and say we're to take less. And we won't. We'll just clem to death first; and see who'll work for 'em then.'

. . .

'And so you plan dying, in order to be revenged upon them!'

'No,' said he, 'I dunnot. I just look forward to the chance of dying at my post sooner than yield. That's what folk call fine and honourable in a soldier, and why not in a poor weaver-chap?'

'But,' said Margaret, 'a soldier dies in the cause of the Nation – in the cause of others.'

'. . . Dun yo' think it's for mysel' I'm striking work at this time? It's just as much in the cause of others as yon soldier. . . . I take up John Boucher's cause, as lives next door but one, wi' a sickly wife, and eight childer, . . . I take up th' cause o' justice.'

. . .

'But,' said Margaret, . . . 'the state of trade may be such as not to enable them to give you the same remuneration.'

'State o' trade! That's just a piece o' masters' humbug. It's rate o' wages I was talking of. Th' masters keep the' state o' trade in their own hands; and just walk it forward like a black bug-a-boo, to frighten naughty children with into being good.'

(from Chapter 17 'What is a strike?')

2 Make a list of all the words and phrases which Higgins uses to describe: (a) the mill owners; (b) the workers; (c) himself; (d) the mill owners' actions; (e) the workers' actions; (f) his own actions. From this evidence, try to describe Higgins' view of the strike (e.g. by considering who does what to whom).

3 Make a list of all the words and phrases which Margaret uses to describe: (a) the mill owners' possible actions; (b) Higgins' description of his own role; (c) the actions of workers in a strike. From this evidence, try to describe Margaret's view of the strike.

4 What is the difference between Margaret's suggestion that 'the state of trade' might not allow the owners to give the workers the same 'remuneration', and Higgins' response that he is not talking about the state of trade but 'rate o' wages'? How, in Higgins' view, do the owners use the term 'state of trade'?

5 What is the effect of the fact that Higgins speaks in a working-class northern dialect, while Margaret speaks in standard English? Does it make his view of the strike more credible? Less credible? More authentic? Less authoritative?

READING

Burton (1982) 'Through glass darkly: through dark glasses', in Carter (ed.) *Language and Literature*, pp. 195–214.
Fawcett (1980) *Cognitive Linguistics and Social Interaction*.
Halliday (1985) *Functional Grammar*.
*Montgomery (1986) *An Introduction to Language and Society*.
*Williams (1976) *Keywords*.

Section 3

Poetic uses of language

Unit 9   Rhyme and sound patterning

In the process of reading words on a page, we translate visual marks (letters) into mental representations of sounds (phones, or **phonemes**). English uses a 'phonetic–alphabetic script' in which letters stand for sounds, or serve to represent particular patterns of sound. For example, the letter *p* in *pin* stands for a single sound (which we also write phonetically as 'p'); the two letters *th* in *thin* stand for a single sound (which we write phonetically as θ); the letter *i* in *time* stands for a combination of sounds called a diphthong (which we write phonetically as 'aɪ'). We can represent the way a word is made up of sounds using a phonetic script, and so we can compare the letter-spelling of a word with the phonetic structure of the word:

letter-spelling:	thing	queen	come
phonetic-structure:	θɪŋ	kwiːn	kʌm

In this unit we are interested in the phonetic structure of words rather than their spelling. Because of the relatively small number of distinct sounds used in a language, the sounds of a text inevitably recur as we read, making up a kaleidoscope of repetitions and permutations. In casual conversation and most kinds of written texts, these sounds occur for the most part apparently randomly, ordered only by the historical accidents governing which sounds make up which words. But it is also possible for speakers and writers to organize the sounds of the language in more systematic ways in order to achieve certain effects. Many different types of discourse employ sound patterning: poetry, jokes, slogans, advertising, speeches, pop lyrics, rapping, toasting, etc.

THE STRUCTURE OF THE SYLLABLE

In order to be able to analyse the various sound patterns which can occur between words, it is useful to be able to describe the structure of the syllables which make up words. The structure of a **syllable** can be described as 'C–V–C', where C stands for a **consonant cluster** (i.e. any number of consonants, including none) and V stands for one vowel or one diphthong. This pattern can be used to describe syllables as shown below (phonetic symbols are used on the left to represent the words on the right):

C	V	C	
b	aɪ	t	bite
sp	ɔ	t	spot
spl	æ	t	splat
m	əʊ	st	most
	ɪ	n	in
p	eɪ		pay
	aɪ		I

The above words all consist of just one syllable (they are monosyllabic). But words may consist of a number of syllables put together:

C V C	C V C	C V C	
p eɪ	m ɑː	st ə	paymaster
p eɪ	m ə nt		payment
e	l ɪ	f ə nt	elephant

TYPES OF SOUND PATTERN

Sound patterns are formed when there is some form of 'echo' between syllables in words that occur close to one another in space or time (e.g. next to each other, or in the same line, or in the same place in different lines). The various names which literary criticism uses to refer to particular kinds of sound patterning are simply conventional labels for different kinds of repetition and parallelism (see Unit 11). The nature of the echo can be analysed by indicating which elements in the C–V–C structure of the relevant syllables are similar. There are six basic kinds of pattern:

1 **Alliteration** [C–V–C] occurs when there is a repetition of sounds made by the initial consonants or consonant clusters of nearby words (e.g. *boat, big, bad*; or *grow, grand, Greek*); alliteration can also occur where there is a repetition of the first stressed segment within a word (*aggression, ungrateful,* etc.).
   Points to note about alliteration:

(a) As with all the patterns, it is sounds, not letters, which produce the effect. So *city* alliterates with *sandwich*, not with *cauliflower*, and in many dialects the pronunciation of *tin* alliterates with *trip* not with *thin*.
(b) Alliteration can exist between the initial sound of a word and a sound at the beginning of a stressed syllable within another word. So *song* alliterates with *unseen* and *dissociate*, but not with *dancing* (because the stress is on the first syllable – see Unit 10: Rhythm).
(c) Alliteration was a major organizing device in Old and Middle English 'alliterative metre', which required that most or all of the stressed syllables in any line of verse were made up of the same word-initial

sound. An example of a line of fifteenth-century alliterative verse is 'Stark strokes thei stryken on a stelyd stokke.' This was gradually displaced in later poetry by sound patterns at the end of lines (especially rhyme).

(d) Alliteration occurs in the case of word-initial sound clusters (e.g. *spl, tr, pl*) only when the entire cluster is repeated, not when only one part recurs. So *glad* alliterates with *glimmer*, not with *go* or *grow*.

(e) One way of remembering alliteration is to think of the so-called 'three Rs' 'reading, writing and arithmetic' where the three words alliterate. The alliteration between *reading* and *writing* illustrates that it occurs through sound rather than spelling (because the letters *wr* are different from the letter *r* but both correspond to the same sound); *arithmetic* alliterates with both because its *r* sound occurs in the first stressed syllable, rather than the first syllable.

2 **Assonance** [C–**V**–C] occurs when there is a repetition of the same vowel sound – especially in stressed syllables – embedded within nearby words. So *light* is assonant with *wide* and *sign*.

3 **Consonance** [C–V–**C**] occurs when there is a repetition of sounds made by the final consonants or consonant groups of nearby words, as in *bad* and *good*, or *treats* and *floats*. (Note, however, that some critics argue that use of the term consonance is only justified when both the initial and final consonants are repeated, as in *read* and *ride*; it would then be equivalent to pararhyme – see 5 below.)

4 **Reverse rhyme** [**C–V**–C] occurs when the sounds of both the initial consonant or consonant group and the vowel are repeated in nearby words, as in *cash* and *carry*, or *stand* and *stamp*.

5 **Pararhyme** [**C**–V–**C**] occurs when the sounds of both the initial and the final consonant group in nearby words are repeated, as in *send* and *sound*, or *beat* and *bite*. (Notice that this effect is what some critics refer to as consonance – see 3 above.)

6 **Rhyme** [C–**V–C**] occurs when the last vowel and consonant cluster in the word are repeated in nearby words: *cloud* rhymes with *shroud*; *bending* with *sending, demonstrate* with *remonstrate*. Rhyme can occur either within a line of verse (where it is called 'internal rhyme') or at the end ('end rhymes'). 'Rhyme' is sometimes also used to describe the repetition of a V–C combination which is not at the end of a word, as in *action pack*.

Points to note about rhyme:

(a) Some apparent approximations to rhyme result from changes in how the words are pronounced, as in *line* and *join*, or *day* and *tea* (which more or less rhymed with each other during the eighteenth century).

(b) Sounds, not spellings, produce rhyme. So *cough* rhymes with *off*, not with *plough*. (Words like *cough* and *plough* whose spelling suggests they ought to rhyme are called 'eye-rhymes'.)

(c) In some traditional literary criticism, the term 'masculine rhyme' is used where the rhyme consists of a single stressed syllable (*round* and *sound*). The term 'feminine rhyme' in this convention means a rhyme involving two syllables (*yellow* and *fellow*). An alternative and more useful termin- ology is 'single rhyme' and 'double rhyme', since it also permits 'triple rhyme' for a rhyme involving three syllables.

(d) Rhymes at the ends of lines of poetry are usually organized into patterns, or rhyme schemes. A poem's rhyme can be worked out by marking 'a' against the last word of the first line and against all the end words which rhyme with it; 'b' is then used to mark the next rhyme, and so on. Typical patterns which emerge are abab, abba, abcabc, etc. Some poetic genres are defined partly on the basis of their rhyme schemes (e.g. the sonnet, the ballad).

(e) Metrical poetry which does not have end rhymes is called blank verse (this should be distinguished from 'free verse' – see Unit 10: Rhythm).

THE SIGNIFICANCE OF SOUND PATTERNS

So far, we have simply identified possible patterns and presented ways of describing them. In order to investigate how such patterns work as a stylistic resource, we need now to consider what kind of significance or function they might have. Six alternative possibilities are presented below. Each possibility should be considered for each case of sound patterning identified in a text.

1 Patterning may serve no particular function, and be simply the accidental result of a random distribution of the small number of distinct sounds which make up the language. This is especially likely in spontaneous conversation. It is also likely where there is some distance in the text between instances of the sound taken to create the effect: functional sound patterning depends on closeness between the words involved, since readers are unlikely to recog- nize sounds repeated far apart (in other words, functional sound patterning needs to be noticeable or perceptually salient).

2 Patterning may serve a **cohesive** function, bonding the words together as a formulaic or fixed phrase or unit. This can enhance the memorability of an utterance, as in riddles, catch-phrases, slogans and proverbs (*action pack; a stitch in time saves nine; be Indian, buy Indian*).

3 Patterning may have the effect of emphasizing or **foregrounding** some aspect of the text. Sometimes a patterning which involves repetition serves

to emphasize the text, to make it look as though it expresses great feeling, as is often the case in political rhetoric. Sometimes the physical existence of the utterance as a linguistic construct is emphasized, as in the case of tongue twisters such as the alliterative *Peter Piper picked a pot of pickled peppercorns.*

4 Patterning may have the effect of creating or reinforcing a parallelism. In this case, words which are linked together on the basis of shared sounds will also be linked in terms of their meanings (they might have similar or opposite meanings). This technique is common in jokes, advertising and some types of poetry (e.g. Augustan verse). Consider, from this point of view, such phrases as *chalk and cheese* and *cash and carry* or these lines by Stevie Smith from 'The river god' (1962):

> But I can drown the fools
> Who bathe too close to the weir, contrary to rules
> And they take a long time drowning
> As I throw them up now and then in a spirit of clowning

5 Patterning may contribute to a level of **sound symbolism**. Such effects are based on a belief that the sounds which make up words are not arbitrarily related to their meaning, as most linguists think, but are motivated in some way by being loaded with resonance or connotational value.

Points to consider about the idea of sound symbolism:

(a) The linguistic view that the sounds of language are arbitrary is supported by evidence such as the fact that the same meaning is expressed in different languages by words with very different sounds (*tree, arbre, Baum*, etc.), and that the sounds of words change over time. Such evidence suggests that sounds are merely conventional aspects of the formal system of a language.

(b) The view that sounds in language may have symbolic meanings or expressive effects, on the other hand, is based on a musical belief that sound itself carries meaning, as well as on the idea that individual sounds are felt differently because the way we make them with the voice differs for each sound. Consider three types of evidence for this:

    (i) Here are three imaginary but possible 'words': *la, li* and *lor*. If you had three tables of different sizes to label with these words, which would you call which? Research has shown that most people – across a wide range of different cultures – label the small table *li*, the middle-sized one *la* and the largest *lor*. This tendency probably reflects the fact that sounds are made differently in the mouth: *lor* is a 'big' sound (mouth open, tongue back, large mouth cavity); *li*, by contrast, is a 'small' sound (mouth relatively closed, tongue up and forward, etc.).

    (ii) Some groups of words have both their sound and their general area of meaning in common (this effect is traditionally called

onomatopoeia): *clatter, clang* and *clash* all suggest one thing striking against another; *sneeze, snore, snooze* and *sniffle* are all to do with breathing through the nose and might be considered to sound like the actions they refer to (though consider *snow* and *snap* as counter-examples).

(iii) Consider the hypothesis of a gradience of linguistic sounds, from 'hard' through to 'soft'. The so-called hardest sounds include *p, b, t, d, k* and *g* (which all involve completely stopping breath coming out of the mouth, then releasing it suddenly); the so-called softest sounds are the vowels (which do not impede the air-flow out of the mouth at all, but simply reshape it), plus sounds like those produced from the letters *w* and *l*. The idea that words contain hard and soft sounds is sometimes used to make an equation between sound and meaning.

(c) Sound symbolism involves attributing conventional meanings or resonances to sound patterns. In Keats' famous line in 'To autumn' (1820), 'Thou watchest the last oozings hours by hours', the repeated *s* and *z* sounds are often taken to represent the oozing of cider in the press. In a line from Tennyson ('The princess' (1853)), 'The murmuring of innumerable bees', the repeated *m* sounds are taken to represent the sound of bees. These associations of sound and meaning are not fixed: *s* and *z* would instead be taken to stand for the buzzing of bees if they were in a poem about bees. Instead, the meaning helps give the effect of sound symbolism in a poem.

MAKING INTERPRETATIONS ON THE BASIS OF SOUND PATTERNS

Having looked at how sound patterns may function, we need to consider how the identification of sound patterning can be used in ways of reading, and to assess some of the possibilities and problems involved in doing this.

Understanding the conventions of many idioms or genres entails recognizing aspects of their use of sound patterning. Contemporary rapping involves rhyming as one of its main organizational principles; and headlines and advertising slogans have characteristic ways of using sound patterns. Many texts written within established literary traditions draw on conventions of sound patterning (and sometimes sound symbolism) as a compositional resource. Traditions of interpretation of these texts also draw on the same network of conventions. In addition, the conventional register of poetic language has fluctuated throughout its history in terms of its use of sound patterning: some periods and posts have preferred highly complex sound patterning (e.g. Gerard Manley Hopkins), while others (e.g. Wordsworth) have striven to make poetic language as simple and straightforward as possible (see Unit 6: Language and context: register).

Earlier in this unit, we listed six types of local sound patterns which can be formed by neighbouring words in a text. These distinctions and labels are useful in that they enable us to describe sound patterning. But in the actual analysis of texts it often seems that there are no clear-cut boundaries between sound effects. Rhyme, assonance and consonance are mixed together not as a repertoire of separate devices but in a texture of complex and interconnected patterning. Consider, for example, the first line of Samuel Taylor Coleridge's 'Kubla Khan' (1816): 'In Xanadu did Kubla Khan'. If you try to identify all instances of sound patterning in this line, you quickly run into difficulties (including difficulties which are the result of language variation). Does the vowel in 'Khan' assonate with 'Kubla' (and possibly with 'Xanadu'), or does it rhyme with 'Xanadu'?

In attempting to interpret sound patterns, it is useful to distinguish between patterns which serve simply to define a form (such as rhyme schemes and local kinds of ornamentation) and patterns which seem to have expressive or symbolic functions (such as extra memorability or special suggestiveness). The problem with trying to interpret this second kind of pattern is that the expressive or symbolic significance of sound effects cannot simply be read off from a text in a series of mechanical equations between sound and sense (see the examples from Keats and Tennyson above). In poetry, for example, a sequence of words beginning with the same sound may mean one thing in one context and quite a different thing in another. (In a directory or index, such a sequence would have a different kind of meaning altogether.) In interpreting poetry, the context and meanings of the words should have priority; only after considering these is it safe to suggest ways in which the sound might support (or perhaps undercut) the sense.

It is not possible to prove an effect of sound patterning or sound symbolism. Caution is therefore needed in putting forward interpretative arguments based on the connotations or symbolic qualities of sounds. Arguments regarding the expressive or symbolic qualities of sound in a text are persuasive only when they are based on some mutual reinforcement that can be shown between properties of the text at different levels (e.g. between its sounds, grammatical structures, vocabulary, etc.), rather than when appeals are made either directly to fixed symbolic values for sounds, or to a reader's personal sense of a sound's resonance.

Finally, when writing about a text, there is little point in simply listing aspects of its sound patterning (e.g. its rhyme scheme, or the fact that wo words alliterate). Comments along these lines only become interesting when linked to one of two kinds of argument: either in the identification of a genre or form, where for some reason this is in question or worth establishing: or else to support a case for some local interpretation, where the evocative effect of the sound connects with other indicators of what is meant.

ACTIVITY

1 Read the three passages given below.

A (from a letter)

O dear Sir Raph, – I am sory to be the mesinger of so dismall news, for por London is almost burnt down. It began on Saterday night, & has burnt ever sence and is at this tim more fears than ever; it did begin in pudding lan at a backers, whar a Duch rog lay, & burnt to the bridge & all fish street and all crasus stret, & Lumber Stret and the old exchang & canans stret & so all that way to the reaver and bilinsgat sid, & now tis com to chep sid and banescasell, & tis thought flet stret will be burnt by tomorow, thar is nothing left in any hous thar, nor in the Tempell, thar was never so sad a sight, nor so dolefull a cry hard, my hart is not abell to expres the tenth nay the thousent part of it, thar is all the carts within ten mils round, & cars & drays run about night and day, & thousens of men & women carrying burdens.

(from a letter by Lady Hobart to Sir Ralph Verney, dated 3 September 1666, telling him about the Great Fire of London; published in Davies 1934)

B (from a lyric poem)

I did not live until this time
Crown'd my felicity.
When I could say without a crime,
I am not thine but Thee.

This carcass breath'd, and walkt, and slept,
So that the World believ'd
There was a soul the motions kept;
But they were all deceiv'd.

(from Katherine Philips 'To my excellent Lucasia, on our friendship', 1667)

C (from a popular song)

It was the Frogge in the well,
Humble-dum, humble-dum.
And the merrie Mouse in the Mill,
tweedle, tweedle, twino.

The Frogge would a woing ride,
humble-dum, humble-dum.
Sword and buckler by his side,
tweedle, tweedle twino.

When he was upon his high horse set,
humble dum, humble dum.
His boots they shone as black as jet,
tweedle, tweedle twino.

(from 'The Marriage of the Frogge and the Mouse', printed 1611)

2 Fill in the following chart by giving one example of each type of sound pattern from each passage (if any are noticeable or perceptually salient). (We have filled in the first box for you.)

	Text A	Text B	Text C
Alliteration	so sad a sight		
Assonance			
Consonance			
Reverse rhyme			
Pararhyme			
Rhyme			
Rhyme scheme			

3 For each of your examples, try to describe the particular effect(s) conveyed by the sound patterning when the text is read aloud. As a way of doing this, work through the list of different kinds of possible significance of sound patterns provided above.

4 Sound patterning is a matter of sounds, not written forms; but because all three passages were written before the conventions of modern spelling were fully established, some of the words may seem odd in the form in which they appear, and this may create difficulties as you try to assess possible sound patterns. Make a note of the specific kinds of difficulty that arise as a result of spellings in the passages.

READING

*Attridge (1982) *The Rhythms of English Poetry*, Ch. 9, pp. 285–315.
Hymes (1960) 'Phonological aspects of style: some English sonnets', in Sebeok (ed.) *Style in Language*, pp. 109–31.
*Leech (1969) *A Linguistic Guide to English Poetry*, Ch. 6, pp. 89–102.

Unit 10   Rhythm

TYPES OF RHYTHM

Rhythm can be defined as a repeated and regular switching between modes. The modes might be quiet versus loud (as in spoken poetry), or light versus dark (as in the visual rhythm of a lighthouse's signal), or contraction versus expansion (as in the rhythm of the heart), etc. Figure 10.1 shows how some of the many things which can be described as 'rhythm' might be organized into groups. We could add other kinds of rhythm at all levels of this figure. We might be able to find rhythms which can be touched or smelt. Visual rhythms could include waves of all kinds (from waves breaking on the shore, to the 'Mexican wave' produced by crowds in sports stadiums). Natural rhythms could include the regular movement of the tide or the phases of the moon. We might add singing and rapping as further kinds of rhythm made by the voice.

RHYTHM IN SOUND

Rhythm is best thought of as something we experience, but is also a feature of the way we actively organize our experience. Most of the rhythms we hear (e.g. in music) are influenced by features of the sounds themselves, but we sometimes hear rhythm even when it is not physically present in the sounds. For example, a clock actually makes a regular repeated sound (i.e. 'tick-tick-tick . . .'), but is heard as a more rhythmic 'tick-tock-tick-tock . . .' The fact that rhythm is shaped by the way we perceive sounds means that there may be differences in the way different people perceive the same rhythm. What one person hears as a 'falling rhythm' may be heard by another as a 'rising rhythm' (for a definition of these terms, see below). To a certain extent, then, the rhythm of a piece of language is as much in need of interpretation as any of its other features.

RHYTHM IN SPEECH

We have seen that rhythm is based on the perception of differences. In the case of rhythm in sound, the differences between sounds are largely a

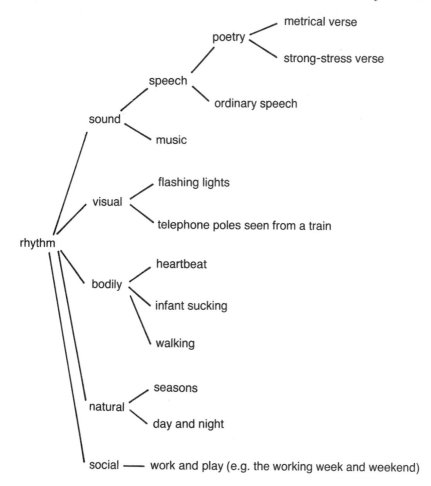

Figure 10.1 A simple classification scheme for types of rhythm

matter of their loudness and/or height and/or length. In speech, these are the features of a vocal sound which determine its **stress** (also called 'accent'). A vocal sound is stressed if it is loud and/or high and/or long compared with the sounds which surround it (which are then unstressed). Stress is a quality not of an individual sound but of the cluster of sounds called a syllable (See Unit 9: Rhyme and sound patterning). Any syllable can carry stress in a sequence of syllables.

In order to be able to analyse patterns of stress (i.e. rhythm) in written texts we need to imagine the sound of a sequence, read it out loud or listen while someone else reads it out loud. It is useful to record what we hear by using a system of marks to differentiate between stressed and unstressed syllables. Because any syllable in a sequence can carry stress, the first task is to mark every syllable (e.g. by putting a dot above the vowel sound of each syllable). In practice, the degree of stress given to the syllables of a spoken utterance will vary considerably, but in order to analyse rhythm it is useful to distinguish three different levels of stress: syllables with no stress (marked by turning the dot into an o), syllables with secondary stress (marked with ') and syllables with full stress (marked with /).

Here are some examples of the analysis of stress distributions in multi-syllable words:

word	syllables	typical stress
	. . .	o / '
specific	spe ci fic	spe ci fic
	. .	/ '
pattern	pa ttern	pa ttern
	. . .	/ ' o
typical	ty pi cal	ty pi cal

Single-syllable words can be stressed, but words which carry little meaning content, like *a, in, the, as,* etc. are usually unstressed.

It is possible to change these typical word stresses. In fast speech, ordinarily stressed syllables may be unstressed; in slow or emphatic speech, on the other hand, certain ordinarily unstressed syllables may be stressed. Moreover, stress patterns change when words are put together. For example, the sentence *I hear the wind sighing* is made up of words with these predicted stress patterns:

o /   o /   / o

I hear the wind sighing

When the whole sentence is spoken, however, it is possible to give some words more stress than others. For example, the *I* might be stressed (perhaps for emphasis) and this would shift the stress pattern in the rest of the sentence:

/ '   o /   ' o

I hear the wind sighing

Alternatively, *hear* and *sighing* can be strongly stressed and the stress on *I* and *wind* de-emphasized:

o /   o '   / o

I hear the wind sighing

It is possible to simplify the way in which we show stresses in a sentence by simply indicating all the syllables, and marking as stressed only those syllables which have strong stress; so we could represent the sentence more simply as:

```
 .  /   .   .   /   .
```

I hear the wind sighing

The convention, which we will use from now on, is that an unstressed or weakly stressed syllable has . above it, while a strongly stressed syllable has / above it.

When pronounced, this sentence illustrates another feature of the natural rhythm of spoken English. English is a **stress-timed language**, which means that the time intervals between stressed syllables tend to be equally long, while the number of unstressed syllables between stresses can vary provided the time interval remains the same length. Thus, in the last pronunciation of the sentence, the interval between the stresses is occupied by two unstresses which are pronounced quite rapidly. This feature of English means that it is relatively rare to find two successive stresses: this may be why *wind* tends to be 'demoted' in the above sentence; when it is stressed, there is an implicit pause between *wind* and *sighing*.

RHYTHM IN POETRY

Its stress-timed nature means that the rhythms of spoken English are relatively flexible and speech rhythms are largely determined by the words chosen and the way they are put together. In many types of poetry, on the other hand, the rhythmic pattern of the lines is decided in advance, and the words are fitted into it. For example, the syllables in the lines of Emily Brontë's 'The wind I hear it sighing' (1846) analysed below conform for the most part to the following predetermined scheme:

```
 . / . / . /
```

In other words, the general pattern of each line is that it should have six syllables, three of which should be stressed, and that it begins with an unstressed syllable. In the most commonly used method of describing poetic rhythms (see below), this pattern is called 'iambic trimeter' (iambic indicates the unstressed–stressed pattern, while trimeter indicates that the line is made up of three groups of this pattern).

The first stanza of the poem may be analysed as follows:

```
 .  /  .  /  .  /  .
```

The wind I hear it sighing

```
 .  /  .    /  .  /
```

With Autumn's saddest sound;

```
/  .   /   .  /  .  /.
```

Withered leaves as thick are lying

```
.   /   .   /   .  /
```

As spring-flowers on the ground.

This text illustrates a number of important points about poetic rhythms:

1   The rhythmic pattern (or **meter**) allows variations of specific kinds (e.g. the iambic trimeter here allows an extra unstressed syllable at the end of the first line). In other words, a poem's rhythmic structure is a pattern of expectation, not an absolute grid which overrides the natural stress patterns of the language.

2   Other variations are possible. The third line does not fit the pattern (it starts with a stress, it has eight syllables and it contains four stresses), but still seems acceptable as a line in the poem. This line would conventionally be described as 'trochaic tetrameter' (trochaic indicating the stressed–unstressed pattern, tetrameter indicating the fact that the line is divided into four instances of this pattern). The lines in each stanza of Brontë's poem follow the same stress pattern (3–3–4–3); this is quite a common form in both popular and literary poetry.

3   Some variations are less likely. The first line could have been the more syntactically regular *I hear the wind sighing*, but its rhythmic ambiguity would not have established the rhythmic pattern as clearly as 'The wind I hear it sighing' does. The natural rhythm of the spoken words must coincide to some extent with the poem's underlying rhythmic structure.

FOUR-BEAT AND FIVE-BEAT RHYTHMIC PATTERNS

According to Derek Attridge (1982), verse in English is written according to two fundamental rhythmic patterns: the four-beat pattern and the five-beat pattern. The four-beat pattern is most obviously realized in lines which have four stressed syllables, but Attridge shows that even lines with two, three or six stressed syllables are variations on the four-beat line. The three-stress line can be seen as a variant on the four-beat line through the notion of 'unrealized' beats. Using the letters 'b' and 'o' under the line to indicate beats and off-beats, the first line of the Brontë poem examined above can be analysed as follows:

```
.   /   .   /   .  /   .
```

The wind I hear it sighing

```
o   b   o   b   o  b   o     (b)
```

In this notation, (b) indicates the unrealized beat. If the poem is chanted out loud while beating out the rhythm, the unrealized beat can be felt at the end of each of the three-stress lines. Our minds seem to be predisposed to arrange rhythmic pulses into patterns of four: allowing for the unrealized beats, Brontë's stanza is arranged in four groups of four (four beats per line, four lines per stanza: called the four × four pattern). This explains why both the extra syllable at the end of the first line and the four-stress third line seem to fit the poem's rhythm.

This four × four pattern is omnipresent in pop songs, folk songs, the blues, hymns, ballads, nursery rhymes and a large proportion of literary poems. The five-beat line is found only in the literary tradition, where it is mainly realized as the 'iambic pentameter' (see below). Its principle feature is that it escapes the insistent four × four pattern and so allows the natural rhythms of the language to emerge (which is why Shakespeare uses it in his plays, and why it is one of the most important and frequently used metrical forms in English); this effect is accentuated when the lines do not rhyme, and iambic pentameter unrhymed verse is called **blank verse**. The opening line of a poem by Margaret Cavendish (untitled, 1653) can serve to illustrate the iambic pentameter pattern:

   . / . / . / . / . /

As I sate Musing, by my selfe alone.

METHODS OF CLASSIFYING RHYTHMIC PATTERNS

There are various opinions about how to classify rhythms in poetry. We present a simplified version of the conventional method (derived from the analysis of classical poetry) together with an alternative terminology. In the conventional method, the sequence of stressed and unstressed syllables is divided into groups (called 'feet'), with one heavy stress in each group. In this system, the definition of **iambic pentameter** is a line made up of a sequence of five feet, where each 'foot' is made up of an unstressed syllable followed by a stressed syllable (. /). In a **rising** rhythm, the stressed syllable is at the end of the foot; in a **falling** rhythm, the stressed syllable is at the beginning of the foot.

The various possible combinations of stressed and unstressed syllables which can make up a foot are classified as follows:

Traditional name	*Stress pattern*	*Alternative name*
iambic foot or iamb	. /	rising duple rhythm
trochaic foot or trochee	/ .	falling duple rhythm
anapestic foot or anapest	. . /	rising triple rhythm
dactylic foot or dactyl	/ . .	falling triple rhythm
spondaic foot or spondee	/ /	
pyrrhic foot or pyrrhic	. .	

The poetry which this descriptive system was designed for is called metrical verse. In metrical verse, the same foot is repeated a fixed number of times (the spondee or the pyrrhic can only be used as an occasional variation on the others). There are eight possible line lengths (their names are derived from the Greek names for the number of feet): monometer (one foot); dimeter (two feet); trimeter (three); tetrameter (four); pentameter (five); hexameter (six); heptameter (seven); octameter (eight).

Metrical verse is also called accentual–syllabic verse, because it involves a fixed number of accents (stresses) in a line, and a fixed number of syllables in a line. For example, an iambic pentameter line has ten syllables and five stresses.

There are other types of poetic meter. English poetry also has accentual or **strong stress** verse, where the number of accents (stresses) are controlled while the unstressed syllables between each stressed syllable (and therefore in each line) can vary considerably. Medieval English poetry like *Sir Gawain and the Green Knight* (anonymous, fourteenth century) is written according to this pattern (with alliteration on the stressed syllables). Most folk and popular poetry is written in strong stress verse in the four × four pattern. Here is an example from the first two lines of a ballad:

.   /   . . / . . / . /

I'll tell you a Tale of my Love and I,

.   / . / . . / .   /

How we did often a milking goe.

Poetry in which both the number of syllables and the number of stresses per line vary to such an extent that no pattern can be found is called **free verse**.

THE COMBINATION OF DIFFERENT RHYTHMS

Some examples where rhythmic systems exist at the same time are:

speech rhythm + poetic rhythm	in spoken poetry
musical rhythm + poetic rhythm + speech rhythm	in a song
sequential visual rhythm + musical rhythm	in a music video
bodily rhythms + musical rhythm	in dance

Sometimes, these rhythms fit with each other (as in dance or song), but other kinds of combinations are potentially discordant with each other. In order to examine the effects of mismatches between poetic and speech rhythms, we return to the line by Margaret Cavendish. The context of the rest of the poem invites us to analyse the line as iambic pentameter:

. / .   / .   / . / . /

As I sate Musing, by my selfe alone

Yet the most natural way of speaking the line seems to be as follows:

```
.  .  /    / .    .  .  /  . /
```

As I sate Musing, by my selfe alone

The speech rhythm here involves giving each important word a main stress and unstressing the other syllables. This produces several mismatches with the expected or underlying poetic rhythm ('sate' is promoted to a stressed position; 'I' and 'by' are demoted). This means that there is a certain tension between the poetic rhythm and the natural-speech rhythm, and if we were to recite the poem aloud we would experience that tension as a dilemma: should we speak the line according to the expected poetic rhythm, should we speak it with the speech rhythm or should we try to compromise? One possible compromise would be as follows:

```
.  /  .    / .    .  .  /  . /
```

As I sate Musing, by my selfe alone

Speaking the line like this places emphasis on 'I', which could be considered appropriate since the poem is about the speaker's melancholy. But it does not emphasize 'by' (as the poetic rhythm would require), since it would make no sense to do so. So in speaking a line of verse we are required to produce interpretations of the rhythm which will compromise between the pattern of expectation and the speech rhythm, and which may also involve interpretations of the meaning at the same time.

With this last point in mind, the next three lines of the poem are analysed below, with the underlying poetic rhythm and one possible speech rhythm given:

```
   .   /     .   /   .   .   .   /   . .      (speech)
   .   /     .   /   .   /   .   /   . /      (poetic)
```

2 My Thoughts on severall things did work upon

Whether we choose the poetic or speech rhythm for line 2 seems to make little difference (there is no compromise).

```
   /    .  /    /  . /    .    /  . /         (speech)
   .    /  .    /  . /    .    /  . /         (poetic)
```

3 Some did large Houses build, and Stately Towers.

Choosing the speech rhythm in line 3 draws attention to the important words 'some' and 'large'; the two stresses next to each other (unusual in English), together with the fact that there is an extra stress in the line, gives a 'weight' to the line which supports its meaning.

```
   /  . /    .    /  .  .  /   /  .           (speech)
   .  /  .    /    .  /  .  /   .  /          (poetic)
```

4 Making Orchards, Gardens, and fine Bowers

In line 4 there is a major mismatch between the poetic and speech rhythms, yet the line sounds acceptably rhythmic and does not seem to jar with the other lines.

This analysis reveals that iambic-pentameter lines are rarely completely regular. In fact, mismatches between speech and poetic rhythms are found in most poetry. A poem's metrical form should be regarded as an underlying structure or pattern of expectation which is set up in order to allow variations to be both foregrounded and meaningful. The above analysis indicates that these mismatches produce tensions which serve to make the rhythm more interesting than an absolutely regular rhythm would be and that these tensions can have effects on the way we interpret the poem (thus variation in rhythm can have both aesthetic and semantic implications).

THE SIGNIFICANCE OF POETIC RHYTHMS

Students and critics often feel the need to relate poetic rhythms to meaning, making impressionistic links between, say, a poem's description of the movement of a boat and the 'rocking' feel of the poem's rhythm. For the most part, such interpretations are best avoided. Poetic rhythms are part of a range of possible sound patterns found in poetry, and the cautions about interpreting sound patterns described in Unit 9: Rhyme and sound patterning, should also be exercised when assessing the significance of poetic rhythms.

ACTIVITY

The following lines are taken from John Milton, *Paradise Lost* book 2, lines 390–402 (1667): they are spoken by Beelzebub and form part of a debate in Hell between the fallen angels.

Well have ye judg'd, well ended long debate,

Synod of Gods, and like to what ye are,

Great things resolv'd; which from the lowest deep

Will once more lift us up, in spight of Fate,

Nearer our ancient Seat; perhaps in view

Of those bright confines, whence with neighbouring Arms

And opportune excursion we may chance

Re-enter Heav'n; or else in some milde Zone

Dwell not unvisited of Heav'ns fair Light

Secure, and at the brightning Orient beam

Purge off this gloom; the soft delicious Air,

To heal the searr of these corrosive Fires

Shall breath her balme.

1 The whole poem is written in iambic pentameter, which means that each line is expected to have the following underlying poetic rhythm:

   . / . / . / . / . /

For each line, first mark the poetic rhythm and then mark a normal speech rhythm above it. The first line might be annotated like this:

   /   .   . /   / / . /   . /   (speech)

     .   /   . /   . / . /   . /   (poetic)

   Well have ye judg'd, well ended long debate,

Some lines will have only one pronunciation (where the speech rhythm exactly matches the poetic rhythm).
2 Now add above each line any compromise pronunciations of the line, between the poetic and the speech pronunciations. For example, another way of speaking the line would be:

   /   .   . /   . / . /   . /   c. 1 (= compromise 1)

   Well have ye judg'd, well ended long debate,

And another way might be:

/   .   . /   / . . / . /   c. 2 (= compromise 2)

Well have ye judg'd, well ended long debate,

3 For each line where there is more than one pronunciation, describe the difference in effect or meaning which the line has when it is pronounced in the different ways.

4 The rhythm of a line cannot always be decided in isolation from the lines which surround it, and there are factors other than the syllabic structure of words which affect rhythm. For example, try to assess the impact of syntax and punctuation on the way you give a rhythm to these lines when you say them aloud.

READING

*Abrams (1988) *Glossary of Literary Terms*, entry on 'Meter'.
*Attridge (1982) *The Rythms of English Poetry*.
Handel (1989) *Listening*, Ch. 11.
Leech (1966) *A Linguistic Guide to English Poetry*, Ch. 7.
Oehrle, Richard (1989) 'Temporal structures in verse design', in Kiparsky and Youmans (eds) *Rhythm and Meter*, pp. 87–119.

Unit 11 Parallelism and repetition

As descriptions of certain features of texts, the terms parallelism and repetition overlap one another. Yet it is worth rehearsing the difference between them if only to understand them more clearly. As its name suggests, repetition is used to describe an exact correspondence between two or more elements of a text (e.g. the repetition of words, as in the chorus of a song). Parallelism is used to describe repetition with difference – that is, a correspondence between textual elements in which there is some degree of repetition and some degree of difference.

Two examples will serve to illustrate repetition and parallelism and the difference between them:

Repetition: 'A horse! a horse! my kingdom for a horse!'

(Shakespeare (1593) Richard III)

Parallelism: Those that I fight I do not hate,
            Those that I guard I do not love

(Yeats (1919) 'An Irish airman foresees his death')

Whereas the first example uses exact repetition of 'a horse', the two lines in the second example repeat some elements (syntax, rhythm, most of the words) in a way which makes us attend to the differences between them. This formal parallelism underlines the fact that the airman's attitude towards those he guards and those he fights is not very different; formal parallelism can signal a parallelism in content.

There are various kinds of parallelism which may occur in texts: between the sounds of words (e.g. alliteration and rhyme), between groups of words (e.g. syntax or rhythm), between characters, between plots, between visual images, etc. In addition, parallelism can also be said to exist when corresponding elements of a text are opposites (e.g. themes of good vs evil in a narrative). In fact, parallelism constitutes the fundamental principle of most of the textual devices and effects examined in Sections 3 and 4 of this book. Rhythm, rhyme and all the varieties of sound patterning are examples of formal parallelism, while metaphor and related figures of speech rely upon various kinds of parallelisms of meaning.

Parallelism and repetition are easily found in all kinds of texts, and there are likely to be many repetitions in any text we look at. When we are writing expository prose (as in the present book), we are usually advised to avoid repetition since it will seem both redundant and unstylish. But the very nature of language means that chance repetition is both inevitable and usually not very interesting: words like *but* and *and* will appear quite frequently because of their functions; in the first sentence of the previous paragraph the word *between* appears five times. Yet in the kinds of text we are writing about (poems, songs, novels, plays, advertisements, etc.), repetition of some kind is often a basic device which contributes to the overall effect. In looking for parallelisms and repetitions, then, we need to ask two questions: (a) Is it worth trying to identify parallelisms in a particular text? (b) How can we decide which parallelisms are interesting or important and which can be ignored?

Before we try to answer these questions we turn to the close analysis of the parallelisms in a particular text in order to illustrate some of the ways in which parallelism works.

IDENTIFICATION AND ANALYSIS OF PARALLELISMS AND REPETITIONS IN A POEM

Our example text is a poem by Margaret Cavendish, Duchess of Newcastle (1653); this is the complete poem:

> *The claspe*
> Give Mee the Free and Noble Stile,
> Which seems uncurb'd, though it be wild:
> Though It runs wild about, It cares not where;
> It shews more Courage, then It doth of Feare.
> Give me a Stile that Nature frames, not Art:
> For Art doth seem to take the Pedants part.
> And that seemes Noble, which is Easie, Free,
> Not to be bound with ore-nice Pedantry.

(*Note:* shews = shows, Stile = style, ore = over).

1 *Repetition of words.* One of the most obvious types of repetition in the poem is that certain words are repeated. If we count the uses of repeated words by writing a number above each occurrence, we see that the most common of the 'important' words is 'seemes' (three uses), and that 'wild', 'Stile', 'Art', 'Noble', and 'Free' are each repeated twice:

<pre>
            1   1   1
Give Mee the Free and Noble Stile,
      1   1
Which seems uncurb'd, though it be wild:
</pre>

                2
Though It runs wild about, It cares not where;
It shews more Courage, then It doth of Feare.
              2   1
Give me a Stile that Nature frames, not Art:
        2   2   (1)
For Art doth seem to take the Pedants part.
              3   2   2
And that seemes Noble, which is Easie, Free,
                            (2)
Not to be bound with ore-nice Pedantry.

2 *Repetition of meanings.* In addition to repetitions of the same words, there are also repetitions of meanings, when there is a grouping of words with similar meanings (e.g. 'free' and 'uncurb'd') or with related meanings (e.g. 'free' and 'wild'). When words can be grouped together because they are associated with each other through their meaning, we can say that their meanings come from the same **semantic field** (*semantic* means 'relating to meaning'). Examples of groups of words in the same semantic field are:

1   Free – uncurb'd – wild – easie
2   frames – bound
3   wild – Nature
4   Art – Pedants, Pedantry
5   seems – shews – frames – Art
6   Claspe (title) – frames

Clearly, some of these six fields also fit into larger fields; 1 and 3 draw on a single larger field (concerning freedom and being natural); 2, 4, 5 and 6 draw on another (concerning the idea of being framed – in more than one sense – by artifice); although they are opposites, 1 and 2 draw on another field (concerning the idea of being bound or unbound). From this, we can see that the semantic fields drawn on by the text involve general thematic oppositions between art and restriction and between nature and freedom. If we treat opposition as a kind of parallelism, we can see that art is paralleled with nature and that restriction is paralleled with freedom. Thus an examination of parallelism may be used to highlight the 'value system' which a text is assuming or promoting: here, nature is being associated with freedom and is preferred over the restrictions of art.

3 *Syntactic parallelism* (see Unit 3: Analysing units of structure). Syntactic parallelism is a good example of repetition with difference. There is at least one syntactic parallelism in the poem (between the first two sentences) on the following pattern:

GIVE – ME – OBJECT –   COMMENT ON OBJECT –

Give   Mee the Free and Noble Stile, Which seems uncurb'd,

Give   me   a Stile   that Nature frames,

DISCLAIMER ABOUT OBJECT

though it be wild

not Art

4 *Rhythmic parallelism* (see Unit 10: Rhythm). Another kind of repetition with difference in this poem involves the fact that different lines have the same rhythmic pattern: the first two lines are both in iambic tetrameter (four-stress, rising duple rhythm), while the next six lines are iambic pentameters (five-stress, rising duple rhythm).

5 *Parallelism of sound patterning* (see Unit 9: Rhyme and sound patterning). There is a complex use of parallelism in the poem involving different kinds of sound patterning, such as alliteration (indicated by italics) and rhyme (indicated by bold typeface):

> Give **M**ee the **Fr**ee and Noble S**tile**,
> Which seems uncurb'd, though it be **w**ild:
> Though It runs *w*ild about, It cares not *wh***ere**;
> It shews more Courage, then It doth of **F**ea**re**.
> Give me a S**tile** that Nature frames, not **Art**:
> For Art doth seem to take the *P*edants *p*art.
> And that s**ee**mes Noble, which is Easie. **Fr**ee,
> Not to be bound with ore-nice Pedantry.

6 *A note of caution.* If we are interested in reconstructing the parallelisms which existed in the text for Cavendish, we need to know something about the language and culture of the time. For example, it is possible that *frames* might have rhymed with *seems* in the seventeenth century, and it would be interesting to know whether there was a potential difference between the pronunciation of 'mee' and *me* (e.g. did the former spelling rhyme with *seems* but not the latter?). A similar problem occurs with the meaning of words. For example, we have put 'wild' and 'Nature' together by claiming that they drew on the same semantic field (something which is natural is also wild), but we would have to check that this meaning of 'Nature' was possible in 1653, because the word has developed many different meanings in its history (see Williams 1976). For indications about how you might begin to find answers to these kinds of question, see Unit 2: Using information sources.

PARALLELISM IN OTHER KINDS OF TEXT

In spoken texts there might be intonational parallelism (e.g. repeated rising or falling intonation on every sentence of a speech). In a novel or play there may be parallelism of events – perhaps realized in a subplot which parallels the main plot (e.g. in Shakespeare's play *A Midsummer Night's Dream* (1596) the subplot and main plot are both about transformation); or there may be parallelism of characters, which may in turn draw on other parallels involving those characters such as oppositions in ethnicity, gender or age. Character parallelism is crucial in Mary Shelley's novel *Frankenstein* (1818), where strong parallels are drawn not only between Frankenstein and the creature he makes, but between Frankenstein and the novel's narrator. Image-based texts like films, videos, paintings and so on may produce and exploit visual parallelisms (of colour, shape, size, etc.). Visual parallelism can also be found in written texts; poets sometimes arrange the layout of poems in order to create visual patterns which form some kind of parallel with the poem's meaning (e.g. George Herbert's poem 'Easter wings' (1633) is arranged symmetrically on the page so that it looks like the wings of an angel).

THE FUNCTIONS OF PARALLELISM

We have seen that parallelism is very common and easy to identify in a text, and we might ask whether it is worth the trouble to describe it in detail. The justification comes when we look at how parallelism contributes to the way texts are built and create meaning. Parallelism has two main functions, one formal (adding to the look or sound of a text), the other semantic (adding to a text's meaning).

1 Parallelism holds a text together by setting up formal relations between its various parts. In this way parallelism is a kind of textual glue. In advertisements made up of a photograph and writing, for example, the different media are typically yoked together by some kind of parallelism (see Unit 13: Juxtaposition). Our analysis of the Cavendish poem suggests that poems can be 'glued' together in a number of different ways through parallelism. We might say that 'The claspe' has a high 'density' of parallelism both formally (the frequency and variety of sound-based parallelisms) and semantically (the large number of words which relate to binding/freedom and art/nature).

There are a number of ways in which we could think about the density of parallelism in 'The claspe'. We might ask whether it is unusually dense for poems of its time, or whether, as a representative poem from the mid-seventeenth century, it differs in density from a representative poem from a century earlier or a century later. This might assist an investigation of how poetic register differs in different periods. If we were interested in possible differences between women's and men's writing, we might compare its density with the density of a male-authored poem of the same time. Or a reader might ask whether the highly organized patterns of parallelism in the poem contradict its speaker's celebration of 'the Free and Noble Stile'. Thus the density of parallelisms within poetry is not just a general and obvious fact, but a subtle and interesting issue in its own right.

2 Parallelism inside a text contributes to the way texts create meanings and draw upon parallelisms operating in the culture which surrounds them. In 'The claspe', for example, the parallelisms build a repeated thematic opposition (itself a parallelism) between nature and art, which is made parallel in the poem to another thematic opposition between unboundedness and boundedness. There are meanings created by the text, but they draw upon parallelisms which exist in the cultural context: the opposition of nature and art is a fundamental one in British culture (though the way it is understood varies through history), and the poem is simply adopting this already-existing parallelism and putting it to use. (Remember this opposition when you do the activity at the end of this chapter).

When a text brings two words or phrases together in formal parallelism it stimulates us to consider whether there are parallelisms in their meanings; for example, in these lines from 'Epilogue to the Satires' by Alexander Pope (1738), 'shame' and 'fame' are formally parallel (they rhyme), and this invites us to consider the possible parallelism between these usually very different concepts (see Unit 9: Rhyme and sound patterning):

> Let humble ALLEN, with an aukward Shame,
> Do good by stealth, and blush to find it Fame.

This function of parallelism suggests that the conventional distinction between form and content is a problematic one.

There are other less central functions of parallelism.

3 Parallelism can make a text easier to remember (e.g. a chorus, a repeated phrase or refrain, a patterning of events); this is particularly important in oral literature, where texts exist by virtue of being remembered.

4 Parallelism can create expectation and excitement and is often used for emotive and persuasive effects; this rhetorical function is clear in the syntactic and intonational parallelism of political speeches:

> No government owns the law. It is the law of the land, the heritage of the people. No man is above the law and no man is below it. . . . Obedience to the law is demanded as a right, not asked as a favour.
>
>   (Margaret Thatcher, Party Conference Speech (1984))

Shakespeare often reproduces this feature of political speeches. In *Henry V* (1599), the king rouses his troops before the battle of Agincourt (against overwhelming odds) by first offering money to any man who wishes to go home, saying that

> We would not die in that man's company
> That fears his fellowship to die with us.

This is, of course, an attempt to persuade the soldiers that it would be honourable to die in such company, and its use of parallelism contributes to that end; this is reinforced shortly afterwards by the king's most persuasive (and parallelistic) description of those who will join him in battle: 'We few, we happy few, we band of brothers'.

In a Christian context, influenced by the bible, syntactic parallelism is also associated with authority and divine inspiration; this is because the Hebrew poetry of the Bible is highly parallelistic and English translations of the Bible often retain this feature. The Psalms provide good examples of this (the following is from Psalm 135, 1611 translation):

> They have mouths, but they speak not;
> Eyes have they, but they see not;
> They have ears, but they hear not

The relation between the conventional symbolic connotations of parallelism and its inherent emotional impact is a complex one, making it extremely difficult to distinguish between them.

5 Formalist critics argue that parallelism is a fundamental constitutive feature of the formal patterning which distinguishes literature from other kinds of discourse. Such critics value parallelism because of the way it tends to foreground or draw attention to the text itself independently of content or meaning (see Jakobson 1960; Leach 1969).

6 Parallelism seems to be pleasurable in itself. The nursery rhyme, a traditional type of text which gives pleasure to children, is named in a way which emphasizes a parallelism (rhyme) as a fundamental part of the genre.

WHICH PARALLELISMS SHOULD WE LOOK AT AND WHICH SHOULD WE IGNORE?

For the Cavendish poem, we counted the repetitions of what we thought of as semantically important words, but we did not count the five uses of 'it'. This illustrates an important point and problem: not all parallelisms are worth considering. It is usually possible to find a large number of parallelisms in a text, but not all of them will be worth the effort. Our decision about which parallelisms to look for is determined partly by whether they are salient. If two repeated elements are too far apart we are unlikely to identify them as being in parallel (e.g. alliterating words need to be close to each other). Because we hear words like *the* and *it* all the time, we are less likely to notice their repetition in a text than words like *nature* or *art*. If we are interested in looking at the way in which a text creates meaning, we would attend only to those parallelisms which a reader would notice and which seem to be meaningful.

But potentially overriding this is another issue, which is that we look for the parallelisms which are of interest to us in relation to a particular goal. Grammatical words like *the* and *it* will not fit into semantic fields because they do not have the right kind of meaning; hence we will not list them if we are interested in semantic parallelisms. But we might in fact trace how often *the* is repeated in a text if we were interested in the density of definite reference (which *the* carries out). In this way, the analysis of parallelisms is like many descriptive activities. In that our description is partly influenced by what we are looking for or expect to find.

ACTIVITY

One reason for the close analysis of a text is to trace the complex ways in which cultural values and ideologies are embodied in texts (in both form and content). The purpose of this activity is to look at the ways in which beliefs about gender can be expressed through parallelism (which we take to include repetition, comparison, opposition, reversal, etc.).

1 Read the following poem several times until you feel you have generally understood it.

	Community	(see note below)

1 Good we must love, and must hate ill,
2 For ill is ill, and good good still,
3   But there are things indifferent,
4 Which we may neither hate, nor love,
5 But one, and then another prove,   ('prove' = 'test')
6   As we shall find our fancy bent.

7 If then at first wise Nature had
8 Made women either good or bad,
9   Then some we might hate, and some choose,
10 But since she did them so create,
11 That we may neither love, nor hate,
12   Only this rests, All, all may use.

13 If they were good it would be seen,
14 Good is as visible as green.
15   And to all eyes itself betrays:
16 If they were bad, they could not last.
17 Bad doth itself, and others waste,
18   So, they deserve nor blame, nor praise.

19   But they are ours as fruits are ours,
20   He that but tastes, he that devours,
21   And he that leaves all, doth as well:
22   Changed loves are but changed sorts of meat.   ('meat' = 'food')
23   And when he hath the kernel eat,
24   Who doth not fling away the shell?

(John Donne; first printed in 1633)

Note: 'Community', according to the *OED*, had the following meanings at this time: (1) common ownership; (2) a quality of character in common; (3) social intercourse; (4) any common occurrence; (5) a group of people living in the same society; (6) a prostitute.

2 Draw a circle around every word (e.g. every pronoun) which names 'woman', and a box round every word which names 'man' (e.g. in lines 8 and 9 you circle 'women' and 'some' and box 'we'). This should help you in deciphering the poem.

3 Now identify different types of parallelism in the text. Where you are uncertain about whether a parallelism exists or not (e.g. whether two words would have rhymed in 1633), put a question mark next to it. Identify the types of parallelism by:

(a) annotating the text (writing numbers above repeated words, drawing lines between rhymes, underlining alliterations, etc.); use clearly distin-guished annotations for different types of parallelism;

(b) making lists (e.g. under the heading 'semantic fields' you could list words with associated meanings, under the heading 'rhythmic parallel-ism' you could list numbers of all lines which are rhythmically parallel, under 'structural parallelisms' you could write out sentences and phrases with similar syntax, etc.);

(c) writing down the parallelisms in meaning, including those created by figurative language (it is particularly important to do this for all parallel-isms which involve women as one element, all parallelisms which involve men as one element, and all parallelisms which involve nature as one element).

4 You have now made a fairly exhaustive description of certain aspects of the text and are able to begin an analysis of the way in which the text works to produce specific meanings. Carry out this analysis as follows:

(a) Look through your data to see if there are any formal parallelisms (involving sound, shape, syntax, etc.) which create or draw attention to parallelisms in meaning.

(b) Identify any places in the poem where you would expect parallelisms, but the parallelism does not occur (e.g. where you might expect but do

not get a sound pattern, rhythm, repeated word, word from a specific semantic field, meaning-parallelism, etc.); suggest reasons for each case (n.b. there may be no identifiable reason).
(c) Does the poem develop or draw upon any general parallelisms? If so, are any of the conventional elements of the equations missing?

5 Based on what you have now done, try to describe (a) the way men are represented in the poem, and (b) the way women are represented. Are there any differences in these representations? How does parallelism contribute to this?

READING

Cruse (1986) *Lexical Semantics* (on meaning relationships between words).
Halliday and Hasan (1976) *Cohesion in English,* Ch. 6 (on word repetition and association through meaning).
*Jakobson, Roman (1960) 'Linguistics and poetics', in Lodge (ed.) (1988) *Modern Criticism and Theory,* pp. 32–57.
*Leech (1969) *A Linguistic Guide to English Poetry,* Ch. 5.
Williams (1976) *Keywords.*

Unit 12 Deviation

Intelligible communication in speech or writing depends upon chaining together units of structure (e.g. words and phrases; see Unit 3: Analysing units of structure) according to certain rules. The sum of these rules makes up what linguists call the 'grammar' of a language, which describes all the patterns that sentences in a language are likely to have. For the linguist, it must be noted, these rules or norms are not the same as the kinds of prescriptions that are sometimes made about usage, such as

Don't split your infinitives.
Don't use double negatives.
Say 'It is I' rather than 'It's me'.

Prescriptive rules such as these are arbitrary attempts to control everyday usage and have little to do with the underlying rule system whose continuous background operation is an important guarantee of everyday intelligibility. When small children are learning language, for example, it is not the superficial prescriptive rules but the underlying rules which provide the grounds for communication.

Types of linguistic rule

Linguists distinguish at least three broad types of underlying linguistic rules:

1 rules of substance to do with the organization of sounds in speech (or letters and punctuation in writing);
2 rules of form relating to words or vocabulary and how they are combined into grammatical sentences;
3 rules of meaning which enable the words, when put together, to have a predictable meaning.

For the linguist, writing a grammar of a language ultimately consists of stating what rules govern the operation of the language under these three basic headings. In everyday usage, or course, not all of the rules are followed all of the time. Careful examination of everyday speech reveals a high degree of 'rule breaking' (little of which may be noticeable at the time) – slips of the tongue, false starts, unfinished sentences and so on. When children are learning the language, they build up the rule system over time, making interesting mistakes on the way. Moreover, when the personality is under great stress, as in certain kinds of psychic breakdown, control of the rule system may be partly lost.

In all these cases, deviation takes the form of errors which constitute impediments to communication. But it would be a mistake to dismiss all linguistic deviation in 'everyday' language usage as due to error. The 'mistakes' that children make are often interesting in their own right, and children derive pleasure from playful linguistic deviation. This pleasure is continued in adult life through word play, puns, figures of speech and so on. Because of this, the distinction which is often made between 'conventional' everyday usage and 'literary' deviation is a problematic one. Nevertheless, rule breaking in literature differs from deviation in everyday usage in that it occurs in regular, systematic ways – some of which we now examine.

CONVENTION AND DEVIATION IN LITERATURE

Literature often appears to separate itself from other uses of language by deliberately distorting the rules of everyday communication. At the same time, it would not be true to say that literature always and inevitably depends upon deviation. It is more accurate to view the literary institution as operating upon a spectrum constituted by degrees of linguistic deviation, so that some authors, periods and genres are more deviant than others.

The pleasure we experience from linguistic deviation in everyday language depends upon our knowledge of the conventions of ordinary usage: deviation only becomes pleasurable and interesting when we know what it deviates from. The same is true of literary deviation, which derives its impact from our sense of the way it deviates from two sets of conventions:

(a) the conventions of ordinary usage;
(b) the conventions of the literary system itself.

What is at first deviation and 'original' in literature can quickly become conventional – which is why writers continually invent new kinds of deviations in the attempt, as Ezra Pound put it, to 'make it new'.

Deviation in rules of substance

In a society such as late twentieth-century Britain, literature exists primarily as a body of printed works rather than as a set of oral performances. Since its principal mode of expression is written rather than spoken, it follows that where we get deviation at the level of substance this is primarily a matter of typography, layout, punctuation and spelling. Poetry routinely adopts modes of layout that are peculiar to itself – relatively short lines indented on the page, and so on. But this has itself become a poetic convention against which even more extreme deviations can be measured. The following poem by Edwin Morgan, for example, takes liberties with many aspects of substance simultaneously – principally, features of typography, layout and punctuation:

Message clear

```
    am                i
                                        if
i am                         he
        he r         o
        h      ur    t
        the re              and
        he      re     and
        he re
    a                   n   d
        th   e   r           e
i am       r                     ife
                        i n
            s       ion and
i                       d     i e
    am    e res    ect
    am    e res    ection
                        o           f
        the                       life
                        o           f
      m    e             n
            sur e
        the               d     i e
i              s
            s    e t    and
i am the    sur            d
    a    t    res     t
                        o           life
i am  he r                       e
i a               ct
i          r   u    n
i   m    e e       t
i                 t           i e
i           s    t    and
```

```
i am th            o       th
i am     r              a
i am the    su       n
i am the    s        on
i am the  e    rect on           e if
i am        re            n     t
i am          s           a           fe
i am          s    e    n     t
i       he  e                   d
i       t e  s      t
i             re               a d
   a    th re               a d
   a          s      t on                  e
   a    t    re               a d
   a    th r             on                e
i                resurrect
                              a        life
i am                      i  n         life
i am          resurrection
i am the resurrection and
i am
i am the resurrection and the life
```

Perhaps the most deviant feature of this text is the way in which the conventional method of indicating the boundaries between words in the written medium has been violated by using spaces within words as well as between them. Moreover, not only do the spaces seem to be randomly distributed with no respect for word boundaries, they also vary in length. This deviation makes the text difficult to read and understand, and it is only when we reach the end that we realize that all the lines are variations on the final line, with letters removed. If, now, we ignore the spacing in each line we can construct words and phrases such as 'i act', 'i am the sun', etc., which are subtly related to the final message – 'I am the resurrection and the life'. The title ('Message clear') can be understood in various ways (it might initially seem an ironic comment on the struggling reader), but one obvious reading of it is that the 'message' becomes 'clear' only when you 'get the message'.

Deviation of substance is not restricted to poetry but may also be found in novels – as you will see if you leaf through novels such as Laurence Sterne's *Tristram Shandy* (1759–67) or Alasdair Gray's *Lanark* (1981).

Deviation in rules of form: vocabulary

This occurs in literature when new words are deliberately created for particular effect. This may be done in various ways, but the most straightforward strategy is simply the pasting of words or elements of words together into new combinations. Many words in the language have already been built up in this way:

fortunate	=	fortune+ate
unfortunate	=	un+fortune+ate
unfortunately	=	un+fortune+ate+ly
breakfast	=	break+fast
straightforward	=	straight+forward

We can see from these examples that even small elements such as *un-*, *-ate* and *-ly* can have a fairly predictable meaning in the structure of a word: *un-* usually means 'not'; *-ate* usually suggests 'quality'; and *-ly* usually suggests 'manner'. These basic patterns of meaning and word construction allow us to make sense of words that we have never encountered before. When Gerard Manley Hopkins in 'Wreck of the Deutschland' (1875) refers to the sea as 'widow-making, unchilding, unfathering deeps' it is clear that he is emphasizing in a particularly compressed fashion the way in which the sea can take husbands from their wives, children from their parents and fathers from their children. Similarly, when T.S. Eliot in *The Waste Land* (1922) puts a neologism (a new word) in the mouth of the blind seer Tiresias, who says 'And I Tiresias have foresuffered all', our knowledge of the conventional function of *fore-* means that we are able to derive a meaning for 'foresuffer'. (Tiresias is presumably claiming that his prophetic powers mean that he not only 'foresees' events but also suffers or endures them before they occur.) Thus we can usually make sense of deviations through our implicit knowledge of the underlying conventions of the language. These principles enable the production and understanding of puns in everyday life, and they help us at least to attempt to interpret the radical deviations in word formation found in James Joyce's *Finnegans Wake* (1939):

> I have just (let us suppraise) been reading in a suppressed book – it is notwithstempting by measures long and limited – the latterpress is eminently leglligible and the paper, so he eagerly seized upon, has scarsely been buttered in works of previous publicity wholebeit in keener notcase would I turf aside for pastureuration.

In this example, Joyce uses 'portmanteau' words (the term is introduced by Humpty Dumpty in Lewis Carroll's *Alice in Wonderland* (1865), and means that several meanings are packed into one word, like a portmanteau bag). 'Notwithstempting', for example, can be read as both 'notwithstanding' and 'not tempting'.

Deviation in rules of form: syntax

Efficient communication depends not only on the choice of words but on how they are arranged in sentences. Indeed, there are strong constraints on the ways in which words can be put together into sentences if they are to make sense. These constraints are called the syntax of the language and all language users are subject to them. The importance of syntactic conventions in English can be demonstrated by how relatively small shifts in word order and combination can significantly alter the meaning of sentences:

This is the ten o'clock news
Is this the ten o'clock news

Poets, no less than other language-users, have to subscribe to syntactic constraints if they are to be understood; even when they deviate from them, they depend upon our knowledge of the conventions they break in order to achieve their effects. Syntactic inversions are quite common in poetry and are partly used in order to conform to a rhyme scheme:

Silent is the house: all are laid asleep:
One alone looks out o'er the snow-wreaths deep.
                            (Emily Bronte, 'The Visionary', 1846)

A more straightforward (but less effective) order would be:

The house is silent' all are laid asleep:
One alone looks out over the deep snow-wreaths,

These are fairly minor deviations from normal word order when compared with the following poem by e.e. cummings:

swi(
          across!gold's

rouNdly
)ftblac
kl(ness)y

a-motion-upo-nmotio-n

Less?
          thE
(against
is
)Swi

mming

(w-a)s
bIr

  d,

This is not an easy text to make sense of on a first reading, since it is deviant on more than one level. At the level of substance, for instance, the normal conventions of graphology and typography have been subjected to severe distortion. At the level of form, affixes such as *-ness*, *-ly* and *-less*, have become detached from the items with which they (most probably) fit, and words have become interrupted internally by other words. In addition, normal word order has been severely disrupted, so much so that it is difficult to reconstruct an easily intelligible alternative with any degree of confidence. But one plausible order would be as follows:

> The bird is/was a black motion swimming swiftly against/across/upon gold's motionless roundness.

If we assume it to be a poem about a bird silhouetted in flight against the orb of the setting sun ('gold's roundness'), what has been gained by scrambling the more normal word order that could have been adopted? In literature, such extreme disruption of syntax conventionally suggests psychological immediacy – the rendering of the actual process of perception or cognition as it happens. This seems to be the case here: it is as if the process of unravelling the syntax mimics the process of recognizing – out of a jumble of impressions – the flight of a bird across the face of the sun.

Deviation in meaning: semantics

All the earlier cases of deviation have consequences for meaning and interpretation; breaking the rules of punctuation, for instance, affects the way we read and make sense of the text in which it occurs. However, it is also possible to find cases of direct manipulation of conventional meanings in themselves. Joseph Heller's novel, *Catch 22* (1961), is particularly rich in this kind of deviation. Set during the Second World War, it gets its title from a paradox called 'catch 22' which is used by the authorities in the novel to keep US airmen flying an ever increasing number of bombing missions. Although airmen can appeal to be grounded on grounds of insanity:

> There was only one catch and that was Catch 22, which specified that a concern for one's own safety in the face of dangers that were real and immediate was the process of a rational mind. Orr was crazy and could be grounded. All he had to do was ask; and as soon as he did, he would no longer be crazy and would have to fly more missions. Orr would be crazy to fly more missions and sane if he didn't, but if he was sane he would have to fly them. If he flew them he was crazy and didn't have to; but if he didn't want to he was sane and had to.

Conventionally, the expressions 'sane' and 'crazy' are opposite in meaning. Part of the fascination (and the humour) of *Catch 22* is the way in which it constructs conditions under which such opposites can both be true at the same time. Love and hate are conventionally opposite in meaning, yet the novel tells us that 'Dunbar loved shooting skeet because he hated every minute of it and the time passed so slowly.' Many examples of semantic deviation in the novel are structured in two parts like jokes:

Doc Daneeka was Yossarian's friend
and would do just about nothing in his power to help him

This profusion of semantic anomalies in the opening chapters of *Catch 22* helps to create the impression of a world in which war has undermined the rational basis of social and moral action.

Another, more fundamental, way in which literature produces and exploits semantic deviation in meaning is through its use of figurative language, since figures of speech (or tropes) can be thought of as deviations from literal meaning (see Unit 13: Metaphor, and Unit 14: Irony). Figures of speech play a large part in other kinds of discourse, but they tend to become conventional and we lose our sense of their 'deviance'. In literature, on the other hand, figurative language tends to be newly created and makes us aware of the way it deviates from literal usage or conventional figures.

Literature as deviant in the way it describes the world

Perhaps the most fundamental kind of deviation which characterizes literature stems not so much from its manipulation of linguistic conventions, but from peculiarities in the way it relates to the world at large. These peculiarities include (a) the way that literary texts construct imagined worlds; (b) the way that literary texts construct imagined speakers; (c) the way that literary texts address imagined addressees.

Many kinds of discourse – news, problem pages, research reports, gossip, even advertising – operate under certain conditions of truth; we expect their assertions to be true, or at least to amount to reasonable claims. Literature, on the other hand, is full of what look like assertions about the world but which actually contradict our everyday sense of what the world is like. Literary discourse, then, is deviant in the sense that it claims to refer to things in the world, but we are not expected to take those claims seriously. Take, for instance, the opening sentence of George Orwell's novel *Nineteen Eighty-Four* (1949):

It was a bright cold day in April and the clocks were striking thirteen.

To a British readership, the notion of there being a bright cold day in April may be completely unremarkable, but the fact that the same sentence tells us that 'the clocks were striking thirteen' serves to place the events of the novel outside that readership's everyday world (since clocks in public places in Britain do not habitually strike thirteen). Furthermore, although when it was written the title of the book looked forward to a date in the future, the past tense of the first sentence refers backwards as if to events which have already happened. Yet most readers would not interpret the first sentence as the beginning of a factual record of events but would realize that Orwell's point was that such events could conceivably come to pass.

It is not just the way that literature refers to things which do not necessarily exist that marks its peculiarity as a discourse. The narrators of novels and the speakers of poems can be as fictional as the events which are presented. When Julian Barnes uses a woodworm to retell the biblical story of Noah's Ark from an unusual angle in *A History of the World in 10½ Chapters* (1989), he follows a long tradition of using non-human narrators in literary narratives. Similarly, the speaker of Sylvia Plath's poem 'Elm' (1962) is a tree.

In the case of poetry in particular, literature's whole mode of address turns out to be deviant since it typically addresses someone (or something) other than the reader. During the Romantic period, for instance, it was possible in the context of a poem to address directly a rose, or a skylark or even a piece of pottery (a Grecian urn):

O Rose, thou art sick

(Blake, 'The sick rose' (1794))

Hail to thee blithe spirit!

(Shelley, 'Ode to a skylark' (1820))

Thou still unravished bride of quietness

(Keats, 'Ode on a Grecian urn' (1820))

Addressing entities that are incapable of talking back may have become a fairly unremarkable literary convention, but it is worth noting how deviant this is by comparison with everyday conditions of discourse. We might swear at the cat when it gets under our feet, but we do not write an elaborate note to it – not, at least, unless we are writing poetry.

EFFECTS AND IMPLICATIONS OF LITERARY DEVIATION: DEFAMILIARIZATION

We have seen that literature is a discourse which reworks the conventions and codes of the language and is potentially deviant in a range of different dimensions. But this does not mean that literature has nothing to say about the ordinary world we live in. On the contrary, its use of deviation allows us to see our world from unfamiliar and revealing angles (Russian formalist critics called this effect **defamiliarization**). The philosopher Wittgenstein is credited with saying that 'the limits of my language are the limits of my world'. In everyday communication we are usually content to leave intact the limits of our language and therefore of our world. Literature, by contrast, extends the boundaries of our taken-for-granted world and allows us to think and feel it afresh by systematically deviating from conventional linguistic practices and habitual modes of expression. Literature may be seen as a domain of linguistic experiment in how to say new things by bending the rules of the system. By subverting the commonsense bonds between utterances and their situations of use it allows us to explore new kinds of identity and forms of relationship.

ACTIVITY

1 For each of the following phrases, choose an appropriate word (or phrase) to fill the blank:

_____ is a pleasant country
_____ is wintry
_____ is the very weather, not _____
love is a deeper _____

2 Now compare your choices with those made in the following poem by e.e. cummings:

yes is a pleasant country:
if's wintry
(my lovely)
let's open the year

both is the very weather
(not either)
my treasure,
when violets appear

love is a deeper season
than reason;
my sweet one
(and april's where we're)

3 Circle all the deviant words and answer the following questions:

(a) Do any of the deviant words have anything in common with each other
     (e.g. what kinds of words are they)?
(b) What are the differences between the phrases you made and those in
     the poem?

4 In addition to these semantic deviations (deviations in rules of meaning), list any deviations in:

(a) rules of substance (i.e. in the letters and punctuation);
(b) rules of form (i.e. how the words are combined together).

5 Are all features of the poem deviant? Do any of the following features appear conventional or fall into regular patterns?

(a) rhythm;
(b) rhyme;
(c) address;
(d) punctuation;
(e) syntax.

6 Assuming that you find some aspects of the poem deviant and some conventional or regular, think of answers to the following:

(a) Why does the poem use deviation at all?
(b) Why is everything in the poem not deviant?
(c) What is the effect of using deviation in some aspects and being conventional or regular in others?

READING

Erlich (1969) *Russian Formalism: History–Doctrine*
Garvin (ed. and trans.) (1964) *A Prague School Reader in Aesthetics, Literary Structure and Style.*
*Leech (1969) *A Linguistic Guide to English Poetry,* Chs 2 and 3.
Lemon, L.T. and M.J. Reis (eds) (1965) *Russian Formalist Criticism,* especially the chapter by Shklovsky (1921) 'Sterne's *Tristram Shandy*: stylistic commentary', pp. 25–57.

Section 4

Reading figures of speech

Unit 13 Metaphor

LITERAL AND NON-LITERAL LANGUAGE

In this and the next unit we look at various uses of non-literal language which as literary devices are collectively called **figurative language**. Certain kinds of figurative language are traditionally called **tropes**; these include metaphor, simile, metonymy and synechdoche (which we discuss in this unit) and verbal irony (which we discuss in Unit 14).

A spoken utterance or written sentence potentially has two fundamentally different sorts of meaning: a literal meaning and (sometimes) an implied, non-literal meaning. Meaning is interpreted in two steps:

(1) by decoding its literal meaning;
(2) then by inferring its implied (non-literal) meaning.

Literal meaning is a meaning which is fixed – always the same, predictable and shared by speakers – for a particular word or group of words. The English word *two*, for example, has a literal meaning, referring to a particular number; and the English word *cat* has a literal meaning, referring to a particular type of animal. Most words have meanings of this kind. When words are put together into phrases and then into sentences, their individual literal meanings combine to form a collective literal meaning. So the meaning of *two cats* is predictable from the individual meanings of the words *two* and *cat*. In this way, a sentence (which is made up of words) has a literal meaning formed from the literal meanings of the words which compose it.

Many sentences also have non-literal meaning, however, which can be called their **implied meaning**. If someone asks you what the time is and you say 'five-thirty', your utterance may well not be literally true (it might be 5.28 or 5.31 etc.). But the hearer can compensate for this: s/he can interpret what you say by adding 'approximately' in her or his head as you speak. The words *five-thirty* can accordingly mean 'approximately five-thirty'. If you and that person are about to go to a film, and s/he asks what the time is and you say 'too late', s/he can add a meaning 'too late to get to the film on time'. You did not literally say this; but s/he can work out that this is a meaning you intended. This process of adding meanings, or building additional meanings out of literal meanings, is called **inferencing**; s/he infers a meaning from your statement.

A figurative word, phrase or sentence is an example of non-literal meaning, and so is interpreted by inferencing, which involves the addition of meanings not literally present in the text. These meanings come from the reader or hearer or viewer, who supplies the meanings from what s/he knows. Because different audiences know different things, so ironies, metaphors, etc. may be interpreted differently by different people.

We can illustrate the distinction between literal and figurative uses using the example of the word *dead* which can be used literally or figuratively. When words are used or interpreted literally, they are understood at face value. If someone says 'Winston Churchill is dead', we take the word *dead* at face value, assuming it simply means 'no longer alive'. A figurative use or interpretation, on the other hand, assumes that a word or phrase should be understood in terms of another, figurative meaning. If someone says 'I feel dead today', it makes no sense to take the utterance as literally true; instead, it has to be interpreted figuratively – typically, as a way of emphasizing how tired the person is. The word *dead*, then, can be used and understood in two different ways: either literally or figuratively.

Signals of figurative language

How do we decide whether to take a statement literally or figuratively? If a trope is being used, it is usually signalled in some way; if there is no signal, we usually read literally. Signals that language is being used figuratively can be of two kinds: textual and contextual.

A textual signal is given by there being something unusual about the piece of language itself, regardless of the situation it is used in. Most often, such a signal is that the language cannot make literal sense; we understand *I feel dead* figuratively, for instance, because it is difficult to imagine any context in which *I feel dead* could be meant literally.

A contextual signal, on the other hand, is given when, although the words themselves make literal sense, the context in which they are used suggests that they are somehow inappropriate, and require a further process of interpretation. This is often the case with verbal irony.

The distinction between literal and figurative is complicated, however, by the fact that many statements can make sense both literally and figuratively. The claim, *Winston Churchill is dead* is evidently true on a literal level, but in the context of a discussion of the British character, *Churchill is dead* may mean that a particular warlike attitude, or so-called 'bulldog spirit', has disappeared. The decision whether to interpret an utterance figuratively or literally (or even both at once) is not always easy, even when we take both textual and contextual signals into account.

METAPHOR

The word *metaphor* comes from a Greek word *metaphora*, meaning 'to transfer' or 'to carry over'. Metaphor occurs when a word or phrase in a passage is clearly out of place in the topic being dealt with but nevertheless makes sense because of some similarity between it and what is being talked about. To interpret the word or phrase, we automatically look for the element of similarity and transfer it into the new context. In doing this, we interpret metaphorically.

When Paul Simon sings 'I am a rock' (1966) we are unlikely to think that he is made of stone or wonder how a rock can sing. Rather, we select those aspects of a rock which might also characterize how the singer may feel or want to represent himself and transfer them to the new context. The metaphor which results is effective because, in describing psychological experience in terms of a 'rock', it vividly transfers our associations of rock – such as hardness, isolation, imperviousness – to the singer (there is also an allusion here to the metaphorical use of the term *rock* in the Bible, which adds or suggests further possible meanings for Simon's phrase).

Analogously, in the statement *by the year 2000 manufacturing will be dominated by industries now at an embryonic stage,* the word *embryonic* does not initially appear to fit in a discussion of industry and manufacturing (because literally it is a term for the offspring of an animal before birth or emergence from an egg). To make sense of *embryonic* in this unusual context, we select those parts of its meaning which allow us to interpret the word in a discussion about industry. *At an embryonic stage* becomes a figurative way of saying that the industries of the future are as yet at a rudimentary level of development. The idea of natural gestation is also transferred into the new context, however, and we are therefore invited to see the development of industry as in some way a natural process; this offers us a reassuring sense that the new industries are to be welcomed. In this way, metaphor can significantly affect how we perceive or respond to what is being described.

Simile

Simile is a category of metaphor in that, as its name suggests, it draws attention to a similarity between two terms. But whereas in metaphor the link between the terms is implied, in simile it is made through an explicit textual signal (*like, as,* etc.). Simile does not, strictly speaking, always entail figurative language, since both terms of a simile can often be understood literally. The simile *the sky is like a polished mirror,* for example, invites the listener or reader to imagine how the sky might actually appear like a polished mirror. This difference between simile and metaphor can be demonstrated by turning the simile into a metaphor. If we say *the sky is a polished mirror* this formulation can no longer be understood literally; we know that the sky is not really a polished mirror, though it might look like one, and therefore *polished mirror* has to be read metaphorically,

Metonymy

Metonymy (Greek for 'a change of name') is distinguished from metaphor in that, whereas metaphor works through similarity, metonymy works through other kinds of association (e.g. cause–effect, attribute, containment, etc.).

The sentence *Moscow made a short statement* makes sense only if we understand it figuratively, taking *Moscow* to stand for the leaders of the Soviet Union. This figure is possible not because of any obvious similarity between the city and the people, but because the two are associated with each other (one is the place where the other lives and works). Metonymies can be formed through many different kinds of associative link. Typical dress, for example, can be used metonymically to stand for those who wear it: if someone says 'a lot of big wigs came to the party', we understand *big wigs* to refer to 'important people' (a metonymy which probably derives from the fashion among the upper classes in earlier centuries in Europe of wearing elaborate wigs in public – a practice still followed by judges and barristers in court).

Synecdoche

Synecdoche (Greek for 'taking together') is a subcategory of metonymy. It occurs when the association between the figurative and literal senses is that between a part and the whole to which it belongs. *Farm hands* is a common synecdoche for workers on a farm; *a new motor* comes to mean 'a new car' by using one part of the car, its engine, to stand for the whole. (Note that the *big wig* is not a part of the person to which it belongs, and so would not be called synecdoche; instead, it is simply associated with the person.)

ANALYSING METAPHORS

Tenor, vehicle, ground

A metaphor consists of two terms or levels: the figurative and the literal. I.A. Richards (1936) proposed that the literal level should be called the **tenor** and the figurative level the **vehicle**. In Paul Simon's metaphor, the vehicle or metaphorical term is 'rock' (since this word cannot be taken literally); the tenor (what is actually being talked about) is 'I' (the singer). In the discussion of future industries, the vehicle is 'embryonic' and the tenor is what is literally being said about the state of industries – something like 'at an early stage of development'. The process of transference through which metaphor works can only take place if there is a link between the context in which a word is normally used and the new context in which it is applied; Richards suggested that such a link should be called the **ground**. In the case of metaphors, the ground is one of similarity; with metonymies, the ground involves some other kind of association such as the one thing being next to or inside the other.

Explicit and implicit metaphors

In an explicit metaphor, one thing is described as if it were another thing. 'I am a rock' is an explicit metaphor. This is not only because both its tenor ('I') and its vehicle ('rock') are specified within the text; it is also because a link is explicitly made between tenor and vehicle by the use of the verb *to be* ('I am a rock'). Bob Dylan's suggestion that 'time is a jetplane – it moves too fast' (1974) is another explicit metaphor. In this case, as well as providing the tenor ('time'), the vehicle ('jetplane'), and a form of the verb *to be* ('is') which links the two, the phrase also specifies the ground of the metaphor (time can be called a jetplane because they both 'move too fast'). This is in fact an unusual metaphor because it makes the ground explicit; in most cases the ground must be inferred.

In contrast to explicit metaphors, an implicit metaphor occurs when one word or phrase stands directly in place of another. One half of the comparison (the tenor) is absent, and so remains implicit. The suggestion that certain industries are at an embryonic stage includes the vehicle or metaphorical term ('embryonic'), but it leaves the reader to infer what the tenor is. The vehicle has been substituted for the tenor which would otherwise have appeared in its place in the sentence.

Metaphors using different parts of speech

So far, many of the metaphors we have looked at involve nouns. But other parts of speech (see Unit 3: Analysing units of structure) can also be used as metaphors, as the following list shows:

Noun: 'time is a *jetplane*'
                             (Bob Dylan, 'You're a big girl now' (1974))
   'You are the *apple* of my eye'

Verb: 'time us *running out*'
   'the hour glass *whispers* to the lion's roar'
                                   (Auden, 'Our bias' (1940)

Adjective: '*golden* skin'
          'a *wooden* performance'

Adverb: Thistles dried to sticks in last year's wind
         stand *nakedly* in the green,
         stand *sullenly* in the slowly whitening,
         field.
                    (Adrienne Rich, 'Toward the solstice' (1977))

Classifying metaphors

Besides classifying metaphors according to the parts of speech they involve, it is also possible to classify them according to the types of transference of meaning they employ (see Geoffrey Leech 1969). A **concretive metaphor** uses a concrete term to talk about an abstract thing. Examples include *the burden of responsibility* and *every cloud has a silver lining*. Religious discourse often uses concretive metaphors to make abstract ideas more vivid: heaven is frequently referred to as if it were a place or a building – 'In my Father's house there are many mansions.' An **animistic metaphor** uses a term usually associated with animate things (living creatures) to talk about an inanimate thing. Examples include *the leg of the table* and *killing a bottle*. A **humanizing** or **anthropomorphic metaphor** (sometimes called **personification**) uses a term usually associated with human beings to talk about a non-human thing. Examples include *the hands of the clock* and *the kettle's sad song*. Humanizing metaphor is connected with the **pathetic fallacy** (the idea that the world reflects or participates in one's emotions); *the kettle's sad song* might be used as a way of indicating a character's mood by implicitly describing how s/he perceives the kettle's sound.

Extended metaphor

When a piece of language uses several vehicles from the same area of thought, it is possible to speak of extended metaphor. Extended metaphor is a common literary device. Marvell, in 'A dialogue between the soul and body' (1681), talks of the soul's relation to the body as follows:

O who shall from this dungeon raise
A soul enslaved so many ways?
With bolts of bones, that fettered stands
In feet; and manacled in hands

Taking the once commonplace metaphor of the body as a prison of the soul, Marvell extends it by selecting a series of vehicles concerned with imprisonment ('dungeon', 'enslaved', 'bolts', 'fettered', 'manacles'), and transferring them to the human body.

Mixed metaphor

Books on 'good style' generally condemn the use of mixed metaphor (the combination of two or more metaphors whose vehicles come from different and incongruous areas) because they can have unintentionally ludicrous effects. For precisely this reason, jokes often exploit mixed metaphor (e.g. *I shall make no bones about the skeletons in the cupboard*). M.H. Abrams (1988) claims that mixed metaphor in poetry can have a functional effect – as in the following lines from *Hamlet* (1601):

To be, or not to be: that is the question;
Whether 'tis nobler in the mind to suffer
The slings and arrows of outrageous fortune,

Or to take arms against a sea of troubles
And by opposing end them

(III, i, 56–60)

Hamlet mixes his metaphors in this passage since he represents the struggle between the individual and fortune as a battle (fortune has its 'slings and arrows' and the individual may 'take arms'), but takes his next metaphor ('sea') from a completely different area. In literal terms it is evidently ludicrous to imagine taking a sword to fight the sea. But Abrams suggests that this mixing of metaphors might be a symptom of Hamlet's troubled mind. It is also possible to suggest that it underlines the futility of trying to resist 'outrageous fortune'.

THE SOCIAL IMPLICATIONS OF METAPHOR

Metaphor and language change

Metaphor is crucial to the way language changes, and can be seen as a process of change in action. New metaphors are constantly being developed whenever a new area of experience or thought needs new descriptive terms (see Unit 4: Language and time).

When a new term is needed, the tendency is to make the unfamiliar familiar by borrowing terms from other fields (so forming metaphors) rather than to invent new terms. *The greenhouse effect* involves a metaphor which figures the global system of the earth as a giant greenhouse. This might help us to understand an unfamiliar idea, but it may also work to domesticate the effect in question and thereby reduce our sense of alarm.

Gradually, however, metaphors become overfamiliar and cease to be recognized as metaphors at all. When this happens, they lose their power to confront us with their effects as metaphors. Everyday language is full of terms which would once have required a metaphorical interpretation, but which are now so familiar that they produce no effect at all. A speaker of English would not normally be conscious of producing two (very different) metaphors in claiming that *things are looking up for the team since the landslide victory last week*. Yet both *things are looking up* and *landslide* have to be understood as metaphors since they cannot be taken literally in the context.

Words and phrases which are metaphorical, but cease to be treated as if they are, are called **dead metaphors** (notice, incidentally, that the phrase *dead metaphor* is itself a dead metaphor). Some dead metaphors can be revived, nevertheless, if we draw attention to the fact that they are metaphors. We can temporarily revive the metaphorical nature of *made my blood boil* by extending the metaphor: *it made my blood boil and steam come out of my ears.*

It is sometimes suggested that literature can be distinguished from non-literary discourse because literature uses language metaphorically, while non-literary discourse uses it literally. A more useful way of thinking about how metaphor is used, however, is to imagine a 'spectrum' of language types, ranging from discourses which consist mostly of literal usages and dead metaphors through to discourses which are highly conscious in their use of new and vivid metaphors.

The persuasive effects of metaphor

Metaphors can be used to reinforce our images of the world, or to challenge them. Figurative language can significantly affect our attitude towards the topic under discussion, and is capable of affecting us even (or perhaps especially) if we do not consciously recognize that it is being used. This is possibly why it is so common in advertising, politics and journalism. The rhetorical purpose or implication of a metaphor can usually be grasped, nevertheless, by thinking about the connotations (implied meanings) it brings to its new context, and then asking what effects those connotations are likely to have on the way we perceive or respond to what is being talked about (see the examples of *embryonic* and *greenhouse* examined above).

Terms of address used primarily or exclusively by men to address women include *honey, baby, doll, hen,* etc.: all dead metaphors, figuring women as food, immature, playthings, animals, etc. These metaphors figure women in ways which reinforce conventional images and attitudes, and therefore both reflect and reproduce those conventions. Drawing out the implications of such metaphorical 'terms of endearment' can contribute to exposing the way such conventions are embedded in our language in a wide range of dead metaphors.

When metaphor works against convention, on the other hand, it can operate as a powerful challenge to established ways of thinking. Wallace Stevens puts the point the other way round: 'Reality is a cliche from which we escape by metaphor.' Rather than promoting a conventional way of seeing the world, a metaphor which draws attention to itself as a metaphor can make demands on our power of creative interpretation. At the end of Norman MacCaig's 'Fetching cows' (1965), for example, the speaker produces a metaphor which demands that we reconsider the sentimental way we often regard farm animals and that we think instead about how we use them as sources of food:

> The black cow is two native carriers
> Bringing its belly home, slung from a pole.

Each time such challenging metaphors are produced, the way language maps the world is altered. Domains which the language usually keeps separate are momentarily fused, and new meanings are brought into existence.

Metaphor in history

Historically, metaphor has served both radical and conservative purposes. This is reflected in shifting attitudes towards it in the history of literature in English.

In the neoclassical period (*c* 1660–1790), poetry was widely thought of as a process of retelling truths which were generally shared and accepted – or, as Alexander Pope puts it in his *Essay on Criticism* (1709), 'What oft was thought, but ne'er so well expressed'. This outlook can be thought of as a conservative one in that it emphasizes the reflection of existing meanings rather than the creation of new ones. In this period, metaphor was distrusted as a potentially falsifying device whose use ought to be sanctioned by social convention or 'decorum'. Although metaphor could be used to 'dress' or embellish accepted and acceptable truths, care was to be taken to keep it subservient to that end. It was even suggested in 1670 that an Act of Parliament should be introduced forbidding the use of 'fulsome and luscious' metaphors.

The Romantic poets, by contrast, thought of metaphor not as an embellishment of thought but as the means of imaginative thought itself. They argued that poetry should not be restricted to saying old things in new ways, but could be made capable of creating new thoughts and ideas; this view was influentially formulated in Shelley's 'A defence of poetry' (1821):

> [The language of poets] is virtually metaphorical; that is, it marks the before unapprehended relations of things, and perpetuates their apprehension, ... if no new poets should arise to create afresh the associations which have been thus disorganized, language will be dead to all the nobler purpose of human intercourse.

In this view, thoughts and ideas do not exist prior to metaphor; rather, they are produced by metaphor. Far from presenting 'what oft was thought', poetic metaphor 'disorganizes' conventional analogies in order to reveal relations which were 'unapprehended' beforehand. As such, metaphor can be seen as an agency through which it becomes possible significantly to transform our perceptions of the world. And since 'poetic' metaphor, in Shelley's sense, is not necessarily confined to poetry, it is possible to generalize from his suggestion to the idea that producing, responding to and analysing metaphor is a form of active participation in the circulation and criticism of meanings in society.

ACTIVITY

Part A

1 Read the following pieces of text and then carry out the operations below (for definitions, see the exposition above).

(a) Open cast mining rapes countryside.
(b) An aged man is but a paltry thing,
     A tattered coat upon a stick.

> (Yeats, 'Sailing to Byzantium' (1928))

(c) The plot is so thick the spoon stands up in it.
(d) I was left for dead by the fastest wheels on the road.
(e) After a somewhat leaden opening, the play's fluid plot captivated the audience.

2 Identify as many uses of figurative language as you can in the above examples. In each case, say what kind of figure is involved (metaphor, metonymy, synecdoche, simile, etc.).

3 For each figure, identify where appropriate: (a) the vehicle; (b) the tenor; (c) the ground.

4 For the metaphors, say whether they are (a) explicit or implicit; (b) dead, revived or fresh; (c) extended or mixed; (d) concretive, animistic or humanizing.

5 Make a note describing a purpose for each figure. Ask youself: what connotations does the vehicle carry over into the new context? How does the figure influence our perception of the thing being presented?

Part B

6 Read the following poem by Langston Hughes (1951).

Harlem

What happens to a dream deferred?

Does it dry up
Like a raisin in the sun?
Or fester like a sore –
And then run?
Does it stink like rotten meat?
Or crust and sugar over –
Like a syrupy sweet?

Maybe it just sags
Like a heavy load.

Or does it explode?

7 Identify as many uses of figurative language in the poem as you can.

8 Is there a pattern in the way the poem uses a metaphor and simile?

9 Is the word 'dream' a metaphor? If so, what is it a metaphor for? (The title and the date might help you here.)

10 What do the metaphors and similes in the second section of the poem (from 'Does it dry up' to 'syrupy sweet') suggest might happen if the dream is deferred?

11 What does the metaphor and simile in the third section suggest?
12 What does the metaphor in the fourth section suggest? (What is the effect of the fact that the last metaphor breaks with the metaphor–simile pattern?)
13 Referring to your analysis of its figurative language, try to summarize the poem's meaning.

READING

*Abrams (1988) *A Glossary of Literary Terms*, entry on 'Figurative language'.
Hawkes (1972) *Metaphor*.
Jakobson, 'Two aspects of language and two types of aphasic disturbances', in Jakobson and Halle (1956) *Fundamentals of Language* (extracted in Lodge (ed.) (1988) *Modern Criticism and Theory*).
Lakoff and Johnson (1980) *Metaphors We Live By*, especially pp. 3–40.
*Leech (1969) *A Linguistic Guide to English Poetry*, pp. 147–65.
Lodge (1977) *The Modes of Modern Writing*.
McLaughlin, 'Figurative language', in Lentricchia and McLaughlin (1990) *Critical Terms For Literary Study*, pp. 80–90.
Richards (1936) *Philosophy of Rhetoric*.

Unit 14 Irony

Irony is one of the non-literal uses of language in which we say one thing but mean another; as such, it is classified along with metaphor, metonymy, etc. as a trope (see Unit 13: Metaphor). Irony is also often thought of as a type of **tone**, a particular way of speaking or writing, which is a matter of general style and can be widespread in a text (whereas metaphors are often discrete small parts of a text).

VERBAL IRONY

The most common type of irony is **verbal irony**. In verbal irony (*verbal* is to do with words) there appears to be something odd or wrong with the words and what they literally mean; so we must interpret the text by finding another meaning for it.

The following is an example of verbal irony, from Solomon Northup's autobiography *Twelve Years a Slave* (1854):

> The softest couches in the world are not to be found in the log mansion of the slaves. The one where I reclined year after year was a plank twelve inches wide and ten feet long.

The term 'mansion' is literally untrue as a name for the home of a slave; moreover, 'log mansion' is an inappropriate combination of words since mansions are not normally made from logs. In order to make sense of passage, you must in your imagination substitute a word like *hut* for 'mansion'. So the sentence is not literally true. When a piece of text says something which is not literally true, it might be a metaphor, a lie, ironic, etc. 'Mansion' is not a metaphor here, because the hut has very little similarity to a mansion. But 'mansion' is not a lie either, because it is self-evidently untrue (there is no attempt at deception). What makes this text ironic, rather than anything else, is the type of relationship between the actual meaning 'hut' and the stated meaning 'mansion'. The meanings are not simply opposites; the opposition is significant, in that it calls attention to the difference in living conditions between slaves and masters (who did live in mansions), and foregrounds the poor living conditions of slaves. While in a metaphor we substitute one word or phrase for another on the basis of significant similarity between the literal meaning and our supplied meaning, in irony we substitute on the basis of significant differences.

Looking at the passage again, we can see that there are other ironies. The first sentence is ironic in its (false) implication that there are couches in slaves' houses (even though they are not 'the softest couches in the world', the implication is nevertheless that they exist). Once again, there is a significant difference between the truth we supply and what the text says. A further irony in the first sentence comes from the implication that we (the readers) should be surprised by what is being said – that the softest couches in the world are not in slaves' houses; this is presented as though it is new and interesting information (whereas in fact we already know this). The irony lies in the relationship between our actual knowledge and the ignorance attributed to us by the text; if we really know this – and it is clear that we do – then why do we not do something about slavery?

SITUATIONAL IRONY

Verbal irony is deliberate. In contrast, dramatic irony and structural irony (which we will discuss now) are intended by an author but the characters involved are unaware of them. These come under the general term **situational irony**.

In **dramatic irony** the audience knows something significantly different from what the characters believe, as in this example from Aphra Behn's play, *The Rover* (1677):

Pedro: ... Sure I had dwelt forever on her bosom –
But stay, he's here.
[Enter Belvile dressed in Antonio's clothes.]
Florinda (aside): 'Tis not Belvile; half my fears are vanished.
Pedro: Antonio!

Here the audience knows that the character is Belvile, but the characters believe him to be Antonio. The consequence of this misunderstanding involves Florinda (who loves Belvile) refusing to marry him, thinking him to be Antonio.

In **structural irony** the text as a whole, or a large part of the text, is unreliable if taken literally. Instead, an alternative interpretation, which is not made explicit (but is implied), is true. Often a text is structurally ironic because it is told by an unreliable narrator, such as an uneducated child (Henry James, *What Maisie Knew* (1897), Mark Twain, *Huckleberry Finn* (1885)), someone mentally handicapped (book 1 of William Faulkner, *The Sound and the Fury* (1929)), a foreigner (Tama Janowicz, *A Cannibal in Manhattan* (1987)), etc. In these types of structural ironies, the text sometimes uses the naive narrator as a moral centre, and her or his failure to understand the events of the novel illustrates the moral corruptness of the events. As in many cases of irony, it is not the hidden truth which is important, but the difference between the apparent meaning and the true meaning.

MECHANISMS OF IRONY

We will now look more closely at some of the techniques of irony, beginning with verbal irony. We begin with an extract from George Eliot's novel *Middle-march* (1871):

> Some who follow the narrative of his experience may wonder at the midnight darkness of Mr Dagley; but nothing was easier in those times than for an hereditary farmer of his grade to be ignorant, in spite somehow of having a rector in the twin parish who was a gentleman to the backbone, a curate nearer at hand who preached more learnedly than the rector, a landlord who had gone into everything, especially fine art and social improvement, and all the lights of Middlemarch only three miles off.

We can summarize part of what this passage is literally saying as follows: 'Given the social environment in which he lives, it is surprising that Mr Dagley (the farmer) has remained ignorant.' But if we leave it at this, we seem to be misreading the passage. A better reading would be something like: 'The social environment has failed in its obligation to educate (people like) Mr Dagley, though the civilized people who are at fault are very pleased with themselves.' We know that the literal meaning is not reliable because of the presence of the words 'somehow', 'everything', 'all', 'only'. These words have the effect of overemphasizing what is being said, and so drawing attention to it. What makes them excessive is that their presence needs to be explained; we can account for their presence as a clue to the reader that what they are saying is not plausible (hence it needs excessive emphasis). We reach this second reading basically by inverting the first meaning. (For further discussion of this text see MacCabe 1979.) This is a very common process in irony. Irony is often created by being overemphatic in saying something (e.g. 'Yes! I'd *really* like that!' when what you mean is that you would not like it at all).

Overemphasis is one mechanism of verbal irony. Another is internal inconsistency. Internal inconsistency might occur in a narrative which does not make sense, in which case we might have a structural irony where the narrator is shown not to have seen the truth. Or it might be an inconsistency in style (which might signal a verbal irony). A common example of this second type is where the **register** (see Unit 6) of the text changes unexpect-edly; in this case, we say that the voice of the text is inconsistent. In Henry Reed's poem 'Naming of parts' (1946), there are at least two registers: some of the lines are spoken as if by a military instructor (e.g. 'And tomorrow morning, / We shall have what to do after firing'); some as if by a dreamy romantic (e.g. 'Japonica / glistens like coral in all of the neighbouring gardens'). Yet there is no explicit change of speaker. In this case, the irony comes from the fact that the two juxtaposed registers express irreconcilable values and world-views. There is no immediately obvious overall world-view which the poem can give rise to; the poem can only be unified by taking it as an attack on the military world from the perspective of the poetic world. This is not the literal meaning of the poem but an ironic meaning which we have to construct. Register shift is not the only source of stylistic inconsistency. It can also arise when there is a change of rhythm, or un-expected alliteration, or when a rhyme fails to materialize.

IRONY WHICH DESTABILIZES

In many cases of irony, it is not only clear that the text is ironic, it is also clear what the implied meaning is; but there are cases of irony where it is difficult to pin down the intended meaning. The following text, from Flann O'Brien's novel *At Swimm Two Birds* (1939), illustrates this:

> As I advanced, he hailed me, utilizing a gesture of the purpose. He chewed thickly, pointing to the play. The craft of billiards was unfamiliar to me but in politeness I watched the quick darting of the balls, endeav-ouring to deduce from the results of a stroke the intentions which preceded it.
>
> Gob, *there*'s a kiss, said Brinsley.
>
> *Extract from Concise Oxford Dictionary: Kiss, n. Caress given with lips; (Billiards) impact between moving balls; kind of sugar plum.*
>
> Diverting his attention with difficulty from the affairs of the table, I persuaded him to peruse my manuscript, a matter of some nine pages.

This is an internally inconsistent text. Three registers are juxtaposed: the elaborate and academic style of the narrator, the colloquial speech of Brinsley and the definitional language of the dictionary entry. Moreover, the presence of the dictionary entry is unexpected; it does not appear to be narrated by anyone – it just appears in the text. Within the dictionary defi-nition, too, there is a juxtaposition of different meanings, with a particularly absurd effect coming from the third. Instabilities like these suggest that the literal reading of the passage is insufficient, because it does not explain the inconsistency: a literal reading, for example, might involve the idea that the dictionary definition is supplied as an aid to the reader, but the fact that the dictionary definition makes an unexpected appearance then has to be taken as a warning that the definition functions in some other way, and that there is an irony at work.

But what is the irony? At least two readings are possible: first, that Brinsley's speech is being mocked by its juxtaposition with the dictionary; or alternatively, that the dictionary is being mocked by juxtaposition with Brinsley's speech. (Is the 'I' of the passage also possibly mocked by this juxtaposition?). There seems to be no clear way of deciding which of these readings is warranted (the text does not guide us in our inferencing here) (see Unit 15: Juxtaposition).

In historical terms, it is possible to generalize a little from the difficulty we face here. In the Northup and Eliot texts discussed earlier in this unit the intended meaning seemed clear; but in O'Brien's, it is not. This difference is characteristic of a general historical difference between much nineteenth- and twentieth-century writing: nineteenth-century realist writers (see Unit 22: Realism) tended to write texts which convey authoritative and decisive world-views; twentieth-century modernists, on the other hand, typically wrote texts which do not convey a specific, authoritative or unified world-view. (Modernists in this sense include James Joyce, Virginia Woolf, T.S. Eliot, Ezra Pound, Djuna Barnes, Flann O'Brien, the Monty Python comedy team, Gertrude Stein, Orson Welles and many others; but note that all twentieth-century writers are modernists; many make the same use of irony as the nineteenth-century realists.) Irony is one of the devices used by modernists to create texts which cannot be read literally, and where a final, implied meaning remains elusive.

ACTIVITY

The passage quoted below is the beginning of Oscar Wilde's play *The Importance of Being Earnest* (first performed in 1885).

1 List four ironies which occur to you as you read the text. Label them as either verbal irony or situational irony. Within situational irony, identify whether your examples are dramatic irony or structural irony. If you have difficulties naming the types of irony, try to explain why.

2 For each example of irony, indicate what the apparent (or literal) meaning is, and then formulate the hidden or implied meaning. Remember that the irony may be carried by an implication or presupposition rather than what has literally been said, so you may have to work out what the implication or presupposition is before you can describe the relevant apparent or literal meaning.

3 For each irony, describe how you know irony is present (it could be a feature of the text, or it could come from your own general knowledge, etc.).

4 The extract is written to be performed. Suggest, for each case of irony, one way in which performance might affect it by emphasizing it further, by changing its meaning or by reducing or even completely removing it.

5 Does irony work in a consistent way throughout the whole passage, or are there many different and inconsistent ironies? Answer this question by describing the functions of the ironies in the text. Here are some possibilities (there are others; and some of these are related, so the same irony could have several functions at once):

   to undermine the speaker;

to give authority to the speaker;

to create an ambiguous and unresolvable meaning;

to express a particular world-view;

to make a moral point.

First Act

Scene

Morning-room in Algernon's flat in Half-Moon Street. The room is luxuriously and artistically furnished. The sound of a piano is heard in the adjoining room.

[LANE is arranging afternoon tea on the table, and after the music has ceased, ALGERNON enters.]

A: Did you hear what I was playing, Lane?

L: I didn't think it polite to listen, sir.

A: I'm sorry for that, for your sake. I don't play accurately – anyone can play accurately – but I play with wonderful expression. As far as the piano is concerned, sentiment is my forte. I keep science for Life.

L: Yes, sir.

A: And, speaking of the science of Life, have you got the cucumber sandwiches cut for Lady Bracknell?

L: Yes, sir. [Hands them on a salver.]

A: [Inspects them, takes two, and sits down on the sofa]: Oh! . . . By the way, Lane, I see from your book that on Thursday night, when Lord Shoreman and Mr Worthing were dining with me eight bottles of champagne are entered as having been consumed.

L: Yes, sir; eight bottles and a pint.

A: Why is it that at a bachelor's establishment the servants invariably drink the champagne? I ask merely for information.

L: I attribute it to the superior quality of the wine, sir. I have often observed that in married households the champagne is rarely of a first-rate brand.

A: Good heavens! Is marriage so demoralizing as that?

L: I believe it **is** a very pleasant state, sir. I have had very little experience of it myself up to the present. I have only been married once. That was in consequence of a misunderstanding between myself and a young person.

A: [languidly]: I don't know that I am much interested in your family life, Lane.

L: No sir; it is not a very interesting subject. I never think of it myself.

A: Very natural, I am sure. That will do, Lane, thank you.

L: Thank you, sir.

[LANE goes out]

A: Lane's views on marriage seem somewhat lax. Really, if the lower orders don't set us a good example, what on earth is the use of them? They seem, as a class, to have absolutely no sense of moral responsibility.

[Enter LANE]

L: Mr Ernest Worthing.

[Enter JACK. LANE goes out]

A: How are you, my dear Ernest? What brings you up to town?
J: Oh, pleasure, pleasure! What else should bring one anywhere?

READING

*Leech and Short (1981) *Style in Fiction*, pp. 277–80.
MacCabe (1979) *James Joyce and the Revolution of the Word*.
*Muecke (1970) *Irony and the Ironic*.
Sperber, D. and D. Wilson (1986a) 'Loose talk', *The Proceedings of the Aristotelian Society* (n.s.) 1985/6: 153–77.
——— (1986a) *Relevance*.

Unit 15 Juxtaposition

VERBAL JUXTAPOSITION

Juxtaposition in its simplest sense means placing side by side. In this sense, juxtaposition is generally relevant to most communicative activity, which usually depends upon the quite precise placement of one communicative element beside another. Sentence construction, for instance, relies upon observing close constraints in the way words are put together. Quite fundamental changes in meaning can result from simple changes in the ordering or placement of items in a sentence (see Unit 3: Analysing units of structure). But the term juxtaposition can also refer to a special rhetorical device which involves more than the straightforward placement of communicative elements next to each other. Juxtaposition in this sense can be defined as:

the combination of two or more elements in such a way that the connecting links between them are suppressed, and where there is some degree of surprise or puzzlement in their close placement.

Some of these features of juxtaposition are displayed quite clearly in Japanese haiku poems such as the following (these are translations):

Haiku 1

Harvest moon:
On the bamboo mat
Pine tree shadows.

Haiku 2

Wooden gate,
Lock firmly bolted:
Winter moon.

Each poem consists of three short lines, and in both cases the sense of the poem comes to rest on three separate elements – 'moon', 'mat' and 'shadows' in one; 'gate', 'lock' and 'moon' in the other. These elements are simply juxtaposed, and the links between them are not very obvious. Neither of the poems forms complete or coherent sentences and so the connections ordinarily present in sentences are not given. This means that the reader is required to make an effort to fill in the gaps and spell out the connections between the main elements. This effort is accentuated by the division of each poem into two sections around a major punctuation mark – a colon. In each case there is only an implicit connection between the elements on either side of the colon. Although it is possible to see a causal relation between a harvest moon and pine-tree shadows, the lack of explicit connections forces the reader to make an imaginative leap. The connection between a locked wooden gate and a winter moon demands an even greater imaginative effort. Both poems simply juxtapose a natural image with a human one – a harvest moon and a bamboo mat, a bolted gate and a winter moon – in ways which create a tension between the first and second part. Haiku poems typically revolve around a tension or puzzle produced by juxtaposing (without further explanation) natural phenomenon with an event or object more closely related to the human world. This can be seen in two further examples:

Haiku 3

Spring rain:
Soaking on the roof
A child's rag ball.

Haiku 4

Overnight
My razor rusted –
The May rains.

These poems seem to invite the reader to supply a causal connection between their elements; thus they could be taken as implying something like:

A child's rag ball was soaking on the roof *because of* the spring rain

Overnight my razor rusted *because of* the May rains

But although this seems to 'explain' the poems, it does so by limiting their suggestiveness and reducing the multiplicity of possible connections between the elements. Leaving the precise relations between elements un-expressed seems actually to increase the communicative possibilities of these short poems; the very disparity of the elements which have been juxtaposed generates – in the absence of explicit connections – a kind of communicative charge.

Although these poems were originally written in Japanese in the seventeenth and eighteenth centuries, it is not difficult to find similar techniques at work in twentieth-century poetry written in English. Here is an example from Ezra Pound (1916):

L'art, 1910

Green arsenic smeared on an egg-white cloth,
Crushed strawberries! Come let us feast our eyes.

In fact, it is not surprising that Pound's poem is reminiscent of haiku; this poem was written when Pound was a leading figure in the 'imagist' movement (roughly 1910–20) in which a group of writers in Britain and the United States attempted to develop a new form of poetry which was strongly influenced by haiku (especially its use of stark, unexplained juxtaposition). This new form of poetry can be seen as an early example of modernism – a period (1910–40) of experimentation in all the arts in which the juxtaposition of very different elements was a characteristic technique. Much of T.S. Eliot's poetry (such as *The Waste Land*, 1922) juxtaposes a wide range of different kinds of linguistic material (quotations from Wagner's operas, biblical language, diaries, language heard in a public house, etc.). This process is related to the technique used in the pictorial arts in the same period called **collage** (which the *OED* describes as 'an abstract form of art in which photographs, pieces of paper, string, etc., are placed in juxtaposition and glued to the pictorial surface'). (See Unit 17: Genre, for further discussion of collage.)

VISUAL JUXTAPOSITION: FILM

The use of juxtaposition in order to set up a collision or tension between communicative elements is not limited to verbal texts. In a film, two very different scenes or images may be juxtaposed by immediately succeeding one another. The Soviet director, Sergei Eisenstein, argued that the way shots are combined into series is central to the way films work. In most films, it is not hard for the viewer to make the imaginative connection between images. The strand of cinematic development associated with commercial cinema and Hollywood uses a style of editing that aims at continuity and smoothness of transition between shots. In contrast, the aesthetic possibility of juxtaposition is an important organizing concept in certain kinds of film practice such as Soviet cinema in the years immediately after the Russian Revolution of 1917. Early Soviet cinema, particularly that of Eisenstein, attempted to produce collisions rather than continuity between sequential shots in order to create quite startling juxtapositions. Eisenstein called this the principle of **montage**, and argued that by introducing a gap or tension between successive images it was possible to generate meaning beyond that contained within the shots themselves. For instance, in two famous images from consecutive shots in Eisenstein's film *Battleship Potemkin* (1925), the first image is a medium close-up of a woman's face wearing pince-nez or glasses, and the second image presents the same woman, but now the eye is bleeding and the pince-nez is shattered. The overall effect is that of a shot hitting the eye, even though the latter action is not explicitly displayed. These images are part of a larger episode, commonly referred to as the 'Odessa steps sequence', in which soldiers brutally attempt to put down a popular uprising. Images of boots marching down steps and of rifle volleys are intercut with images of a child's pram rolling unattended down the steps and a small boy being trampled underfoot (see Plates 1–4).

As well as creating a powerful sense of movement and confusion, these stark juxtapositions encourage the viewer to make the connection between the soldier's actions and the suffering of the defenceless people. In this way, montage as a collision between images can here be seen as replicating larger contradictions between contending social forces. Indeed, juxtaposition for Eisenstein was part of a self-consciously Marxist approach to film making, not only emphasizing conflict between images but (like Bertolt Brecht in the theatre) also demanding the active interpretative engagement of the audience.

SERIAL AND SIMULTANEOUS JUXTAPOSITION

Juxtaposition in film, video and television mostly works by exploiting a sense of surprise or shock achieved by juxtaposing successive images. Thus these media may be said to use temporal or serial juxtaposition. The images from Eisenstein's film are good examples of serial juxtaposition, since their meaning depends on the order in which the elements are presented; any change in the order either changes the meaning or results in nonsense.

Juxtaposition is also used in other kinds of media which are not temporal but spatial (e.g. photographs, paintings, cartoons, etc.). In such cases, the juxtaposed elements are simultaneously present for interpretation and the order in which they are read seems not to affect the overall meaning. We can therefore say that such media use simultaneous juxtaposition. (You might want to consider whether juxtaposition in a written text is serial or simultaneous: we read serially – one word after the other – but all the words are present on the page at the same moment and can be read in a different order.)

Any visual composition, of course, is likely to contain an organization of elements placed side by side. In this sense whatever occurs within the same visual frame has been 'juxtaposed', if only in rather weak terms. But, as we argued earlier, the notion of juxtaposition is more usefully applied to instances where the connection between elements seems arbitrary or not immediately obvious and where the reader or viewer is called upon to make the imaginative connection. Magazine advertising often uses juxtaposition in the sense we are using it here. The advertisement in Plate 5, for example, juxtaposes two basic elements within the image – a bottle of cognac and a diamond-encrusted watch.

At first sight, there is no obvious reason why such objects should be put together. Indeed, the very absence of an obvious connection poses a puzzle

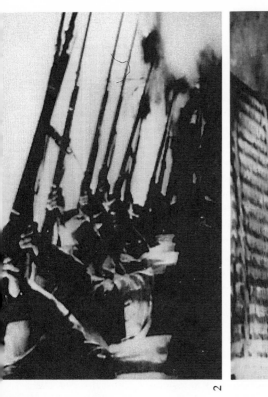

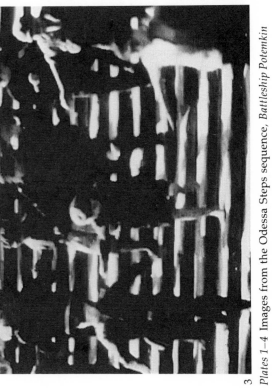

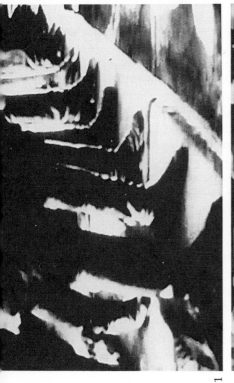

Plates 1–4 Images from the Odessa Steps sequence, *Battleship Potemkin*

to the reader, an enigma that requires some interpretative effort to solve. One way of connecting the items is supplied by the accompanying text in terms of the time it takes to produce each object: 'It takes 1000 painstaking hours to create a half million pound watch. And 300,000 hours to make Henessy X.O.' Since the brandy is said to take much longer to produce than the watch, we are presumably invited to assume that it is a much more luxurious item and has more cultural value (even if it is less expensive) than the watch.

Since juxtaposition here invites the reader to compare (or contrast) the juxtaposed items, we can suggest that visual juxtaposition works in a similar way to metaphor (see Unit 13). This idea is borne out in the example in Plate 6, in which a gilt-framed art object is juxtaposed with a bottle of whisky.

There is no immediately obvious connection between paintings and scotch whisky. However, the title and subject of the painting proves to be 'The Famous Grouse', which in turn operates as the trade mark for the brand of whisky being advertised. The art object and the whisky are therefore linked by virtue of their names and the shared image of the bird (as well as by the fact that grouse and whisky share the same 'country of origin'). These visual and verbal links invite us to transfer selected attributes of the art object to the commodity being advertised (just as a metaphor demands that we transfer selected attributes from vehicle to tenor). Since the painting has a title and a signature (in the bottom left-hand corner) and is exhibited in an ornate frame, we are invited to think that it has great aesthetic value and to transfer that quality to the whisky. The painting's title also tells us that the grouse is 'noted for its character and distinguished appearance', and we are expected to understand that this is also true of the whisky. As if to underline the parallel between painting/bird and whisky, the caption suggests that both maintain a certain quality 'in an age of change'.

In the examples of juxtaposition examined earlier, it was noticeable that juxtaposition operates by generating meanings that are somehow 'beyond' or 'between' the elements that are juxtaposed. In the haiku and imagist poems, the lack of a definite connection between images seems to open them up to a multiplicity of interpretations. However, when elements are juxtaposed in an advertising image, the accompanying text often plays an important role in fixing a preferred reading of the image. In the advertisements examined above, the captions prevent possibilities such as 'Hennessey is as tough as diamonds' or 'This grouse is looking for his whisky.' This suggests that juxtaposition is both a powerful and an unpredictable device to use, since advertisers often find it necessary to control the possible interpretations it might generate.

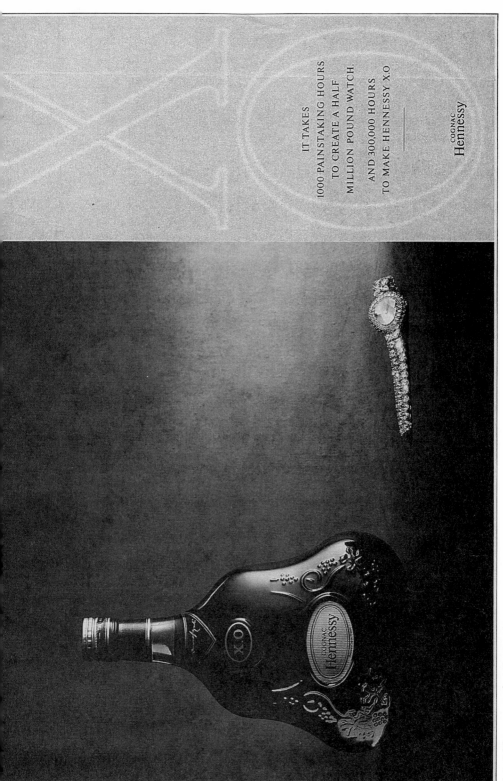

Plate 5 Hennessy advertisement

Plate 6 The Famous Grouse advertisement

THE EFFECTS OF JUXTAPOSITION

It is not possible to predict one single effect for all cases of juxtaposition, but we can point to a range of characteristic, sometimes overlapping, effects. We have already seen that juxtaposition tends to open up a plurality of possible meaningful connections between juxtaposed elements precisely because simple and straightforward connections are omitted. Juxtaposition can also produce a characteristic sense of tension or incongruence, as in Pound's imagist poem given above: 'Green arsenic smeared on an egg-white cloth. / Crushed strawberries!' This incongruence typically demands that the reader make some effort of comprehension.

Juxtaposition can therefore be thought of as a rhetorical strategy. We have already seen that in some instances juxtaposition works in a way similar to metaphor. This is supported by a humorous serial juxtaposition which is often used in films: the first image typically shows two people beginning to make love and is then cut to images of volcanoes erupting or fireworks exploding. The juxtaposition of the second image with the first asks us to imagine that there is a metaphorical relation between the couple's lovemaking and eruptions of fireworks (the second image becomes a metaphor for the first one).

Some of the other effects of juxtaposition can be summarized as various kinds of irony (see Unit 14).

1 *Tragic irony*: An example of tragic irony may be found at the end of Shakespeare's *King Lear* (1606), where Edmund's dying attempt to revoke his command that Cordelia be murdered and Albany's supplication 'The gods defend her!' is immediately juxtaposed with Lear's arrival carrying Cordelia dead in his arms:

> Edmund: He hath commission from thy wife and me
> To hang Cordelia in the prison, and
> To lay the blame upon her own despair,
> That she fordid herself.
> Albany: The gods defend her! Bear him hence awhile.
> [Edmund is borne off]
> [Enter Lear with Cordelia dead in his arms; Edgar, Captain and others following]
> Lear: Howl, howl, howl.

The juxtaposition of Cordelia's death (and Lear's reaction to it) with Albany's prayer ('The gods defend her!') reinforces the tragic effect here and ironically casts doubt on the very efficacy of prayer. Thus one of the effects of juxtaposition is to undermine or call into question one element through the immediate proximity of the other.

2 *Comic irony*: Sometimes the incongruity of the juxtaposition leads to a humorous effect. In radio broadcasting, accidental mixing between alterna-

tive sources (e.g. from live studio talk to prerecorded announcements or commercials) can lead to unintended juxtapositions, as in the following examples:

> 'It's time now, ladies and gentlemen, for our featured guest, the prominent lecturer and social leader, Mrs Elma Dodge . . .' (*Superman cut in*) . . . 'who is able to leap tall buildings in a single bound'.

> 'So remember, use Pepsodent toothpaste, and brush your teeth . . .' (*Cut in to cleaning product commercial*) . . . 'right down the drain!'

In these examples it is important that the cut-in text provides a grammatically well-formed completion of a sentence begun in the initial text, even though its topic in each case is discordantly at odds with that already established by the initial text. Humorous juxtaposition is often deliberately employed as a textual strategy in comic texts (as in the mixing of different registers: see Unit 6: Language and context: register).

3 *Destabilizing irony*: When elements from recognizably different texts are deliberately, rather than accidentally, mixed in with each other, a sense of irony can be created which goes beyond calling one element into question by its juxtaposition with another. In the following example from *Ulysses* (1922), James Joyce intersperses the description of a place with fragments of a formulaic prayer:

> Stale smoky air hung in the study with the smell of drab abraded leather of its chairs. As on the first day he bargained with me here. As it was in the beginning, is now. On the sideboard the tray of Stuart coins, base treasure of a bog: and ever shall be. And snug in their spooncase of purple plush, faded, the twelve apostles having preached to all the gentiles: world without end.

'Drab abraded leather', 'base treasure of a bog', 'snug in their spooncase of purple plush' are phrases unlikely to occur outside the context of literary descriptions. On the other hand, the fragments 'As it was in the beginning, is now . . . and ever shall be . . . world without end' clearly belong to a prayer. These two types of text (or the two registers they use) normally operate in very different contexts, the sacred and the secular, but here they are starkly juxtaposed. It would simplify matters if we could claim that this juxtaposition merely calls the prayer into question by inserting it into a secular context. But counterpointed, as they are in this passage, the sacred and the secular simultaneously call each other into question. One way of understanding the presence and relevance of the prayer fragments in the passage is to suppose that they form the contents of the consciousness of the first-person narrator (see Unit 19: Point of view), but there is no explicit signal that this is the case, no reporting clause such as 'The unchanging nature of the room recalled to mind the oft-repeated formula like some ironic echo: "As it was in the beginning, is now ..."' In addition, the weaving together of these different strands of text blurs the boundaries between description of external objects and events and internal states of consciousness. But it also – and perhaps more interestingly – destabilizes the text, so that we are no longer certain where different parts of it are coming from. There is no longer a single, authoritative, narrative voice making clear to us where one element or fragment stands in relation to another.

ACTIVITY

Part A

1 Cut-up poems are made by juxtaposing elements drawn from two or more pre-existing texts in order to create effects of tension or incongruity. Quoted below are two extracts from Adrian Henri's 'On the late late massachers stillbirths and deformed children a smoother lovelier skin job', which is presented as a 'Cut-up of John Milton Sonnet XVIII On the late Massacher in Piedmont / TV Times / CND leaflet'.

(a)

> The seven-day beauty plan:
> Avenge O Lord they slaughter'd saints, whose bones
> Will cause up to 1 million deaths from leukaemia
> Forget not, in thy book record their groans
> Now for the vitally important step. Cream your face and neck a
>   second time
> No American president world-famous for beauty creams
> responsible for the freedom and safety of so many young offenders
> TODAY'S MEN OF ACTION
> The Triple Tyrant Macmillan Kennedy Watkinson
> The West governments are satisfied as to the moral necessity to
>   resume Racing from Newmarket

(b)

> This baby's eyes and nose had merged into
> one misshapen feature in the middle of its
> forehead, lost 6' from Hips
> sufferers can now wear fashion stockings
> Early may fly the Babylonian wo
> followed by
> TOMORROW'S WEATHER
> The Epilogue
> close down.

2 Relying on features of language and style, try to identify the source of each phrase or line (i.e. whether it is from Milton's sonnet, the *TV Times*, or the CND leaflet).

3 Pick out three examples of juxtaposition and try to describe the effect of each one.

4 What is the overall effect of the use of juxtaposition in this extract from the poem?

Part B

5 Construct a cut-up poem of your own by (a) selecting two short texts (one of which should be a poem); (b) cutting them up into fragments; and (c) weaving them together in order to achieve effects which are similar to Henri's poem.

For the best results do not use two texts of the same type (two poems, or two adverts, etc.). The reason for choosing a poem as one of your source texts is to help establish a semblance of poetic form in your cut-up poem, but the other text needs to be significantly different in order to create effects of tension and incongruency. Use the same wording as the original texts but you need not use the whole of each text nor follow their original order.

When you have finished your cut-up poem, try to answer the following questions:

6 What guided your choice of texts?

7 How did you decide where to divide them up into fragments?

8 What principles guided your attempt to reconstitute them as a cut-up poem (e.g. why did you use the material you included? Why did you not use other material? Why did you juxtapose the material in the way you did?).

9 What kind of overall effect do you think you have achieved?

READING

Eisenstein, Sergei 'The cinematographic principle and the ideogram', in Mast and Cohen (eds) (1979) *Film Theory and Criticism*, pp. 85–100.
—— 'A dialectic approach to film form', in Mast and Cohen (eds) (1979) *Film Theory and Criticism*, pp. 101–22.

Unit 16 Intertextuality and allusion

ALLUSION

An 'allusion' occurs when one text makes an implicit or explicit reference to another text. Allusions may vary from the explicit (where an actual quotation is made and signalled with quotation marks) to the implicit (where no signal is given and the original wording is changed to suit the new context). Thus the opening of Wordsworth's *The Prelude* (1805) implicitly alludes to the end of Milton's *Paradise Lost* (1667) without actually quoting from it:

> The earth is all before me: with a heart
> Joyous, nor scared at its own liberty,
> I look about, and should the guide I choose
> Be nothing better than a wandering cloud,
> I cannot miss my way.

> (*Prelude*, I, 15–19)

> The World was all before them, where to choose
> Their place of rest, and Providence their guide;
> They hand in hand with wand'ring steps and slow,
> Through Eden took their solitary way.

> (*Paradise Lost*, XII, 646–9)

Allusion as a means of establishing a relation to a cultural or literary tradition

Allusion serves to place a text within the textual network which makes up a cultural tradition. Because of this, allusion can be used simply as a way of adding cultural value to a text. This is a common device in advertisements. For example, the following captions appeared in the *Observer* magazine of 8 May 1988 (try to work out what each caption is alluding to and write the original wording in the right-hand column):

CAPTION	PRODUCT/FEATURE	ALLUDING TO?
'A room of my own'	Renault	
'If Chocolate be the food of Gods, Heaven must be in Birmingham'	Cadbury's Bourneville chocolate	
'She who dares, wins'	fashion feature	
'Quilts for all seasons'	*Observer* special offer	

One of the reasons for making such allusions is that they are thought to invoke some of the cultural connotations of the source text and, by a process of transference, bestow them on the product being promoted: thus, in the first example (which has a picture of a woman in a Renault car), women are being encouraged to buy this car by suggesting that it will grant them some of the independence which Virginia Woolf was seeking for women in *A Room of One's Own* (1929). Such allusions can also serve to flatter readers – giving those who recognize the allusion the illusion of being superior to those who don't even realize that an allusion is being made. The Cadbury's advertisement therefore implies that it is only 'highly cultured' people – those with the 'good taste' to recognize an allusion to Shakespeare (see the first line of *Twelfth Night*) – who will fully appreciate Bourneville chocolate.

Varieties of allusion

Texts may allude to other texts in a variety of ways:

1   Through a verbal reference to another text (as in the example discussed above where *The Prelude* refers to *Paradise Lost* through a similarity of phrasing).

2   Through epigraphs (a quotation at the beginning of the text). T.S. Eliot's poem 'The hollow men' (1925) has an epigraph taken from Conrad's *Heart of Darkness* (1899/1902): 'Mistah Kurtz – he dead': this invites the reader to look for a significant relationship between the poem and the novel – which is perhaps that both texts suggest there is a hollowness at the heart of European 'man' in the twentieth century.

3   Through names of characters: thus the name Stephen Dedalus (the central character in James Joyce's *A Portrait of the Artist as a Young Man* (1914–15)) refers to Daedalus, a character in Greek mythology who 'made wings, by which he flew from Crete across the archipelago ... his name is perpetuated in our daedel, skilful, fertile of invention' (*Brewer's Dictionary of Phrase and Fable*).

4   Through choice of titles: thus the title of William Faulkner's novel *The Sound and the Fury* (1929) is an explicit allusion to Macbeth's despairing claim that life is nothing but 'a tale / told by an idiot, full of sound and fury, / Signifying nothing' (Shakespeare, *Macbeth* (1606) V, 5, 26–8).

Allusion in film, television and music

The process of allusion is not confined to literature and advertisements, but may be found in most cultural and artistic forms. A television series like Dennis Potter's *The Singing Detective* (1986) derives a lot of its humour by alluding to earlier television programmes and genres (see Unit 17: Genre). Music may allude to earlier music (e.g. Stravinski's allusions to Bach, or the Beatles' allusion to the French national anthem and 'Greensleeves' in 'All you need is love' (1967)). Woody Allen's films frequently make allusions to literature and to other films: *Play it Again Sam* (1972) is a striking example, which makes a series of allusions to *Casablanca* (1943). Francis Ford Coppola's film *Apocalypse Now* (1979) exists within a complex network of allusions to Joseph Conrad and T.S. Eliot. It is in essence a rewriting of Conrad's *Heart of Darkness* (1902), but towards the end the Kurtz character (played by Marlon Brando) reads Eliot's poem 'The hollow men' (1925) – which reverses the relationship between *Heart of Darkness* and 'The hollow men' noted earlier.

Allusion signals a relationship between texts

An adequate reading of a literary text will need to recognize the significance of the ways it interacts with earlier texts. We need to look for common ground between the text which makes the allusion and the source text. This involves trying to work out the similarities and differences between the two texts which are momentarily brought together by the allusion. By choosing the title *The Sound and the Fury*, Faulkner is presumably inviting us to compare Macbeth's nihilistic despair with the events and themes of his novel. In *A Portrait of the Artist*, the name Stephen Dedalus invites the reader to look out for parallels between the novel and the story of Daedalus; is there some connection with the notion of flight? Or is the emphasis on Stephen's aspirations to be an artist (skilful, fertile of invention)? Or with failure (since Icarus, his son, dies)? Or with the father–son relation (death of the son partly because the father's ingenuity and foresight fails)? A reading which approached the novel with this range of questions in mind would probably find that each of them is relevant in some way.

A way of reading allusions

Thomas Hardy's novels can often seem overloaded with allusions, but some of them are charged with a significance which an adequate reading cannot afford to pass by. In *Tess of the D'Urbervilles* (1891), for example, Alec D'Urberville, Tess' eventual seducer, makes an allusion which, if she had spotted it, might have allowed Tess to avoid her tragedy. Early on in the novel, Tess' impoverished parents sent her to work for a rich family whom they mistakenly think they are related to. Tess' new employer, Mrs D'Urberville, who knows nothing of the suspected kinship, sets her to work looking after her poultry and bullfinches. One of the responsibilities involved in looking after the bullfinches is to whistle to them in order to 'teach 'em airs.' Alec, Tess' so-called cousin, spies her vainly attempting to practise whistling and takes this as an opportunity to flirt with her:

> 'Ah! I understand why you are trying – those bullies! My mother wants you to carry on their musical education. How selfish of her! As if attending to these curst cocks and hens were not enough work for any girl. I would flatly refuse if I were you.'
>
> 'But she wants me particularly to do it, and to be ready by tomorrow morning.'
>
> 'Does she? Well then – I'll give you a lesson or two.'
>
> 'Oh no, you won't!' said Tess, withdrawing towards the door.
>
> 'Nonsense! I don't want to touch you. See – I'll stand on this side of the wire-netting, and you can keep on the other; so you may feel quite safe. Now, look here; you screw up your lips too harshly. There 'tis – so.'
>
> He suited the action to the word, and whistled a line of 'Take, O take those lips away'. But the allusion was lost upon Tess.

The editor of the Macmillan edition of Hardy's novel provides an endnote which tells us that Alec is alluding to the first line of the Page's song in Shakespeare's *Measure for Measure* (1604), Act IV, scene 1. But this information, in itself, is not enough to allow us to understand the full import of the allusion. Without an understanding of the significance of the song in the context of *Measure for Measure* the allusion remains lost upon us as well as upon Tess. It is only when we compare the situation in Tess with the situation in the text being alluded to that the significance of the allusion becomes apparent. Peter Hutchinson (1983) makes a succinct analysis:

> The narrator may be suggesting that Tess is simply ignorant of the source. . . . If we too are ignorant of this, we may assume that the reference is merely a means of contrasting Alec's worldliness with Tess's simplicity and uncultured existence. This is certainly part of its function, but the fact that the narrator terms the whistling an 'allusion' may suggest that the original context of the song has some bearing on the present situation. In retrospect [when Tess has been seduced by Alec and abandoned by Angel Clare] we can see that it clearly does: the Boy sings these lines to Mariana when she has become a seduced and abandoned victim.

Thus the fact that the allusion is lost upon Tess proves fatal for her; for the reader, to understand the allusion will add to our sense of the text's tragic irony (once we know how the novel ends).

It is possible to identify at least three separate stages in this analysis of the allusion in *Tess of the D'Urbervilles*:

1 The first step is to recognize that an allusion has been made in the first place. In Hardy's novel, this is made easy because we are told that 'the allusion was lost upon Tess', but not all allusions are so explicit. To a certain extent the ability to spot an implicit allusion is largely dependent on the reader having read the text being alluded to (thus the reader will have the feeling of having read something vaguely similar and will proceed from there). But spotting an allusion is not so wholly dependent on chance as this suggests; it is often possible to detect the presence of an allusion because it will usually stand out in some way from the text that surrounds it – perhaps through differences of style or register (see Unit 6: Language and context: register). For example, Ernest Hemingway quotes the seventeenth-century poet John Donne in the title of his novel *For Whom the Bell Tolls* (1940); but we do not need to know this fact in order to recognize that the title uses a more archaic and 'literary' phrasing than Hemingway usually employs.

2 The second task is to trace the allusion. In the example from *Tess* the editor does this job for us, and in some instances we will be familiar enough with the allusion to go straight to the original text. But in most cases we will have to do some detective work. Books in the reference section of most libraries will be of use in this (see Unit 2: Using information sources). If we have a hunch who the original author is, we might go straight to a con-cordance of the works of that author (though not many authors have had concordances made of their work). In most instances, however, the first recourse might be to a dictionary of quotations. For example, we could trace the allusion in *Tess* in the following manner: (a) decide which is the key word ('lips' in this case); (b) look up 'lips' in the index of the dictionary, and go to the page number indicated for the quotation and its source. If this fails, it is often a matter of educated guesswork: for example, the name Dedalus might seem vaguely 'classical' or 'mythical' and this might send us to *Brewer's Dictionary of Phrase and Fable* or to a dictionary of classical mythology (see the end of this section for a list of some of the books which might be useful).

3 The third step involves a close reading of the section of the source text in which the word or phrase originally appears, together with some investi-gation of its significance in the text as a whole. At this stage you should try to work out the similarities and differences between the source text and the text being read. This should help you to establish why the allusion is being made and whether there is an ironic or parallel relation between the texts (see Unit 15: Irony, and Unit 11: Parallelism). Only by such a careful con-sideration of the source text (as the example from *Tess* demonstrates) can we be aware of the full implications of an allusion.

INTERTEXTUALITY

'Intertextuality' is used in some literary criticism to describe the variety of ways that texts interact with other texts, and in particular to focus on the interdependence between texts rather than their discreteness or uniqueness. Allusion is a form of intertextuality which works largely through verbal echoes between texts; however, texts may also interact with one another through formal and thematic echoes.

Intertextuality through genre

The very idea of genre – that texts can be divided into different groups according to certain shared characteristics – necessarily involves a degree of interaction between texts (see Unit 17: Genre). No text is an island; any poem, for example, will draw on certain poetic conventions which will distinguish it from prose (even if only to undercut or resist those conventions). The idea that texts belong to intertextual 'families' is even more true of the various subgenres, such as that of the sonnet. The sonnet was developed in Italy and was introduced into English poetry in the sixteenth century. Its first practitioners in English generally followed the formal and thematic conventions established by Italian poets such as Petrarch: thus most sonnets have fourteen lines of iambic pentameter arranged into an elaborate rhyme scheme and have a male speaker who addresses his words to a woman he loves or is trying to woo. Although the thematic range of the sonnet has been greatly extended since then, the form continues to be associated with male passion. Thus Edna St Vincent Millay's sonnet 'I, being born a woman and distressed' (1923), is intertextually related to the sonnets of the past not only because it conforms to the formal requirements of the sonnet, but because it reverses and flaunts these thematic conventions:

> I, being born a woman and distressed
> By all the needs and notions of my kind,
> Am urged by your propinquity to find
> Your person fair, and feel a certain zest
> To bear your body's weight upon my breast;
> So subtly is the fume of life designed,
> To clarify the pulse and cloud the mind,
> And leave me once again undone, possessed.
> Think not for this, however, the poor treason
> Of my stout blood against my staggering brain,
> I shall remember you with love, or season
> My scorn with pity, – let me make it plain:
> I find this frenzy insufficient reason
> For conversation when we meet again.

Millay's speaker is clearly a woman who informs a man she has had sex with that she is so far from feeling eternal love for him that she feels no urge even to make conversation with him when they meet again. Part of the impact of the poem arises from the fact that the woman rejects the role conventionally ascribed to women in such situations. But its full impact can only be registered by a reader who realizes that it uses the sonnet form in order to transgress those thematic conventions we have come to expect in sonnets. Thus part of the meaning of the poem derives from the intertextual relationship it sets up between itself and the sonnet tradition.

Intertextuality through parody

A second way in which intertextuality occurs specifically through genre is in parody, satire and mock forms. These subgenres rely upon intertextual relations with other genres for their effect. For example, Alexander Pope's *The Rape of the Lock* (1712/14) depends upon the reader's familiarity with the conventions of the epic genre which it mocks. Thus the poem opens:

> What dire offense from amorous causes springs,
> What mighty contests rise from trivial things,
> I sing – This verse to Caryll, Muse! is due

These lines echo the ritualistic opening gesture of the epic mode – an example of which can be seen in the opening lines of *Paradise Lost*:

> Of man's first disobedience, and the fruit
> Of that forbidden tree, where mortal taste
> Brought death into the world, and all our woe,
> With loss of Eden, till one greater man
> Restore us, and regain the blissful seat,
> Sing, heavenly Muse . . .

As its opening indicates, *The Rape of the Lock* uses these epic conventions in order to treat a 'trivial' social event as if it were an epic matter.

From these examples, we can see that part of the significance of a literary text exists not within itself but in the relationships it sets up with other texts. These examples also show that the intertextual dimensions of cultural texts can only have effects and meaning through the active knowledge which a reader brings to them. Thus Pope's poem has a much-reduced impact on readers unfamiliar with the tradition it parodies.

The changing role of intertextuality

Between the Middle Ages and the end of the eighteenth century education in Britain was limited to a privileged minority and was based in the study of the literature of ancient Greece and Rome (the 'classics'). Authors assumed that their readers would recognize allusions to the 'authorities' (the classics, Aristotle, the Bible), and tradition was valued at least as much as innovation. For example, in the 'neoclassical' period (roughly 1660–1790), authors demonstrated their respect for classical writers by writing thematic and formal imitations of them (Andrew Marvell (1681) 'An Horatian ode upon Cromwell's return from Ireland'; Alexander Pope (1733–9) 'Imitations of Horace'; etc).

In the Romantic period (roughly 1790–1830), however, with its emphasis on 'originality' in a period in which literacy and education in the vernacular (i.e. not using the classical languages) began to increase, the importance of the 'classics' as authorities began to dwindle. The relation of authors to past texts became less that of reverential imitation and more an attempt to break with the past. Wordsworth's allusions to *Paradise Lost*, for example, both acknowledge Milton's importance and register Wordsworth's rebellion against him.

Intertextuality and originality

The fact of intertextuality and allusion thus raises questions about originality: how far do literary texts originate in an author's mind and how far are they composed out of other literature? In modernist literature (roughly 1910–40), allusion becomes a constitutive principle of composition. If T.S. Eliot's *The Waste Land* (1922) is read alongside the notes Eliot printed with it, we get a sense of the poem as a collage of quotations from and allusions to other texts. In the so-called postmodernist period (roughly 1960 to the present), writers such as Angela Carter (e.g. *The Magic Toy Shop* (1967)) and Umberto Eco (e.g. *The Name of the Rose* (1980)) seem to have set aside attempts to be original in the narrow sense in order to participate in an intertextual free-for-all in which the possibility that all writing is allusive and/or intertextual is celebrated for its own sake.

Post-structuralist accounts of intertextuality

Traditional literary criticism is often concerned with the texts which influenced a particular writer: influence is most usually established through tracing allusions. If an editor spots an allusion, s/he will typically say something like 'Keats is thinking of Shakespeare's Venus and Adonis here.' But this assumption begs a number of questions: how do we know that? What if the allusion were unconscious? Or accidental? or created by the editor's own associations? What if texts inevitably interact and reading is necessarily an intertextual process? For post-structuralist theorists such as Julia Kristeva and Roland Barthes, all language usage is inevitably intertextual in several senses: first, because individuals don't originate or invent language – it always exists before we do; and second, because without pre-existing forms, themes, conventions and codes there could be no such thing as literature at all. For Barthes, 'a text is . . . a multi-dimensional space in which a variety of writings, none of them original, blend and clash. The text is a tissue of quotations drawn from the innumerable centres of culture' (1977: 146). Such a theory of intertextuality is radically different from traditional understandings of the functions and significance of allusion.

ACTIVITY

1 Read the following sonnet by Edna St Vincent Millay (1930):

> I dreamed I moved along the Elysian fields,
> In converse with sweet women long since dead:
> And out of blossoms which that meadow yields
> I wove a garland for your living head.
> Danae, that was the vessel for a day
> Of golden Jove, I saw, and at her side,
> Whom Jove the bull desired and bore away,
> Europa stood, and the Swan's featherless bride.
> All these were mortal women, yet all these
> Above the ground had had a god for guest;
> Freely I walked beside them and at ease,
> Addressing them, by them again addressed,
> And marvelling nothing, for remembering you,
> Wherefore I was among them well I knew.

2 Assuming that the speaker of the poem is a woman addressing her male lover, try to work out what she is saying about him (one of the clues is that in the final couplet she seems to compare him to Jove).

3 Identify as many cases of allusion as you can by:

(a) circling all the words and phrases (including names) which you think may be allusions;
(b) finding out what they are allusions to by looking them up in appropriate sources (see below or see Unit 2: Using information sources).

4 Having done 3, you should now have discovered what the 'Elysian fields' are, and have found out about Jove's relationships with three 'mortal women'. Using this information, try answering question 2 again. Is your answer any different from what you gave earlier?

5 Is the poem making a compliment to the man or is it doing something else? How do the allusions support your answer?

READING

Abrams (1988) *A Glossary of Literary Terms*, entries for 'Allusion', 'Intertextuality', 'Parody'.
*Barthes, Roland (1968) 'The death of the author', and (1971) 'From work to text', in, for example, Barthes (1977) *Image – Music – Text*.
Bate (1970) *The Burden of the Past and the English Poet*.

Bloom (1973) *The Anxiety of Influence.*

Eliot, T.S. (1919) 'Tradition and the individual talent', in, for example, Eliot (1953) *Selected Prose.*

—— (1922) *The Waste Land* (including Eliot's notes). (Anthologized in most collections of Eliot's poetry.)

Gilbert and Gubar (1979) *The Madwoman in the Attic.*

Hutchinson (1983) *Games Authors Play,* pp. 57–60.

Renza, Louis A. 'Influence', in Lentricchia and McLaughlin (eds) (1990) *Critical Terms for Literary Study,* pp. 186–202.

Examples of the kinds of reference books useful in tracing allusions (see Unit 2: Using information sources): concordances (e.g. to Shakespeare and to the Bible); *Dictionary of Quotations; Halliwell's Film Guide; Dictionary of Mythology, Folklore, and Symbols; Allusions in Ulysses; Dictionary of National Biography; Brewer's Dictionary of Phrase and Fable.*

Section 5

Aspects of narrative

Unit 17 Genre

In the most general sense 'genre' simply means the sort, or type, of a text: poem, thriller, novella, sonata, horror movie, tragedy, etc. The term presents serious difficulties, nevertheless, as soon as we begin to consider the questions it raises. Is there a fixed number of sorts of text? And how can this be decided? Do the formal elements of a text themselves signal how to label it, or is our classification a result simply of our own expectations or individual perceptions? These questions pose issues which stretch far beyond the obvious convenience of being able to sort texts into types (e.g. for marketing, educational or critical reasons). In fact, they raise deep questions about the relationship between fixed, formal properties of a text and relational properties which are the result of our ways of seeing or thinking about it.

Attitudes vary towards creating texts within established genres. In some periods and places, it is thought a valuable achievement to produce a good 'generic text', such as a detective thriller, or a highly stylized but not especially original pop ballad. In other circumstances, this aspiration is widely dismissed as simply imitative and formulaic, lacking in individual creativity and imagination. So the concept of genre contributes to the ways texts are produced, received and circulated in society, but its contribution is not fixed. Rather, that role alters, under pressure from prevailing concepts of originality, taste and audience demand. Understanding the role of genre in ways of reading involves, therefore, not only working out how texts are classified and defined; it also means grasping how systems of classification fit into aesthetic and social frameworks regarding how texts are created, used and evaluated (see Unit 16: Intertextuality and allusion).

SORTING TEXTS INTO TYPES

The word *genre* comes from Latin *genus,* meaning 'kind' or 'type'. (*Genus* is still used to describe types in the classification of species.) Clearly, notions of kind or type depend on some system of criteria for distinguishing members of one class from members of another; and it is this we will examine first.

Classification on the basis of formal arrangement

The formal properties (see Unit 3: Analysing units of structure) of texts are often thought of as a suitable basis for classification. Sonnets have fourteen lines and follow distinctive stanzaic and rhyme patterns (Petrarchan, Spenserian, Shakespearean, etc.). The more general distinction between poetry, drama and fiction (derived historically from Aristotle's classical distinction in *Poetics* between lyric, epic or narrative, and drama) is also based on formal differences. Poetry typically involves rhythm and other kinds of sound patterning; fiction does not, necessarily, but does involve narrative. Drama involves characters speaking and acting in relation to each other. (For Aristotle, distinguishing between genres was primarily a matter of who speaks: lyrics are uttered in the first person; in epics or narrative, the narrator speaks in the first person, then lets characters speak for themselves; in drama, the characters do all the talking.) Using such formal distinctions to classify texts is very common. But such classifications are not always watertight. What of verse drama? Narrative poetry (as in ballads)? Dramatic monologue?

Classification on the basis of theme or topic

Sometimes subject matter is taken as the basis of a genre. The pastoral, for instance, involves concern with country life; the 'whodunnit' focuses on a concern with resolving an enigma in the narrated story; biography relates events in a life; science fiction explores possible future or alternative worlds; war poetry is concerned with war; etc.

Classification on the basis of mode of address

There is also a possibility of labelling texts in terms of how they address their readers or audience. Some texts involve direct address to a reader or audience (e.g. letters, newscasting). Others have a specific addressee named in the text but are arranged to be overheard (e.g. odes, chat-show discussion, most drama). Sometimes variation between modes of address takes place within a form. Essays addressed to 'Dear Reader' are introduced into narratives in some eighteenth-century novels; and radio genres such as phone-in items and quiz interludes are embedded in larger formats.

Classification on the basis of attitude or anticipated response

Sometimes what a text is about overlaps with an attitude or emotion conventionally adopted towards the subject matter. Pastoral often implies not just concern with country life, but also a reflective mode; elegies – although originally defined on the basis of the meter they used – are primarily concerned with lamenting deaths (and often take the form of pastoral elegies, spoken by shepherds); war poetry has a complex history both of jingoistic and anti-war traditions, combined in explorations of notions of patriotism, moral values and loyalty. Each of these popular stereotypes of a genre focuses less on formal properties, or on subject matter, than on a mood created and the anticipated reaction of an audience.

DECIDING WHAT GENRE A TEXT IS IN

Genre as an expression of conventional agreement

How do you know whether a particular film, for example Kevin Costner's *Dances with Wolves* (1991), is a western? If we followed the methods just outlined we might decide this on the basis of aspects of the text and its reception. But another way of deciding is to look at the other films which are agreed conventionally to be westerns, and to compare *Dances with Wolves* with those. Here, the identification of a genre would rely not on precise definition but on conventional agreement. Certain films are westerns because people agree (without formal analysis) that they are westerns. Particular genres are often likely to emerge in this way – as names for perceived groups of texts, rather than as theoretically designed categories on the basis of formal features. Thus we might say that only on the basis of general consensus can specialist analysis take place, in which case any attack on conventional understandings of genre by formal analysis would undermine the viability of the concept of genre.

Genres: prototypes and history

If it is not possible to determine the genre of a text by rigorous tests based on stable criteria, it is nevertheless possible to appeal to notions of expectation and prototypical cases. Some genres depend on specific texts, which are thought to be exemplary cases of the genre; Sophocles' *Oedipus Rex* (c. 420 BC) is often appealed to as an exemplary tragedy, with other texts defined as tragedies to the extent that they are similar to this play. This view of genre, where there is a prototype and various other texts which are more or less close to this prototype, enables texts to be assigned to genres even when they do not have all the features from that genre. (In the same way, an ostrich which cannot fly is nevertheless part of the genre of 'bird', as a result of its partial resemblance to prototypical birds like sparrows or robins – which can fly). Thus it is possible for a text to be a horror film, while evoking laughter rather than fright, if it uses other conventions of the form; and it is possible for a novel to have no discernible narrative, if it works with or exploits our expectation that it should.

Notions of the typical or 'prototypical' are not fixed, however. Alongside difficulties presented by what appear marginal cases, there is the fact that generic conventions come to us as a historical legacy, shaped and reshaped by the complex history of production and circulation of texts, as well as changing attitudes towards them. We might think of a 1930s western like John Ford's *Stagecoach* (1939) as prototypical, and of the revisionist westerns of the 1950s onwards as getting part of their meaning from their deviation from that prototype; however, it now seems to be the case that the revisionist westerns themselves are the typical type of western, and so we would argue that the prototype has changed to something like Sergio Leone's *Once Upon a Time in the West* (1969). Genres are always being redefined by actual practice, even when there is no deliberate attempt to modify or undermine generic conventions.

FUNCTIONS OF GENRE

Why, however, do people want to divide texts into groups, and who in fact does it? Why should a system of genres ever emerge?

Genre as a framework for a text's intelligibility

One view of these questions is that genres create expectations that govern how a text is likely to be understood or construed. In this respect, genre is a major dimension of the tacit knowledge, or body of interpretative assumptions and techniques, we draw on in reading. The genre of a novel, for example, determines the degree of realism to be expected from it, and the genre of a performance guides the audience's responses concerning the significance of costume, character and choice of particular ways of speaking or moving.

Genre as a reflection of the nature of human experience

In this view, texts can be classified into genres which reflect their relation to fundamental human experiences; the distinction between tragedy and comedy is often made along these lines. The theory of archetypal genres (particularly associated with Northrop Frye (1957)) belongs here, where four selected genres (romance, comedy, tragedy, satire) are claimed to correspond to the four seasons. One problem with these views is that they tend to have little to say about the emotional functions of less traditional or less high-cultural genres, such as the twelve-bar blues, the performance pop-video or the road movie (e.g. *Easy Rider*). This view seems, then, to work by an initial broad generic distinction between serious forms (corresponding to human experience) and non-serious forms.

Genre as a promotional device

In this view, genres are part of a classification necessary to identify product range. They label different audience tastes and wishes (for news, detective fiction, quiz shows, romance, etc.). In particular, genres allow audiences to predict and plan kinds of experience for themselves, and to repeat the kinds of pleasure or entertainment they have previously enjoyed. Television scheduling displays this type of thinking (indeed, schedules are divided into segments largely on the basis of such a classification); so does the layout of library and bookshop shelves.

Genre as a way of controlling markets and audiences

This view overlaps with the last, but extends it by suggesting that genres do not so much reflect audience wishes as create them. In this sense, they are part of a process of controlling the production of entertainment and directing culture markets. By trading on what has been successful, formulas are adopted which can be confidently invested in. This view of genre is seen by some people as leading towards a detrimental standardization of cultural products into predictable forms (Hollywood's decisions about which films to finance is often thought to follow this pattern).

DEFEATED EXPECTATIONS: EXPLOITING GENRE THROUGH COLLAGE AND PASTICHE

Two common ways of combining genres together are collage and pastiche. In **collage**, various genres (or features of genre) are placed alongside one another, and so implicitly joined together. Such collage can be used, as it commonly is in modernist texts, to set up a process of contrastive judgement which results from the juxtaposition of different voices or quoted texts (see Unit 15: Juxtaposition, and Unit 16: Intertextuality and allusion). A **pastiche** text is similar in that it imitates a text or texts from other genres, but clearly signals that this is what it is doing, often by merging the conventions of one genre with the subject matter of another; in so doing, a pastiche undermines the possibility of a central authoritative point of view or speaking voice.

Techniques of this sort of genre mixing can lead to different kinds of **irony** (see Unit 14). In the case of collage, something in the text – or in our expectations – tells us to respond to one of the genres in the compound as more powerful or persuasive than others. In pastiche, tensions between subject matter and the generic conventions followed can indicate satire, directed either towards the form adopted or the topic.

POSTMODERNISM AND GENRE

The effects of irony in generic compounds and formulaic imitations of genre make possible one major dimension of **postmodernism**. Roughly, post-modernism is the condition believed characteristic of our time in which exposure to language and media so saturates social experience that any act of communication always carries with it the obvious marks of its genre and the constraints its genre places upon it. A postmodern text, accordingly, does not simply communicate its contents to its reader; it also refers to the ways of writing and reading a text. Older texts can also be read in a post-modern way: for example, Wordworth might have described his own Romantic poem as 'a spontaneous overflow of powerful feelings', but we could read his poems instead as texts about the creation of themselves as examples of the Romantic poetic genre.

While postmodernism claims that direct access to human experience is problematic, it is not an alienated and despairing claim, but a celebration. It aspires to ways of enjoying – and finding a new agenda for – creative and interpretative activity. That agenda involves seeing how texts build on, subvert and play with conventions of texts and their contexts, rather than reaching out for personal or social messages. Accordingly, the notion of genre is foregrounded in postmodernist work, especially as regards forms of pastiche or highly allusive writing. Attention to genre becomes a pre-condition of reading anything. Reading has to involve asking such questions as: what references to conventional genres, or to particular other texts, does a text make? You can only read a text through reading its relationships to a history of other texts: that is, its intertextuality.

GENRE AND WAYS OF READING

The most obvious importance of the idea of genre, as part of a skill of critical reading, involves seeing conventions in a text instead of assuming the text to be a kind of unmediated human expression or way of getting at social meaning or truth. At the very least, this means recognizing that human creativity, and the particular meanings texts create, are not fully 'original', but are built by exploiting already-existing resources or patterns. This is true at the level of individual sentences, where words and constructions lie ready for use. It is true in terms of ideas: comparisons, themes and topics form stock resources within a society's repertoire of symbolic conventions. It is also true in the label we impose on a text: its genre. Finding a pure truth of experience or of society there becomes a virtual impossibility: any attempt to do so speaks more of our networks of generic conventions than it ever can of anything beyond them.

ACTIVITY

This activity explores genre mixing, looking specifically at the genres 'travelogue', 'satire' and 'romance'. The starting point is the observation that two texts mix these genres. Both Jonathan Swift's *Gulliver's Travels* (1726) and Daniel Defoe's *Robinson Crusoe* (1719) could be put into the genre of travelogue. In the *Oxford Dictionary of English Literature*, however, *Gulliver's Travels* is described as a satire, while *Robinson Crusoe* is described as a romance. So we could argue that *Gulliver's Travels* belongs to two genres, satire and travelogue, and *Robinson Crusoe* belongs to two genres, romance and travelogue.

1 Make three lists under the headings 'travelogue', 'satire' and 'romance'. Each list should contain the following:

(a) the features which you think are necessary aspects of texts in each genre (you may have to divide up some of these into subgenres; for example, you may feel that there are different kinds of romance);
(b) examples of texts which you think fit into each of the three genres.

To help you, we append here some definitions; you should not feel bound by them, though; instead, use your own intuitions about the three types of genre. (For example, you may feel that a travelogue need not have pictures.)

travelogue (*The Oxford English Dictionary*): 'A lecture or narrative description of travel, illustrated pictorially.' (The word is first cited in 1903, but it could be taken to describe a genre which had existed unnamed earlier than this.)

satire (*Collins Concise English Dictionary*): '(1) a novel, play, etc., in which topical issues, folly, or evil are held up to scorn by means of ridicule. (2) the genre constituted by such works. (3) the use of ridicule, irony, etc., to create such an effect.'

romance (*Collins Concise English Dictionary*): '(1) a love affair. (2) love, esp. romantic love idealized for its purity or beauty. (3) a spirit of or inclination for adventure or mystery. (4) a mysterious, exciting, sentimental or nostalgic quality, esp. one associated with a place. (5) a narrative in verse or prose, written in a vernacular language in the Middle Ages, dealing with adventures of chivalrous heroes. (6) any similar narrative work dealing with events and characters remote from ordinary life. (7) a story, novel, film, etc., dealing with love, usually in an idealized or sentimental way. (8) an extravagant, absurd, or fantastic account. (9) a lyrical song or short instrumental composition having a simple melody.'

2 *Gulliver's Travels* is said to be both a satire and a travelogue; *Robinson Crusoe* is said to be a romance and a travelogue. Here we have examples of texts which fit into two genres at the same time. We can represent the possibilities of genre mixing using the following chart:

	Travelogue	*Satire*	*Romance*
Texts in two genres			
Gulliver's Travels	yes	yes	no
Robinson Crusoe	yes	no	yes
....	no	yes	yes

Texts in all three genres

....	yes	yes	yes

Texts in one genre only

....	yes	no	no
....	no	yes	no
....	no	no	yes

Fill in the chart, giving several examples for each of the seven choices (if you can find any).

3 Look at your list of the features of each genre. Can you explain, using this list, why certain links between genres should be possible. (For example, does the same or a related feature turn up in more than one genre?)

4 Is there any pattern to genre mixing, or is it just random chance that some texts mix genres and some do not? The kinds of pattern you might look for include whether there are certain historical periods when specific mixed genres become popular, and then perhaps die out again.

5 What general conclusions can you reach on the basis of this activity?

READING

Aristotle (*c* 340 BC) *Poetics* (many editions available; e.g. in Aristotle, Horace, Longinus (1965) *Classical Literary Criticism*).

*Culler (1975) *Structuralist Poetics*, pp. 136–8.

Durant and Fabb (1989) *Literary Studies in Action*, Ch. 5.

Frye (1957) *Anatomy of Criticism*, pp. 158–239.

*Jameson, Fredric 'Postmodernism and consumer society', in Foster (ed.) (1985) *Postmodern Culture*, pp. 111–25.

Rosch, Eleanor 'Classification of real-world objects: origins and representations in cognition', in Johnson-Laird and Wason (eds) (1977) *Thinking*, pp. 212–22.

Watt (1972) *The Rise of the Novel*.

Williams (1966) *Modern Tragedy*.

Unit 18 Narrative

Narratives consist primarily in the telling (by a narrator) of a sequence of connected events. There needs to be some relation (e.g. of cause and effect) between the events of a narrative; and typically it has a particular kind of beginning and a particular kind of ending. Narratives usually have a point; they are told for a purpose. These are the general characteristics of narratives, which we will look at below.

The theoretical study of narrative is typically concerned with what some – perhaps all – narratives have in common. For example, many narratives begin in a similar way (e.g. with someone leaving home), or have similar roles for characters (e.g. the killed partner whom the hero must avenge). In this way, narratives can be viewed as constructions using recycled parts; we look at some of these parts in a later section of this unit.

THE GENERAL CHARACTERISTICS OF NARRATIVES

A narrative strings together a series of statements about things happening. We can distinguish the actual events taking place in the world (or which are claimed to have taken place, in fiction) from the way those events are told in the narrative. Pioneering work in this area was done by the Russian formalist critics (e.g. Viktor Shklovsky, writing in the 1910s and 1920s) who made the following distinction:

what happened	vs	how it is told
'story'		'narration'

We can think of the narration as drawing upon the story. One reason for making this distinction is in order to examine the way in which a narrative re-orders events. Where a text includes a flashback, for example, the order of events in the story (historical time) is obviously not the same as the order of events in the narration (narrated order).

When the narrator draws on the story (or pretends to draw on the story – fictional narratives do not correspond to any real story) to create the narration, s/he creates a narrative which, broadly speaking, 'makes sense'. Reality need not make sense, but a narration usually does; this is an important distinction to draw, because we can think of narrations as ways of making sense of the world around us through telling stories about it. 'Making sense' can mean a number of things. The narrative may make sense because it tells us something we want to know, need to know, expect to know, have heard before, etc.; thus a point or message can often be extracted from a narrative. (Sometimes this point is explicitly made; for example, in a concluding moral.) The narrative may also make sense because it is coherent. Coherence in a narrative amounts to our recognition that we are being told one unified story – which means that we understand why we are told every event, we understand how events fit together and if there are any substories inside the main story, these substories make sense in terms of the overall story, perhaps as commenting on it (e.g. subplots in a Shakespeare play or a story one character tells another).

A narrative is always told by someone. The narrator is not necessarily the same as the author of the book which contains the narrative: the author is a real person; the narrator is simply the 'voice' to whom the words of the narrative are attributed; a single novel might contain several narrators (see Unit 19: Point of view). Because narrators are fictional constructions, it is possible to invent narrators who are fantastic in various ways; so an animal may be a narrator, or a dead person (the film *Sunset Boulevard* is narrated by a drowned man). We might think of the narrator as a point of view embodied in a character, who can, if wished, represent the author; although sometimes the voice of a narrative or its point of view are not clearly expressed as a character – this is often the case in a film, and thus it is sometimes difficult to identify a narrator in a film.

Narratives are typically about change. We can think of a change like this:

situation A   changes to   situation B

The changes are often brought about by human actions, and the notion that actions are causes which have effects is an important part of many narratives. Often in a narrative the changes that take place – particularly the important ones – can be understood in terms of situation A being a lack or disruption, which is filled or resolved by situation B. So we can think of many narratives as having changes like this:

situation A   changes to   situation B
lack   leads to   restoration

The lack may occur when a family member leaves home; this lack may be restored when a family is reunited at the end (it need not be exactly the same people; the crucial point is that a lacking family is replaced by a restored family). Or the lack may be the theft of an object, which is hunted and finally recovered. The lack may be a personal lack; the hero or heroine may begin in ignorance and end in wisdom, or begin in isolation and end in community. There are many other variations on the pattern of lack and restoration, and the movement from one to the other is often the driving force of a narrative.

One very important aspect related to the unity and coherence of a narrative is its achievement of closure. **Closure** is the 'tying up' of the narrative, whereby loose ends are dealt with, problems solved and questions answered. The restoration of a lack is a form of closure. Few narratives are completely without closure (if they are, we think of them as experimental or avant-garde), though because most narratives involve plenty of lacks and plenty of restorations, there is typically some lack of closure – a few issues (though not usually central ones) may not be resolved. Sometimes the narrative ends with closure but at the very end of the text a new lack may open up again; the text in its conclusion opens up a new narrative (perhaps leading to a new text – a sequel – which will bring closure to the lack which begins that new narrative).

Narratives are often 'bracketed' or 'framed' by text which is not integrally part of the narrative. For example, an **orientation** may precede the narrative proper and a **coda** may conclude the narrative proper. The orientation is the introduction, before the narrative begins, which often functions to tell the reader/viewer/listener that a story is about to begin. Two examples of orientating are 'Once upon a time . . .', and in a film the camera travelling over the city towards a particular locality. The coda is the conclusion, after the narrative proper has finished (e.g. 'And they all lived happily ever after').

We can exemplify some of these points by looking at some aspects of the narrative of N. Scott Momaday's novel *House Made of Dawn* (1966), about a young American Indian man after the Second World War and his relationship with his culture. As in many narratives, the novel is concerned with an interior change in the hero from lack to fulfilment (in this case the change is emphasized by the fact that the narrative is constructed to parallel an all-night healing ceremony). The novel is divided up into a one-page prologue and four numbered sections. The prologue is echoed in the last page of the novel in that both parts describe a runner (the hero); they are somewhat distinct from the development of events in the narrative, and we could call one the orientation and the other the coda. After the orientation, the narrative begins with the return home of the hero from the war; we can interpret this as an inversion of the common opening in which the hero leaves home. Normally, leaving home is seen as disruptive, but in this novel the hero is unable to fit into the home which he returns to, and so his return is the creation of a lack or a disruption. At the end of the novel, the hero walks out of the village, so providing a mirror-image of the beginning. But now he is integrated into the culture. In the prologue (the orientation) he runs alone; at the end he runs with others. These lacks and closures are to do with movement between the village and the surrounding landscape (a culture–nature opposition: see Unit 11: Parallelism and repetition); the closure of the novel involves the unifying of the two, a unity expressed in the title *House Made of Dawn*.

THE BUILDING BLOCKS OF NARRATIVES

Many different narratives may be built from the same basic components. By components we mean types of character and types of event, and – more abstractly – types of lack and restoration, and ways of getting the narrative from beginning to end.

The characters in a narrative are the individuals involved in the described events. A character can be associated with a particular role; roles are repeated from story to story (e.g. the princess, the police detective, the town drunk, the monster) – particular roles are usually part of particular genres. In addition to thinking about a character as filling a particular role, we can also see a character as having a particular function in the narrative; the convention (following the work of the Russian theorist Vladimir Propp) is to say that the character *is* the function. For example, the character 'Dirty Harry' may play the role of 'the rogue police detective' and may be the function 'hero'. Functions are one of the reusable building blocks of narrative. How do we decide that a character is a particular function? Propp decides on the basis of the character's involvement in specific types of event; for example, for Propp the hero is the character who, in the fairy tales under discussion,

> is forbidden to do something;
> is sent off to resolve a lack;
> acquires a magical object;
> fights the villain;
> is marked (e.g. injured, or given something like a ring);
> is pursued;
> arrives somewhere unrecognized;
> is married and ascends the throne;
> and so on (Propp lists many more).

We could say that Dirty Harry is a hero (is the hero function) because in the film narratives he is involved in a number of these kinds of event.

Propp lists seven functions, not all of which are clearly useful in all narratives (Propp was looking at Russian fairy-tales), though one in particular, 'the donor', has been the source of much interest. A character and sometimes also an object is particularly important in enabling a narrative to move from lack to fulfilment. **Donor** (=giver) is the name given to this character, and typically the donor(-function) will give the hero(-function) some object which enables the hero to conclude the narrative by restoring the lack. In Propp's fairy-tales the gift is often magical (a cloak of invisibility or a special weapon), but if we move beyond fairy-tales to more realistic narratives we still find that there may be something magical about the gift (e.g. it may function unexpectedly, like a Bible carried in a shirt pocket which deflects a bullet). A typical type of donor is an old person who gives the hero (-function) something in exchange for a favour. Sometimes the gift is simply information (as when the dying character in a thriller gasps out crucial information with her or his last breath).

By looking at a wider range of texts than fairy-tales we could add to or modify Propp's list of typical events. One modification could involve the final part of the narrative, which Propp describes as 'The hero is married and ascends the throne'. While few non-fairy-tales end their narratives in this way, it is nevertheless the case that many narratives end with a man and woman coming together, and also with institutional success of some kind; thus we could adapt Propp's typical event to 'The hero/ine finds a partner and gains institutional success'. We could also change the gender-specificity, which is drawn from folk-tales; a woman can equally well play the hero-function, and a man could play the princess-function (the beloved of the hero, or in this case of the heroine). Furthermore, roles and functions can be played by a group rather than an individual; examples would be the anonymous 'Indians' in a western, or the working class in a realist novel.

WAYS OF READING NARRATIVE

In this unit we have taken a view of narrative significantly influenced by the Russian formalists (Shklovsky and Propp). This way of reading narrative is useful for emphasizing the distinction between the conventions and building blocks of the story and the ways these are shaped into the narration. It is also worth noting, however, that the 'story' itself is often at the heart of culture in its widest sense: social meanings, beliefs, structures and conventions. Narratives permeate culture as a way of making sense, packaging experience in particular ways for particular groups and audiences.

One example of putting this to use in analysis is as follows. As part of the self-representations and imaginings of a culture, an individual can be classified on the basis of some characteristic – race, ethnic group, gender, age, sexuality, size, skin colour, disablement, etc. It is interesting to look at the relationship between a particular classificatory characteristic of a character and the function played by that character in the narrative. For example, in many contemporary American films a Black (African–American) character has the function of donor. The donor typically has little presence in the narrative (usually appearing briefly) but has a crucial role in enabling it to develop and come to a conclusion. In any particular film we could interpret the use of a Black donor as making a historical claim: that Black Americans function as donor for the development of the 'narrative' of the US economy. Or we could interpret it in terms of a contradictory position taken by the film with regard to racism, since it enables racial discrimination at the level of employment (the actor gets a small part) while carrying a positive message at the level of meaning (without this Black character the narrative could not be resolved).

Another interpretive possibility is to look at closure in a narrative. Does it take place or not in a particular narrative (or do we find a partial failure of closure?). This is of interest in telling us whether the narrative claims that all is well with its fictional world. Hence the existence or non-existence of

closure often reveals a moral or ideological position. For example, if a narrative can be closed by the major male and female characters getting married,
the narrative potentially carries a message about the virtues of marriage.
Along similar lines, we could look at what constitutes or causes a 'lack' or a
disruption in the terms of a particular narrative: if the absence of the father
at the beginning of a film constitutes its initial lack, then the narrative
means that nuclear families should stay together.

ACTIVITY

In many narratives, there is one character who is singled out as the most
important – as the hero or heroine. Your task in this activity is to think of
some narratives which you know (if you are working in a group, try to pick
narratives which you all know), and to look at whether there are similarities
in the way a particular character becomes identifiably the hero or heroine.

1 Choose and write down the titles of four narratives (novels, films, television programmes, poems, etc.).
2 For each narrative, write down the name of the person you would
consider the hero(-ine), that is, the most important character. If you are in
doubt, write down more than one name.
3 For each name you wrote down, look at what characteristics the character
has, using the following guide. (Your eventual aim is to find which characteristics are linked with this character being the hero/-ine.)

(a) Say when the character first appears in the text and when s/he last
     appears. In connection with this, comment on whether the character is
     involved in the initial lack and/or the closure.
(b) Name the actions which the character carries out, and the things which
     happen to the character. (As a suggestion, see Propp's list, above, for
     some actions which involve heroes in fairy-tales; the character might,
     for example, be chased.)
(c) Describe any interaction with other characters who could be identified
     as 'villain', 'donor', 'princess', etc. (The terms need not be taken liter-
     ally; the character-function called 'princess' could be played by the
     hero's girlfriend, or for that matter the heroine's boyfriend).
(d) List other characteristics which you think might be relevant in defining
     a particular character as the central one (e.g. in a film it may be
     important that a particular actor plays the character).

4 Now compare the four narratives with each other; make a list of main-
character (hero/-ine) characteristics from a–d above which are found in
more than one narrative. This list now gives you a preliminary indication of
the common narrative characteristics of a hero/-ine. You have taken a first
step in building your own analysis of the structures of narrative.

READING

Barthes, Roland (1977) 'Introduction to the structural analysis of narratives', in Barthes *Image–Music–Text*.

Ellis (1982) *Visible Fictions*, pp. 62–76 and 145–59.

Jameson (1981) *The Political Unconscious* pp. 126–8. (Jameson adapts Propp.)

Propp (1968) *Morphology of the Folklore* (worth skimming through and reading selectively).

*Toolan (1989) *Narrative* (a good all-round introduction).

Unit 19 Point of view

'STORY' AND 'NARRATION'

In most theories of narrative two main dimensions or levels are identified. The first consists of the basic events or actions, in the chronological order in which they are supposed to have happened, together with the circumstances in which the actions are performed. This level is sometimes referred to as the **story**. The second level comprises the techniques and devices used for telling the 'story' to the reader. This latter level is sometimes referred to as **narration**. In effect, these two levels may be seen as corresponding to the distinction between the tale itself and the manner in which it is told – a distinction which is based upon our intuitive recognition that the same tale can be told in different ways. (See Unit 18: Narrative.)

POINT OF VIEW AND NARRATION

The term 'point of view' in the discussion of prose fiction has been used in a variety of ways (see Fowler 1986). It can be used fairly literally to refer to visual perspective – the spatial position and angle of vision from which a scene is presented. It can also be used to designate the ideological framework and presuppositions of a text (e.g. 'the point of view of the emergent bourgeoisie' or 'a male perspective'). Finally, it can be used as a term for describing and analysing basic types of narration – the relation of the teller to the tale in any narrative. It is this relationship – between point of view and narration – that will be examined in this unit.

The simplest distinction that we can make in point of view is between two types of narration: a first-person 'I-narration' and a third-person 'they-narration'.

First-person narration

First-person narration may be found in wide range of novels otherwise different in style and period. Novels such as Daniel Defoe's *Robinson Crusoe* (1719), Charlotte Brontë's *Jane Eyre* (1847), Mark Twain's *Huckleberry Finn*

(1884), Philip Roth's *Portnoy's Complaint* (1967), Alice Walker's *The Color Purple* (1983) are all told in the first person. Indeed, in the case of *Robinson Crusoe*, the very chapter headings emphasize the use of the first person: 'I go to sea', 'I am very ill and frighted', 'I sow my grain', 'I am very seldom idle'. In most of these novels, the I-narrator is also the central protagonist of the tale. First-person narration often seems more subjective than third-person since it seems to position us within the consciousness of the narrating character. But there are ways of reducing this sense of subjectivity. An important subclass of first-person narration involves cases where the narrative is told not by the central protagonist but by a subsidiary character. F. Scott Fitzgerald's *The Great Gatsby* (1922) is a well-known case of this. Although Nick, the narrator, tells the story in the first person, he remains on the margins of the events which involve the central figure – Jay Gatsby himself – whose story is thus told from some degree of narrative distance.

Third-person narration

Third-person narration can be used in such a way that we are not particularly aware of the role of the narrator, who remains outside the action of the tale. In such writing the text seems to operate as a simple window on the events of the story; and, because the role of the narrator is carefully effaced, this mode of narration acquires a reputation for objectivity. The opening of *Lord of the Flies* (1954) by William Golding is of this type, in the way it introduces an unnamed boy, who is carefully observed from without:

> The boy with fair hair lowered himself down the last few feet of rock and began to pick his way towards the lagoon. Though he had taken off his school sweater and trailed it now from one hand, his grey shirt stuck to him and his hair was plastered to his forehead. All round him the long scar smashed into the jungle was a bath of heat. He was clambering heavily among the creepers and broken trunks when a bird, a vision of red and yellow, flashed upwards with a witch-like cry; and this cry was echoed by another.

The degree to which this figure – the fair-haired boy – is presented from the outside is emphasized by the difficulty of transforming practically any of the text into the first person by replacing *he/his* with *I/my*. 'My hair is plastered to my forehead', for instance, would sound wrong because *plastered* implies a point of observation outside the figure. Overall, then, this passage uses the third person to maintain a position of apparent objectivity.

Not all uses of the third person, however, are of the same type; and it is important to recognize that there are contrasting possibilities within it, which we may sum up in terms of the following oppositions:

Internal vs. External
Restricted knowledge vs. Unrestricted knowledge

*Internal/External:*The example of third-person narration given above from *Lord of the Flies* observes characters and events from outside. But third-person narration may also work from inside the consciousness of characters by telling us how they think and feel. Much of D.H. Lawrence's *Lady Chatterley's Lover* (1928), for instance, despite its title, adopts Connie Chatterley's perspective rather than that of her lover, Mellors. The following passage, with its emphasis on Connie's feelings, is fairly representative of the novel as a whole:

> Now she came every day to the hens, they were the only things in the world that warmed her heart. Clifford's protestations made her go cold from head to foot. Mrs Bolton's voice made her go cold, and the sound of the business men who came. An occasional letter from Michaelis affected her with the same sense of chill. She felt she would surely die if it lasted much longer.
>
> Yet it was spring, and the bluebells were coming in the wood, and the leaf-buds on the hazels were opening like the spatter of green rain. How terrible it was that it should be spring, and everything cold-hearted, cold-hearted. Only the hens, fluffed so wonderfully on the eggs, were warm with their hot, brooding female bodies! Connie felt herself living on the brink of fainting all the time.

Although the passage, like the rest of the novel, is consistently in the third person, it none the less is devoted primarily to the inner sensations of the person it describes. Indeed, rhetorically, it is structured around a simple, basic opposition in Connie's sensations between warmth and cold (equivalent to life and death). Significantly, it is difficult to read the penultimate sentence as the narrator's comment. It makes most sense as a piece of *free indirect thought* (see Unit 21: Speech and writing) belonging in part at least to Connie herself. Third-person narration, therefore, has the option of being internal (as in the case of Lawrence) or external (as in the case of Golding).

Restricted/Unrestricted: A second distinction may be made in third-person narration between narrators with no restrictions on their knowledge and narrators whose knowledge is limited. We tend to assume that narrators have unrestricted access to knowledge unless there are indications to the contrary. Such indications of limited knowledge are usually signalled by phrases of doubt, such as *it seemed/appeared/looked as if*. The following paragraph, for example, from 'Open House' by Nadine Gordimer, uses several signals of doubt (like 'no doubt' 'somehow' and the question form: 'Hadn't he written a book about the Bay of Pigs?'):

> The voice on the telephone, this time, was American – soft, cautious – no doubt the man thought the line was tapped. Robert Greenman Ceretti, from Washington; while they were talking, she remembered that this was the political columnist who had somehow been connected with the

Kennedy administration. Hadn't he written a book about the Bay of Pigs? Anyway, she had certainly seen him quoted.

It is no accident, of course, that this kind of narrowing down of a potentially omniscient narration should come in a narration that aligns itself strongly with the consciousness of one character, even while remaining third person. It is important to recognize, therefore, that third-person narration need not of necessity remain objective. It can quite easily work from subjective, internal and restricted positions.

FOCALIZATION

We can see, therefore, that the distinction between first-person and third-person narration is not sufficient in itself to account for different types of point of view. An additional complication arises from the fact that most prose fiction is not stable or homogeneous in the point of view which it adopts, so that it can be quite misleading to describe a story as 'told externally in the third person' (which would imply that this was a consistent point of view throughout). Even Ernest Hemingway, who might be thought an exemplar of the external third-person viewpoint, does in practice use a variety of modes of narration, often within the same text, which allow for subjective and internal points of view. Because of this instability in point of view, some accounts of narrative (e.g. Mieke Bal 1985, and Shlomith Rimmon-Kenan 1983) have developed an alternative model using the term **focalization**. Focalization refers to the way in which a text represents the relationship between *who* 'experiences' and *what* is experienced. The one who experiences is termed the **focalizer**, and who or what the focalizer experiences is then called the **focalized**. Focalization falls into two main types: external focalization, where an anonymous, unidentified voice situated outside the text functions as focalizer; and character focalization, where phenomena are presented as experienced by a character within the story.

It is possible, then, to map shifts and tendencies in focalization within any one text by using the following simple notation:

External focalizer	EF
Character focalizer (first person)	CF1
Character focalizer (third person)	CF3
Focalized phenomenon	F

The advantage of the notion of focalization is that it helps to reveal the way a text will shift from sentence to sentence in terms of who is experiencing what and how. Crucial evidence for deciding who is focalizing is the presence or absence of verbs of experiencing such as *look, see, touch, smell,* etc. Consider the following example from Rosamund Lehmann's *The Weather in the Streets* (1936) (the sentences have been numbered):

[1] She [Olivia] ran down to the next floor, telephoned for a taxi, then

opened the door of Etty's bedroom, adjoining the sitting room. [2] Silence and obscurity greeted her; and a smell compounded of powder, scent, toilet creams and chocolate truffles.

In the first sentence Olivia and her actions are focalized from without by an unidentified focalizer. In the second sentence, however, the smell and the silence are impressions that belong to Olivia rather than to the external focalizer of the first sentence. The focalization shifts therefore from external focalization (EF) to character focalization (CF). This can be summed up as follows:

Sentence 1: EF (unspecified) → F (Olivia)
Sentence 2: CF (Olivia) → F (silence, smell, etc.)

Similar shifts can be detected in the following passage from the same book:

[1] Between stages of dressing and washing she [Olivia] packed a hasty suitcase. [2] Pack the red dress, wear the dark brown tweed, Kate's cast off, well-cut, with my nice jumper, lime green, becoming, pack the other old brown jumper – That's about all.

Again, the extract begins as externally focalized, but in the second sentence there is a switch to Olivia's 'inner speech' or thoughts, as she does her packing (presented in free indirect style; see Unit 21: Speech and writing). Moving into the character's consciousness in this way entails a change of focalization from external to character focalization. Here again we can summarize:

Sentence 1: EF (unspecified) → F (Olivia packing)
Sentence 2: CF1 (Olivia) → F (Olivia packing)

On this occasion, the notation helps to highlight not just a shift in focalization, but the way in which Olivia in this passage comes to be focalizer of her own actions. For a moment she is the object of her own subjective consciousness in a way that is both intimate and distanced. In ways such as these the notion of focalization can become an important supplement to notions of point of view, because it prompts close attention to the shifts, developments and balances within point of view within a particular text. *The Weather in the Streets*, for instance, moves between external and character focalization which is centred primarily on Olivia, who figures sometimes as third person, sometimes as first person. These subtle variations help construct her as simultaneously both subject and object of the narrative.

Focalization can in this way be studied in terms of how it is realized from one sentence to another in a text. It may be observed at the level of the form of the text. But focalization at a deeper level is more than this. Patterns of focalization are at once the expression and construction of types of consciousness and self-consciousness. In that respect, *The Weather in the Streets* is very much a novel of the first half of the twentieth century. It is quite distinct, for instance, from *Robinson Crusoe*, even though Crusoe also figures as both subject and object of his own narrative. The relentless 'I' of Crusoe's narrative seems to present the human subject as individual, stable, unified and separate. The shifting patterns of focalization in *The Weather in the Streets*, on the other hand, seem to present an idea of subjectivity as split and dispersed at the very moment that it becomes possible to grasp it in a self-conscious way.

ACTIVITY

The following text is the complete version of a story by Hemingway. It is narrated in the third person and involves two main protagonists, a man and a woman.

A very short story

One hot evening in Padua they carried him up on to the roof and he could look out over the top of the town. There were chimney swifts in the sky. After a while it got dark and the searchlights came out. The others went down and took the bottles with them. He and Luz could hear them below on the balcony. Luz sat on the bed. She was   5 cool and fresh in the hot night.

Luz stayed on night duty for three months. They were glad to let her. When they operated on him she prepared him for the operating table; and they had a joke about friend or enema. He went under the aesthetic holding tight on to himself so he would not blab about   10 anything during the silly, talky time. After he got on crutches he used to take the temperatures so Luz would not have to get up from the bed. There were only a few patients, and they all knew about it. They all liked Luz. As he walked back along the halls he thought of Luz in his bed.   15

Before he went back to the front they went into the Duomo and prayed. It was dim and quiet, and there were other people praying. They wanted to get married, but there was not enough time for the banns, and neither of them had birth certificates. They felt as though they were married, but they wanted everyone to know   20 about it, and to make it so they could not lose it.

Luz wrote him many letters that he never got until after the armistice. Fifteen came in a bunch to the front and he sorted them by the dates and read them all straight through. They were all about the hospital, and how much she loved him and how it was im-   25 possible to get along without him and how terrible it was missing him at night.

After the armistice they agreed he should go home to get a job so they might be married. Luz would not come home until he had a good job and could come to New York to meet her. It was under-   30

stood he would not drink, and he did not want to see his friends or anyone in the States. Only to get a job and be married. On the train from Padua to Milan they quarrelled about her not being willing to come home at once. When they had to say good-bye, in the station at Milan, they kissed good-bye, but were not finished with the   35
quarrel. He felt sick about saying good-bye like that.

He went to America on a boat from Genoa. Luz went back to Pordenone to open a hospital. It was lonely and rainy there, and there was a battalion of *arditi* quartered in the town. Living in the muddy, rainy town in the winter, the major of the battalion made   40
love to Luz, and she had never known Italians before, and finally wrote to the States that theirs had been only a boy and girl affair. She was sorry, and she knew he would probably not be able to understand, but might some day forgive her, and be grateful to her, and she expected, absolutely unexpectedly, to be married in the   45
spring. She loved him as always, but she realized now it was only a boy and girl love. She hoped he would have a great career, and believed in him absolutely. She knew it was for the best.

The major did not marry her in the spring, or any other time. Luz never got an answer to the letter to Chicago about it. A short   50
time after he contracted gonorrhoea from a sales girl in a Loop department store while riding in a taxicab through Lincoln Park.

1 Read through the story and then try altering the mode of narration by transposing the text into first-person narration from the woman's point of view. (Thus, 'Luz sat on the bed' becomes transposed to 'I sat on the bed'.)
2 Write down any peculiar or incongruous sentences that result from this transposition and try and detail the grounds on which they are peculiar.
3 Now transpose the text into first-person narration from the man's point of view. (Thus, 'they carried him up on to the roof' becomes transposed to 'they carried me up on to the roof'.)
4 Note again any peculiarities or incongruities that result.
5 Which transposition of point of view has worked best and why? What does it suggest about the original, third-person mode of narration? Does it involve an implicit bias; and if so, in favour of whom? What other textual mechanisms might support this bias?

READING

Bal (1985) *Narratology: Introduction to the Theory of Narrative.*
Branigan (1984) *Point of View in the Cinema.*
*Fowler (1986) *Linguistic Criticism*, Ch. 9, pp. 127–46.
*Rimon-Kenan (1983) *Narrative Fiction: Contemporary Poetics*, Ch. 6, pp. 71–85.
Scholes (1982) *Semiotics and Interpretation.*
Uspensky (1973) *A Poetics of Composition.*

Unit 20 Narration in film and prose fiction

In the twentieth century there are two culturally dominant ways of experiencing fiction available to us: the visual forms of film (and television); and the prose forms of the novel (and short story). Often the same stories are available in different media, so reinforcing the distinction developed in Unit 18: Narrative, between the story and its mode of narration. In this unit we explore this distinction further, and the similarities and differences in the way film and prose work as media for narration.

A film is based upon an illusion – the illusion of movement. One of the curiosities of the history of cinema is the way in which film's general potential for showing movement quickly became devoted almost exclusively to narrative; by the 1930s 'movies' or 'films' showing in 'picture palaces', 'film theatres' or 'cinemas' had become established as a rival to the novel or short story as a major source of narrative fiction.

Throughout the history of the cinema, film has drawn freely on available narratives that already existed in prose form: Victor Fleming's *Gone with the Wind* (1939), John Huston's *The Maltese Falcon* (1941) and *Moby Dick* (1956), Howard Hawks' *The Big Sleep* (1946), etc. were all taken from novels. Yet in many ways techniques of film narration and prose narration have little in common with each other, apart from the fact that they both tell stories.

INSTITUTIONAL DIFFERENCES BETWEEN FILM AND PROSE NARRATION: CINEMA VERSUS LITERATURE

Prose narrative and film narrative have become institutionalized in quite different ways. Studio-based commercial cinema is a highly capital-intensive institution; the cost of making a commercial film for cinema can run to millions of dollars, using equipment that is costly and capital-intensive. Cinema is also a highly specialized industry, requiring a large number of skilled workers (camera operators, script writers, editors, sound and lighting technicians, etc.), such that the production process can only be understood as a highly collective one involving a large range of people in different capacities. An analogous perspective applies to the process of consumption: complicated publicity and distribution networks provide for the screening of films at advertised times in public auditoria, where they are viewed by an audience who have come together expressly for the purpose.

By comparison, the novel as an institution of cultural production is not nearly so capital-intensive or industrialized. Publishing houses may be large-scale commercial enterprises, but they often depend on more than fiction for their commercial viability. Nor is the production process so heavily centralized as is the case with the film industry. Printing, for example, is routinely subcontracted. In addition, the actual production of the text of a novel is much more individualistic than the production of a film. Novels are 'authored' (see Unit 24: Authorship and intention) and, as such, they issue from a single, unitary source. Responsibility for the words on the page is always assumed to lie with the individual author. (There is nothing in the novel corresponding to the credit sequence in a film.) Authors are also much cheaper as a production entity than a film crew: millions of dollars do not have to be raised in advance in order to begin production on a novel. Significantly, consumption of the prose text mirrors its conditions of production: the reader often reads alone, and responds to the text as an individual.

DIFFERENCES OF MEDIA: FILM VERSUS PROSE

The commercial film has evolved as a self-contained event, presented as a text which lasts about two hours, and as a result must be intelligible at a single viewing. As a visual text, it is based upon the continuous projection of light through moving frames onto a screen, thereby providing a high-definition image typically accompanied by high-quality sound. As a result, it has to be viewed in the dark, with direct appeal to the senses of hearing and vision; but also, typically, projection is continuous and without interruption for the course of the film. As a public event there is therefore no possibility, under normal cinematic conditions, for control by the viewer. Spectators are in no position to vary or control the rate of viewing. Neither interruption nor review is permitted. The spectator is caught up by the event in a continuous process. Two key points emerge from this: first, the spectator's condition – viewing images in darkness – is similar to that of someone dreaming, which favours a high degree of projection of the self into the film, or identification with particular aspects of it; second, as a self-contained but continuously projected event, film in mainstream cinema has evolved under a regime that values easy intelligibility.

The novel, by contrast, presents its stories in the medium of prose writing. This favours an individual mode of consumption. Reading a prose novel is usually a solitary act and apparently allows greater degrees of discretion and control to the reader. The reader can choose the speed of consumption (unlike for a film), and is not required by the environment to pay attention to the text to the same degree, so that variable levels of attention are possible. It is possible to skip parts of the text, and parts of the text can be reread at the reader's convenience.

FORMAL DIFFERENCES: VISUAL IMAGE VERSUS VERBAL SIGN

The most important contrast between film and prose, however, rests on the distinctive features of the two media. The philosopher C.S. Peirce distinguished different ways in which one thing can represent another, and where the relationship was arbitrary he used the term **sign** (so a word can be a sign of a thing), but where the relationship was less arbitrary but instead was based on resemblance he used the term **icon** (so a photograph can be an icon of a thing). (See Unit 8: Language and society, for further discussion of the arbitrary nature of the linguistic sign). As mediums of representation, film is made of icons, while prose is made of signs. Because the film image resembles the portions of reality which it signifies, it has a more immediate relationship to what it depicts. Film's grasp of reality can seem much more direct and easily intelligible.

NARRATION

This basic distinction between words and images is an important point of difference between the two media. Indeed, the differences between film and prose fiction can seem to reduce to a long-established distinction in the study of narrative between 'showing' (mimesis), on the one hand, and 'telling' (diegesis) on the other. It has even been suggested that narrative film can be thought of as 'story' without the level of narration – a tale without a teller. In what follows, however, it is suggested that film can be thought of as a narrative medium – though the mode of narrative is quite different from that in prose.

Despite the differences between them, some important points of resemblance between film and prose fiction remain. These resemblances are best revealed in terms of narration. In the first place, it is not true to claim that film is a non-narrated medium. It is fairly common, for instance, for the soundtrack of a film to include elements of voiced-over first-person narration (as, for instance, in Stephen Spielberg's *The Color Purple* (1985) or Billy Wilder's *Sunset Boulevard* (1950)). More significantly, however, the way in which film is shot and edited together to construct a coherent and intelligible story follows certain basic conventions, which amount to codes of narration, or routine ways of telling, even when a personalized narrator is not evident. Film is not a completely transparent 'window' on the world of the tale; the film image should not be confused with reality. Film images are icons, standing in place of a segment of reality that exists elsewhere. Moreover, the significance of an image always exceeds what it literally depicts or denotes. This broader significance has many aspects, and is conferred on the image in several ways, for instance:

(a)   An image supplied by a shot derives significance from its place in series of shots. This is the classical principle of **montage** (see Unit 15: Juxtaposition).

(b) In mainstream cinema, the image is constantly supplemented by sound. Contemporary cinema typically uses immensely complex, multilayered soundtracks, which interweave several different types of sound, including music (e.g. 'motifs'), ambient or diegetic sound (e.g. traffic, rattling teacups, etc.) and voice/speech (both as character dialogue and voice-over narration).

The organization and sequencing of shots – especially in commercial cinema – are subject to powerful conventions. Most evident, in relation to the presentation of dialogue in the fictional film, is that it is rare in filmed dialogue for characters to address the camera; rather, they are filmed in various degrees of profile addressing each other (as if the camera were not there). This is such a binding convention that 'the look to camera' might almost be described in film terms as 'the forbidden look'. When it does occur, it typically breaks the illusion of naturalism. Examples can be found both in art cinema (in films by Jean-Luc Godard and Ingmar Bergman, for example) and in popular television series (e.g. Glenn Gordon Caron's *Moonlighting*, 1985–9).

The practice of filming dialogue in profile is part of a larger set of conventions built up around an important organizing principle: the **line of action**. In its simplest form, for a scene involving two protagonists, this principle is based on an imaginary line drawn between the two characters. In mainstream cinema it is a basic convention to restrict consecutive shots in the same scene to only one side of this imaginary line. In theory, it might seem possible to set up shots from anywhere within a 360 degree circle around the space in which the filmed action occurs. In practice, however, shots are restricted to half this domain, in conformity with what then becomes known as 'the 180 degree rule'.

In shooting a scene involving dialogue, film makers have available to them a standard repertoire of possible shots. The most common amongst these are mid-shots, medium close-ups and close-ups. At or near the beginning of a scene a mid-shot will occur, in which both characters figure, in order to establish the line of action (sometimes called a two-shot or an establishing shot). As the dialogue proceeds, there is usually a progressive focusing down on the individual protagonists, so that each is shown individually in close-up. At or near the end of a scene, a two-shot or mid-shot is often used as part of the process of achieving closure (signalling that the scene is ending). Within the scene, then, the handling of close-ups is prepared for by the initial establishing shot which gives the line of action; subsequent chaining together of the close-ups develops in a form of visual counterpoint: a shot of one speaker is typically replaced by a shot of the other in a technique commonly known as 'field/reverse-field' or 'shot/counter-shot'. In the clearest cases, the speaker is observed from a position near by, to one side or behind the listener; the position is then reversed when the speaking roles switch, the camera remaining all the time on one side of the line of action. The sequence of stills in Plates 7–9, from David Lean's film of *A Passage to India* (1978), helps to show this at work (see p. 196).

These basic conventions are, of course, honoured as much in the breach as in the observance. They have grown up as routines which provide flexible formats for making what is seen on screen coherent and intelligible; but they are not adhered to in a rigid fashion. The field/reverse-field does not always follow the speaker. Sometimes it includes the reactions of the listener, hence the term 'reaction shots'. Generally, however, these routines provide background norms of presentation which help guide the spectator through the time and space of the narrative, and which the spectator has unconsciously learned to use.

The notion that conventions help to supply or guarantee intelligibility is crucial here. Conventions cue us to expect certain kinds of relationship between shots so that, for instance, if in one shot we (as viewers) see a character gazing out of frame, we then interpret the next shot (whenever possible) as depicting what that character could see from the position s/he occupies. Such apparently simple mechanisms for chaining shots together help to situate us, the viewers, in the temporal and spatial world of the fiction, and to draw us through the narrative. In this way the 'eye' of the camera, as reflected in the angle of shots and the way in which these shots are edited into sequence, is anthropomorphized, or made to seem human. As spectators, we see from positions that could be (and sometimes even are) those of protagonists in the fiction themselves.

It has been argued, in fact, that the position constructed for the film spectator (and the pleasures associated with being a spectator) resemble those of a voyeur – a claim that has been particularly discussed within feminist film theory but which has also been made the subject of conscious attention by film makers themselves in films such as Michael Powell's *Peeping Tom* (1959) and Alfred Hitchcock's *Rear Window* (1954). One significant aspect of the notion of the voyeuristic spectator is that the camera does not just show the action of the story, like some simple recording device; it shows events in a way that is so constructed and edited according to specifiable conventions that it amounts, if not exactly to a narrator, then to some anthropomorphically defined, implied spectator. Indeed, for a feminist film theorist such as Laura Mulvey (1975) the eye of the camera is not merely anthropomorphic, but more specifically masculine, inasmuch as it routinely constructs women within cinema as objects of male desire (see Unit 23: Positioning the reader or spectator).

DIFFERENCES BETWEEN FILM AND PROSE FICTION

Because it operates exclusively through the medium of the verbal sign, the novel can seem somehow more dense in its texture than film. Its relationship to reality can seem more oblique, since the world which unfolds in the novel is not given directly but is developed by the narrator and

Plate 7 A Passage to India: two-shot

Plate 8 A Passage to India: field

Plate 9 A Passage to India: reverse-field

recreated in an active and controlled process of reading which allows for reflection, comparison and the gradual construction of a coherent whole. Patterns of reference and cross-reference may be built up over several hundred pages; and the whole novel may take several hours to read (perhaps ten hours for an average-length novel).

Film, by contrast, can seem more immediate, but perhaps at the same time less dense. In the case of a film adaptation of a novel, the ten hours of reading are replaced by two hours' viewing, which is usually expected to be intelligible at a single screening. This might suggest that film is somehow a less complex, less demanding medium than the prose novel. But it is worth remembering that film is a multilayered medium working with a potent combination of two modalities of expression: image and sound. The image has powerful possibilities for condensing significance: descriptive detail, character and action can be displayed simultaneously within a single shot, whereas prose is constrained by a sequential, piece-by-piece mode of presentation. And the significatory possibilities of the image are further enhanced by the different sorts of potential of soundtrack. The shrinking of consumption time from a novel to a film, therefore, does not inevitably entail simplification or mere reduction.

In all this, however, it is important to note that stories have a constructed nature in whichever medium they are rendered. We have seen that film, no less than prose, depends on the operation of conventions. Such conventions range from those governing the depiction of dialogue to those governing the depiction of a chase or the intrusion into a scene of a sinister onlooker. These filmic conventions are just as crucial for narration in film as are those that govern the representation of thought or speech (see Unit 21: Speech and writing) or the handling of point of view in prose fiction (see Unit 19). Prose is governed by conventions which are linguistic in character. What is less obvious – but no less true – is that film makers also operate according to a kind of language: the language of film.

ACTIVITY

E.M. Forster's novel, *A Passage to India* (1924), was filmed under the direction of David Lean in 1978. In the following activity you are invited to prepare a shooting script from a passage of the novel and to compare it with a simplified shot sequence from Lean's film.

The extract from the novel reprinted below deals with a visit to a site of local interest – the Marabar Caves – by Aziz, an Indian doctor, and Adela Quested, an Englishwoman. Miss Quested is preoccupied with thoughts of her impending marriage to an English colonial officer, Ronny Heaslop. Dr Aziz, a widower, is also preoccupied – but with thoughts of a more mundane character to do with the organization of the trip, for which he feels responsible.

Miss Quested and Aziz and a guide continued the slightly tedious expedition. They did not talk much, for the sun was getting high. The air felt like a warm bath into which hotter water is trickling constantly, the temperature rose and rose.... [Aziz] had never liked Miss Quested as much as Mrs. Moore, and had little to say to her, less than ever now that she would marry a British official.

Nor had Adela much to say to him. If his mind was with the breakfast, hers was mainly with her marriage.... There were real difficulties here – Ronny's limitations and her own – but she enjoyed facing difficulties, and decided that if she could control her peevishness (always her weak point), and neither rail against Anglo-India nor succumb to it, their married life ought to be happy and profitable. She mustn't be too theoretical; she would deal with each problem as it came up, and trust to Ronny's common sense and her own. Luckily, each had abundance of common sense and goodwill.

But as she toiled over a rock that resembled an inverted saucer, she thought, 'What about love?' The rock was nicked by a double row of footholds, and somehow the question was suggested by them. Where had she seen footholds before? Oh yes, they were the pattern traced in the dust by the wheels of the Nawab Bahadur's car. She and Ronny – no, they did not love each other.

'Do I take you too fast?' enquired Aziz, for she had paused, a doubtful expression on her face. The discovery had come so suddenly that she felt like a mountaineer whose rope had broken. Not to love the man one's going to marry! Not to find it out till this moment! Not even to have asked oneself the question until now! Something else to think out. Vexed rather than appalled, she stood still, her eyes on the sparkling rock. There was esteem and animal contact at dusk, but the emotion that links them was absent. Ought she to break her engagement off? She was inclined to think not – it would cause so much trouble to others; besides, she wasn't convinced that love is necessary to a successful union. If love is everything, few marriages would survive the honeymoon. 'No, I'm all right, thanks,' she said, and, her emotions well under control, resumed the climb, though she felt a bit dashed. Aziz held her hand, her guide adhered to the surface like a lizard and scampered about as if governed by a personal centre of gravity.

'Are you married, Dr. Aziz?' she asked, stopping again, and frowning.

'Yes, indeed, do come and see my wife' – for he felt it more artistic to have his wife alive for a moment.

'Thank you,' she said absently.

'She is not in Chandrapore just now.'

'And have you children?'

'Yes, indeed, three,' he replied in firmer tones.

'Are they a great pleasure to you?'

'Why, naturally, I adore them,' he laughed.

'I suppose so.' What a handsome little Oriental he was, and no doubt his wife and children were beautiful too, for people usually get what they already possess. She did not admire him with any personal warmth, for there was nothing of the vagrant in her blood, but she guessed he might attract women of his own race and rank, and she regretted that neither she nor Ronny had physical charm. It does make a difference in a relationship – beauty, thick hair, a fine skin. Probably this man had several wives – Mohammedans always insist on their full four, according to Mrs. Turton. And having no one else to speak to on that eternal rock, she gave rein to the subject of marriage and said in her honest, decent, inquisitive way: 'Have you one wife or more than one?'

The question shocked the young man very much. It challenged a new conviction of his community, and new convictions are more sensitive than old. If she had said, 'Do you worship one god or several?' he would not have objected. But to ask an educated Indian Moslem how many wives he has – appalling, hideous! He was in trouble how to conceal his confusion. 'One, one in my own particular case,' he spluttered, and let go of her hand. Quite a number of caves were at the top of the track, and thinking, 'Damn the English even at their best,' he plunged into one of them to recover his balance. She followed at her leisure, quite unconscious that she had said the wrong thing, and not seeing him, she also went into the cave, thinking with half her mind 'sight-seeing bores me,' and wondering with the other half about marriage.

1 Write out a dialogue for your film scene; then sketch alongside it, in a series of simple cartoons or pictures, how you think the scene should be shot.
2 Compare the shooting-script you have prepared with the actual dialogue and simplified shot sequence in Plates 10–24 (below).
3 What are the main differences between your shooting-script and the given shot sequence. Do they involve different interpretations and realizations of the novel? If so, in what way?

Scene on the Kawa Dol
Miss Quested: It's almost a mirage.

10

Dr Aziz.
May I ask you something rather personal?

You were married, weren't you?

11

Doctor Aziz: Yes, indeed.

12

Miss Quested: Did you love your wife when you married her?

13

Doctor Aziz: We never set eyes on each other till the day we were married. It was all arranged by our families. I only saw her face in a photograph.

14

Miss Quested: What about love?

15

Doctor Aziz: We were man and woman. And we were young.

16

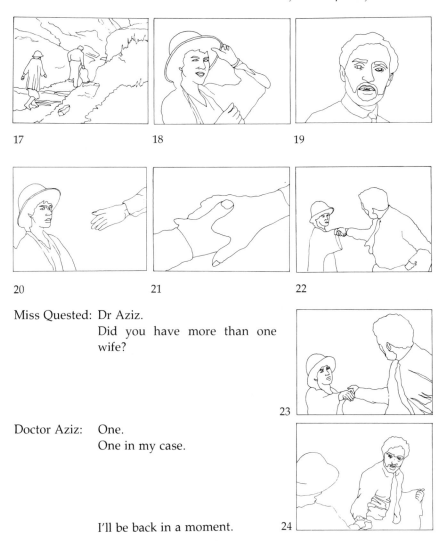

Miss Quested: Dr Aziz.
Did you have more than one wife?

Doctor Aziz: One.
One in my case.

I'll be back in a moment.

Plates 10–24 A Passage to India: scene on the Kawa Dol

READING

*Bordwell (1985) *Narration in the Fiction Film.*
Bordwell and Thompson (1979) *Film Art: an Introduction.*
*Chatman (1978) *Story and Discourse: Narrative Structure in Film and Prose Fiction.*
Cook (ed.) (1985) *The Cinema Book.*
Ellis (1982) *Visible Fictions.*
Giddings, Selby and Wensley (1990) *Screening the Novel.*
Mulvey, Laura (1975) 'Visual pleasure and narrative cinema,' *Screen* 16, pp. 6–18; reprinted in Bennett *et al.* (eds) (1981) *Popular Television and Film.*

Unit 21 Speech and writing

Speech is the primary mode of linguistic expression. As a species we are biologically adapted for speech but not for writing; and as individuals we learn to speak (largely unconsciously) well before we learn to write. Learning to write, in fact, only ever occurs as a result of conscious and deliberate instruction. Human languages have always been articulated in speech; as a mode of expression, writing is by comparison, even with its own long history, a relatively recent form, which even now appears in comparatively few of the world's languages.

In literate societies, nevertheless, our ideas about language are formed largely by our conscious experiences of writing rather than by our everyday experiences of ordinary speech. Yet the two media are very different. Speech tends to operate in conditions of what we can call **co-presence**, particularly in face-to-face settings of an informal type where what we say has to be understood as we say it, often helped by facial expressions and gestures. In such situations, fine adjustments can be made to what we say in the light of immediate and continuous reactions from our interlocutor. Writing, on the other hand, creates a relatively fixed and permanent product, which allows the separation of participants (writer and reader) in time and space. The process of composition may be lengthy, involving several stages and many revisions as the final product takes shape; and because the final product is relatively fixed, the process of interpretation may be extended, deferred and interrupted, involving several readings and rereadings.

These very different conditions under which speech and writing operate can be related to different features associated with the two modes of expression. These different features emerge most clearly if we compare a transcription of a fragment of everyday conversation with how it might have been if it had been composed as written text.

Speech (short pauses are indicated by (.))

> Well you see (.) I'm sure it would have I'm sure it would have been possible
> if they had known anyone who was a post office engineer to install (.) a um er (.) rig

so that the the (.)
where you can actually dial from the from the from that phone (.) er and
if you (.) but that could be you know locked away and the er something
like that (.)
so that you could actually dial from that one
by-pass the coin mechanism

Writing

I am sure it would have been possible, if they had known anyone who
was a post office engineer, to install the type of pay-phone where you
can, if you wish, use a key to by-pass the coin mechanism and still dial
out.

Some of the noticeable features of speech that we typically do not find in
writing are:

1   **pauses** and **pause fillers** (*um/er/erm*);
2   **false starts**, where a phrase or sentence is begun only to be replaced by
    something else ('. . . and if you (.) but that could be . . .');
3   **self-corrections**, where a phrase or sentence is begun and then recycled
    in an amended form ('. . . from the from that phone . . .');
4   **repetitions**, where a phrase is immediately recycled without alteration
    as part of building up to the larger utterance ('(.) I'm sure it would have
    I'm sure it would have been . . .');
5   **response cues**, where the recipient is invited to complete or supply for
    themselves the full sense of the utterance ('. . . but that could be *you
    know* locked away and the er *something like that* . . .').

The presence of such features goes some way to explaining why the spoken
extract appears to be longer than the equivalent written statement. They
also create a misleading impression of lack of fluency – even sloppiness – in
speech. They are, however, integral to the performance of speech in
everyday circumstances. Pause fillers, for instance, are spoken in a characteristic tone which helps to reinforce the signal they give that the utterance
is unfinished and that a momentary hesitation at this point by the speaker
should not be mistaken for the end of a turn. Repetitions are a common
feature of the beginning of a turn, where speakers are competing with each
other to speak. Completion markers point to the active role of the listener in
conversation, and to the way in which background understanding and
shared knowledge can be assumed between people talking to each other –
so much so that it becomes odd, even condescending, to spell everything out
in a completely explicit fashion. Since meanings are shaped, reshaped and
negotiated at the moment of speaking, speech can be seen as a much more
dynamic and participatory mode of interaction than writing.

SPEECH AND NARRATIVE

Story telling – whether in a novel or an everyday anecdote – often relies on the expressive and dramatic potential of speech. In this sense, nearly all narrative depends at some point on the presentation of material as if it were fragments of a spoken dialogue which is being quoted. But in written narrative the features of speech which we noted above – the false starts, the self-corrections, etc. – are rarely retained in this practice of apparent quotation. Instead, specific techniques have evolved in writing in order to introduce and mark the quotation of speech. What is at stake here may be seen in the narrative writing of small children, where ways of embedding speech into writing are still imperfectly controlled. In the following opening to a story written by an eight-year-old child, it is difficult to distinguish who is talking to whom:

> *The tidy house*
> One day a girl and a boy said,
> Is it sping time?
> Yes! I think so. Why?
> Because we,ve got vister.
> Who!
> Jamie and Jason. Here they come.
> Hello, our toby! I havont seen you for a long time.
> Polkadot's outside and the sunflowers are bigger than us
> Mark let's go and see.
> OK.
>
> (Carla, aged 8: cited in Steedman 1982: 42)

In this story, pieces of dialogue are not attributed in any clear way to specific speakers. Toby and Polkadot turn out to be, respectively, a dog and a rabbit belonging to the visitors. Not even the single use of the reporting verb ('said') in the first line successfully discriminates between the two possible speakers ('a girl and a boy'). Careful examination of spatial co-ordinates ('come', 'go', 'outside') suggests that Jamie and Jason are the visitors; if this is the case, Mark is probably the boy. Most of the dialogue, therefore, belongs in all likelihood to the girl and the boy, except for 'Polkadot's outside and the sunflowers are bigger than us', which seems to be said by one of the visitors. But while it is possible to arrive at some sense of who is speaking to whom, it might be argued on the basis of this extract that clear distinction between speakers is not important for young children – that speech is a medley of undifferentiated voices and that identifying the owners of such voices is not important to them. It is more likely, however, that for the eight-year-old child the written mode of story telling has not fully separated itself from oral story telling; the child is still heavily depen-dent on oral strategies. The spoken story, in this respect, has particular strategies available to it that have no direct equivalent in writing: such as changes in voice quality as a way of registering a change of speaker, as in the following case:

> *Trainee doctor's story (on casualty)*
> They come bustin' through the door – blood is everywhere on the walls on the floor
> everywhere
> [raised pitch] It's okay Billy it's okay we're gonna make it
> [normal voice] What's the hell wrong with you?
> We look at him. He's covered with blood yknow? All they had to do was take a wash cloth at home and go like this [pause] and there'd be no blood.

This example reminds us that a common feature of everyday conversational anecdote is the use of different tones of voice in the dramatic re-enactment of dialogue.

TYPES OF SPEECH PRESENTATION IN PROSE FICTION

Writers, however, like the child author of 'The tidy house' above, do not, by definition, have available to them the expressive possibilities of the voice. Instead, various techniques in the written medium are used in the presentation of speech and the identification of speakers. These are highly conventionalized, and it is worth noting that not much attempt is made at fidelity to actual, 'real-time' conversational speech with all its apparent lack of fluency. These techniques may be classified under the following major types.

Direct speech

In direct speech, speech is enclosed within quotation marks and introduced by or presented alongside a reporting clause (*she said/declared/commanded/ asserted*, etc.):

> She said: 'Well there's nothing I can say to that, is there?'
> He leaned forward and said: 'I'm going to give you another chance, Anna'.
>
> (Doris Lessing, *The Golden Notebook*, 1962)

Indirect speech

By comparison with direct speech, indirect speech is presented from a slightly different perspective, with a shift from the perspective of the speaker to that of the narrator. Indirect speech differs from direct speech in the following ways:

1   Quotations marks are dropped.
2   Some kind of subordinating conjunction such as *that* is used.
3   There is a switch from first- and second-person pronouns (*I, you*) to third-person (*she, he, they*).
4   There is a shift in the tense of the verb 'backwards' in time (e.g. from *is* to *was*).
5   Temporal expressions shift backwards in time (e.g. *now* would become *then*).
6   Demonstratives shift from close to distant ones (e.g. *here* becomes *there*).

The piece of direct-speech dialogue from *The Golden Notebook* given above can be transformed into indirect speech, producing the following:

> She said that there was nothing she could say to that. He leaned forward and said that he was going to give her another chance.

Free direct speech

In this case the perspective of the narrator is minimized instead of being emphasized. The reporting clauses are dropped altogether, although the quotation marks are usually (though not invariably) preserved. The first line of dialogue in the example below *could* be treated as direct speech if 'They talked about his work' is taken as a reporting clause. But the remaining speech is in the free direct mode because of the absence of any other reporting clauses:

> They talked about his work. He specialised in leucotomies:
> 'Boy, I've cut literally hundreds of brains in half!'
> 'It doesn't bother you, what you're doing?'
> 'Why should it?'
> 'But you know when you've finished that operation, it's final, the people are never the same again?'
> 'But that's the idea, most of them don't want to be the same again.'
>
> (Lessing, *The Golden Notebook*)

Free indirect speech

This is a mixed form, consisting partly of direct speech and partly of indirect speech, where, because of the suppression of some of the distinguishing signals, it is difficult to separate the voice of the narrator from the voice of the character. In the later stages of the following extract, there is the appearance of what is called **backshifting** of tense ('entrust' becomes 'entrusted'), as well as some pronoun shift ('myself' becomes 'himself'); these characteristic features of free indirect speech re-emphasize the presence of a narrator who filters the speech of characters:

For what? he asked her, with careful scorn. To compete with phrase-
mongers, incapable of thinking consecutively for sixty seconds? To
submit himself to the criticisms of an obtuse middle class which
entrusted its morality to policemen and its fine arts to impresarios.

(James Joyce, *Dubliners*, 1914)

It is a fairly simple matter, involving few changes, to switch the free indirect
speech of this passage into direct speech, thereby emphasizing the perspective of the character:

'For what?' he asked her, with careful scorn. 'To compete with phrase-
mongers, incapable of thinking consecutively for sixty seconds? To
submit myself to the criticisms of an obtuse middle class which entrusts
its morality to policemen and its fine arts to impresarios?'

Free indirect speech is thus an ambiguous mode in that it blurs the distinction between a character's speech and the narrative voice; this ambiguity
has made it attractive to novelists from Jane Austen onwards. Some writers
– such as Joyce in *Dubliners* or Austen in *Emma* (1816) – are especially
known as exponents of free indirect speech. As a technical device it offers
writers a way of presenting words which seem to come from inside and
outside a character simultaneously. Such words can be given the emotional
weight of the character's perspective, while at the same time preserving a
degree of narrative distance or ironic detachment from the character.

Thought and speech

In many respects, thought may be considered as a kind of 'inner speech';
and the major ways of presenting it are much the same as those reviewed
above for external speech.

Thus the different modes of presenting both speech and thought can be
represented in a chart which shows the different degrees to which a
character's speech or thought can be filtered through the narrator:

Free direct speech/ thought	Unfiltered by narrator	('Come here tomorrow.')
Direct speech/thought	Some filtering	(She said to him, 'Come here tomorrow.')
Free indirect speech/ thought	More filtering	(She said to him to come tomorrow.)
Indirect speech/thought	Most filtering	(She said that he was to come there the next day.)

Because of the connection between modes of presentation and relative closeness to or distance from the viewpoint of the character or of the narrator,
modes of presenting speech in prose fiction are more than mere technical
accomplishments. Each possibility has a different effect, and seems to carry
a different value ranging from allowing the character to speak as if in her or

his 'own words' to filtering them through the perspective of the narrator. These different kinds of interplay between the voice of the narrator and the speech of a character make the issue of speech presentation important not just for its own sake but also for the way in which it connects with other topics such as **point of view** in fiction (see Unit 19).

Genre and the presentation of speech

Subtle differences in the presentation of speech can also serve as indicators of **genre** (see Unit 17). Consider, for example, the following reporting clauses which frame direct speech (they are all drawn from within a few pages of each other in one text; the speech itself has been omitted):

'. . . .,' she replied sharply.
'. . . .,' she stuttered.
'. . . .,' she wailed gaspingly.
'. . . .,' he murmured huskily.
'. . . .,' she asked as calmly as she could.
'. . . .,' he said with chilly emphasis.
'. . . .,' he countered silkily.

Readers familiar with the genre will probably instantly recognize these as coming from popular romance (they are quoted from Susan Napier's *The Counterfeit Secretary: a vivid story of passionate attraction,* published by Mills and Boon (1986)). As direct speech, it is genre-specific in the way in which the *manner* of the speech has been foregrounded in the reported clauses through adverbial phrases such as 'gaspingly', 'huskily', 'with chilly emphasis', and so on. Compare these with the following short scene from Nancy Mitford's novel *The Pursuit of Love* (1945):

'*Allô – allô.*'
'Hullo.'
'Were you asleep?'
'Yes, of course. What's the time?'
'About two. Shall I come round to see you?'
'Do you mean now?'
'Yes.'
'I must say it would be very nice. But the only thing is, what would the night porter think?'
'*Ma chère,* how English you are. *Eh bien, je vais vous le dire – il ne se fera aucune illusion.*'
'No, I suppose not.'
'But I don't imagine he's under any illusion as it is. After all, I come here for you three times every day – you've seen nobody else, and French people are quite quick at noticing these things, you know.'
'Yes – I see –'
'*Alors, c'est entendu – à tout à l'heure.*'

Both The Counterfeit Secretary and *The Pursuit of Love* are concerned with emotional attachment, and dialogue in both works as an important vehicle for registering fluctuations in degrees of attachment. This makes the differences in the ways dialogue is handled all the more striking. *The Counterfeit Secretary* uses some free direct speech, but a great deal of the dialogue is direct speech, where information about the manner of the speaker is foregrounded in explicit narrative comment. *The Pursuit of Love* makes much more use of free direct speech, in which the words of characters have to achieve their own significance without being mediated by a direct comment from the narrator. Comparison between the two techniques suggests that, for popular romance, the shifting grounds of emotional attachment may be carried in the manner of the speech as much as by the speech itself. For readers of *The Pursuit of Love*, on the other hand, the ebb and flow of emotional confrontation is to be deciphered in the nuances of the dialogue itself. Such differences function as formal markers of generic distinctness; they may also signal differences in attitudes towards language and meaning in the intended readerships of the two works.

ACTIVITY

Since 'thought' may be considered as a kind of 'inner speech', the presentation of thought – for the purposes of this unit – is treated as similar to the presentation of speech. Direct speech, for example, is similar in its presentation to direct thought – except that the kind of reporting verb will be different:

Direct speech: She said, 'Well there's nothing I can say to that, is there?'
Direct thought: She thought, 'Well there's nothing I can say to that, is there?'

In the following extract from Lessing's *The Golden Notebook*, two characters, Tommy and Anna, are having a confrontation. Tommy is the adult child of Anna's close friend; he is challenging Anna about her writing – specifically about her way of organizing her work in four notebooks.

'Don't put me off, Anna. Are you afraid of being chaotic?'
Anna felt her stomach contract in a sort of fear, and said, after a pause: 'I suppose I must be.'
'Then it's dishonest. After all, you take your stand on something, don't you? Yes you do – you despise people like my father, who limit themselves. But you limit yourself too. For the same reason. You're afraid. You're being irresponsible.' He made this final judgement, the pouting, deliberate mouth smiling with satisfaction. Anna realised that this was what he had come to say. This was the point they had been working towards all evening. And he was going on, but in a flash of knowledge she said: 'I often leave my door open – have you been in here to read these notebooks?'
'Yes, I have. I was here yesterday, but I saw you coming up the street so I

went out before you could see me. Well I've decided that you're
dishonest, Anna. You are a happy person but ...'
'I, happy?' said Anna, derisive.

1 Identify the type of speech presentation in the following segments:

(a) Anna ... said, after a pause: 'I suppose I must be.'
(b) in a flash of knowledge she said: 'I often leave my door open – have you
     been in here to read these notebooks?'

Try to rewrite each segment as indirect speech. Make a note of the changes
that were necessary in order to do so. Compare the original with your
rewritten version: are there any differences between them in terms of
meaning or effect? If so, make a note of what the differences are.

2 Identify the way of presenting speech used in the following segment:

'Yes, I have. I was here yesterday, but I saw you coming up the street so I
went out before you could see me. Well I've decided that you're
dishonest, Anna. You are a happy person but ...'

Try to rewrite the segment as free indirect speech. Make a note of the
changes you needed to make in order to do this. Compare the original with
your rewritten version: do they differ in meaning or effect? If so, how?

3 Identify the way of presenting inner speech/thought used in the following
segment:

Anna realized that this was what he had come to say. This was the point
they had been working towards all evening. And he was going on, ...

Is there any ambiguity about how much of this extract is the character's
thought, and how much is the narrator's report of events? If so, where does
the ambiguity begin? How might you resolve this ambiguity? Try to rewrite
the passage as direct thought ('inner speech'). Compare the original with
your rewritten version: do they differ in effect? If so, how?

4 Substitute your rewritten segments in the original, and read the whole
(rewritten) passage through again. Does it work as well as the original? If
not, why not? If you can offer an answer to this question, you have gone a
long way towards explaining why the writer may have made those particular technical choices in the first place.

READING

Brown and Yule (1983) *Discourse Analysis.*
*Leech and Short (1981) *Style in Fiction,* pp. 318–51.
Montgomery (1986) *An Introduction to Language and Society.*
Ong (1982) *Orality and Literacy.*
Steedman (1982) *The Tidy House.*
*Toolan (1989) *Narrative: a Critical Linguistic Introduction,* pp. 90–145.

Unit 22 Realism

'Realism' as a critical term is traditionally used to refer loosely to texts where the relationship between the text and the depicted reality is felt to be direct and immediate. Examples of realism are typically chosen from genres such as 'the nineteenth-century novel', 'the Hollywood film' and 'popular fiction'. An alternative way of thinking about realism, however, is to see it as marked out by the adoption of specific devices or formal techniques for producing a sense of 'the real'. It is possible, therefore, to make a distinction between **realistic**, commonly used to mean something like 'lifelike', and **realist** in the more technical sense of conforming to conventions for passing something off as real, so that even future-fantasy or science-fiction may be treated as examples of realism.

THE TRADITIONAL VIEW

Realism is both the name of a literary movement involving primarily novels which flourished between about 1830 and 1890 (including, for instance, George Eliot as one of the major British exponents) and a particular **genre** (see Unit 17) of writing which is in some way realistic. This was the view held by realist writers as well as by most critics until recently. Within the traditional view it is possible to see realism either as a direct imitation of the facts of reality, or as a special reconstruction of the facts of reality, for which Eric Auerbach (1953) adopts Aristotle's term *mimesis*. In **mimesis**, while the reader recognizes a version of reality because it includes elements which s/he recognizes, it also produces a more generalized or universalized version of reality than that which the reader habitually experiences, and this is what is thought to be of most value.

In Unit 17 on **genre**, we looked at the possibility of listing characteristics of particular genres. In the traditional view, the characteristics of realism revolve particularly around its subject matter and its message or moral intentions. The subject matter of realist novels is often concerned with the domestic sphere (many realist novels take place inside the home, or are centred around events in the home); most of the events described are not about heroic deeds but are, rather, the ordinary events within the lives of ordinary people, their emotions, their relationships, etc.; and ordinary people are presented as complex and multifaceted. Although realist texts are about individual characters and their lives, their message – often developed in terms of a secular, socially based morality – is presented as if true for all readers.

Language, reality and representation

In such an approach to realism, language is treated as a transparent medium as if it were capable of simply reflecting reality without drawing attention to the way in which it works. However, it is clear that the relation between texts, particularly literary texts, and reality is far more complex than simple reflection or idealization. As Leech and Short argue: 'The myth of absolute realism arises from a mistaken attempt to compare two incomparable things: language and extralinguistic realities' (1981: 152). Realist texts are, after all, primarily verbal constructs, and it is their essentially textual nature which is often ignored in discussions of realism. It is for this reason that some critics have turned to analysing not the relation between words and things but the relation between words.

How traditional realism shapes ways of reading

The traditional view, by which realist texts are assumed to describe the reality of a period or a place, is common in the criticism and teaching of texts, and is often tied up with stereotypical views of the place of particular people in reality. (This notion of the stereotype is also part of the literary practice of realism, relating to the notion of the cultural code, discussed below.) Many texts are assumed to be realist in this sense: for example, women's novels are often read in university courses as though they were autobiographical (drawing upon the stereotypical notion that women are restricted to the private and the personal); or novels by working-class writers are read as documentary descriptions (according to a stereotype in which working-class people see everyday reality as it really is but are unable to transcend that view).

THE STRUCTURALIST VIEW

Structuralist critics such as Roland Barthes (1986) and David Lodge (1977) have helped to shift attention to the textual qualities of realism; and they have stressed that the notion of literary convention is very important in the construction of realist novels. In this view, whether or not a text is realist (that is, has the formal characteristics of realism) is not related to whether it is realistic.

Conventions

Literary texts are generally constructed according to a system of textual conventions or rules; our notion of which genre a text belongs to is largely founded on the recognition of the set of conventions that the text is drawing on (see Unit 17: Genre). When a writer produces a realist narrative, it is against a background set of realist conventions governing the choices which s/he will make; for example, s/he will be constrained by the conventions that events in the text are arranged in a chronological order; that there are 'round', or developed, characters; that there will be a certain type of ending; and so on. Although these conventions of realism can be experimented with and altered, as they invariably are in novels, they nevertheless exist as the basis for construction of the text.

Characteristics of realism

Lodge (1977) suggests that realist texts achieve their effect not so much because they are like reality as such, but because they resemble in their conventions texts which we consider to be non-fictional. He takes two separate descriptions of capital punishment, one by George Orwell, 'A hanging', and one which appeared in the *Guardian* newspaper and argues that Orwell's is in fact a fiction, even though presented as if it were the account of an eye-witness. He then shows similarities between the realist fiction and the non-fictional report: (a) in neither case are features of the language foregrounded so that they become the focus of attention; (b) the narrator does not draw attention to her or his role in interpreting events – the events, rather, seem to speak themselves; (c) there is an emphasis on detailed description of the context of the event (the exact time, place and setting) and of the preparation for the execution. It is not easy, says Lodge, to distinguish one text from the other on the basic strategies that they adopt to depict the event. From this he concludes that realist texts draw on the conventions used to write non-fictional texts in order to convince the reader that they are describing reality. (Orwell's text is a rather extreme version since it reads like an authentic eye-witness account.) Lodge suggests a working definition of realism in literature as: 'the representation of experience in a manner which approximates closely to descriptions of similar experience in non-literary texts of the same culture' (1977: 25).

In a similar way, as discussed in the unit on Speech and writing (see Unit 21), it is clear that dialogue is represented in literature according to a set of conventions rather than with reference to the way that people speak in real life. Many elements of actual speech are omitted when it is represented in text (e.g. hesitation, interruption, etc.) and other elements are included to signal to the reader that they are reading 'real speech' (e.g. inverted commas, the use of colloquialism, etc.).

On the other hand, Roland Barthes (1977) draws attention to the fact that in many classic realist texts there is a proliferation of descriptive detail. Although narratives in general tend to include a descriptive section which sets the scene for the actions to take place, Barthes points to the presence in realist texts of details which seem to be included for the sole purpose of signalling to the reader that it is 'the real' which is being described. For example, in the following extract from *The Well of Loneliness* by Radclyffe Hall (1928), some of the description serves the purpose of setting the principal character within a certain social class (well-timbered, well-cottaged, two large lakes in the grounds, and so on), but other elements seem to be included simply because of the conventions of realist texts.

> Not very far from Upton-on-Severn – between it, in fact, and the Malvern Hills – stands the country seat of the Gordons of Bramley; well-timbered, well-cottaged, well-fenced, and well-watered, having in this latter respect, a stream that forks in exactly the right position to feed two large lakes in the grounds. The house itself is of Georgian red brick, with charming circular windows near the roof. It has dignity and pride without ostentation, self-assurance without arrogance, repose without inertia; and a gentle aloofness that, to those who know its spirit, but adds to its value as a home.

The aside in the first sentence – 'between it, in fact, and the Malvern Hills' – serves no informational purpose as such, and functions simply to give a sense of the real. Similarly, the description of the house as being built of Georgian red brick and as having circular windows seems excessive. These details amount to what Barthes calls **realist operators**; that is, they help to reinforce for the reader a sense that the text is well anchored to some recognizable reality.

Barthes also suggests that many realist texts make use of a **cultural code**, which is a set of statements which must be decoded by the reader according to a set of conventions which the reader already knows and shares with the writer. These are statements which appeal to background knowledge and which either appear self-evident or assume that the reader will recognize and assent to them. For example, *The Well of Loneliness* continues:

> To Morton Hall came the Lady Anna Gordon as a bride of just over twenty. She was lovely as only an Irish woman can be, having that in her bearing that betokened quiet pride, having that in her eyes that betokened great longing, having that in her body that betokened happy promise – the archetype of the very perfect woman, whom creating God has found good.

This information about Anna is presented as if the reader will agree that this description self-evidently fits the stereotype of the perfect woman. The reader is supposed to draw upon background assumptions about the loveliness of Irish women, and to recognize the elements about Anna's eyes and body which the text presents as self-evidently constituting perfection in women. It is presented as information that 'we all know'. In drawing upon this kind of background knowledge we are, Barthes would claim, drawing upon the cultural code, using the term to indicate an organized repository of common-sense wisdom. It is through the cultural code that realist texts confirm certain conventional views of reality (which may have no correspondence in how things actually are); in this, realist texts are creating rather than reflecting realities, and one way of reading realist texts is to see them as shaping (rather than reflecting) our views of the real.

A further convention in realist texts is that they have narrative **closure**; that is, at the end of the narrative, the problems which the text presents are resolved. In nineteenth-century realist novels plots are frequently resolved by death or marriage, and coincidence is a strong motivating factor in the way that most, if not all, of the loose ends of the plot are finally knitted together so that the reader is left with no unresolved questions about the characters. In twentieth-century narrative texts, the resolutions are less complete; writers no longer feel it necessary to employ coincidence to such an extent to bring their narratives to a close. However, for many readers, narrative closure is pleasurable, and they feel unsatisfied if a text leaves them with too many unresolved elements of the plot (see Unit 18: Narrative).

REALIST FILM

Colin MacCabe (1981) has argued that realist films, rather than fully exploiting the potential of film, have largely restricted themselves to the conventions of realist novels.

Characteristics of realist film

MacCabe states that one of the characteristics of realist film is that there is a **hierarchy of discourse** in relation to the truth; by this he means that there may be several narratives or points of view running at the same time through a film and that these narrative strands are not all equal in terms of the way that the audience is supposed to receive them. There is generally one character who is focused on and who is presented as if in a privileged position in relation to truth; this is the character whose statements the audience is led to believe and whose point of view the audience is led to adopt. This can be illustrated by examining a section of the realist film *Saturday Night and Sunday Morning* (1960). The film is shot in black and white and the subject of the film is the life of the working class in Nottingham. In fact, it becomes clear that the discourse which is privileged within the hierarchy is that of the central working-class male figure; in the following sequence, illustrated by stills from the film (Plates 25–35), this figure takes his revenge on an older woman who is portrayed in the film from his point of view.

25

26

27

28

29

30

31

32

33

34

35

The woman is represented as interfering and moralistic (when the hero sees a poor man breaking into a shop, he tries to help him escape whereas her actions result in the man being arrested by the police). He decides to shoot her with an air-gun whilst she is gossiping on the street corner, and the audience is led to collude with this because of the way that his point of view occupies a privileged position in the hierarchy in relation to the woman's point of view. Thus, the audience is supposed to see his perspective on the matter as the truth.

MacCabe also introduces the term 'non-contradictory reality', to describe the way that realist film presents a seemingly coherent vision of reality. There is nothing in this sequence of shots from *Saturday Night and Sunday Morning* to suggest that the situation could have happened in another way. There are very few discordant voices which question the moral view being presented here. Spectators are therefore being induced to take up what MacCabe calls a 'dominant position'; that is, they recognize the hieriarchies of discourses and align themselves with them. In this case spectators align themselves with the hero's point of view, positioning themselves alongside him and adopting a similar dominant position.

MARXISM AND REALISM

Marxist criticism attaches particular importance to questions of realism, although without presenting a unified approach. Within a Marxist frame of reference critics have particularly debated about the progressive or reactionary nature of realism. For some critics, such as Georg Lukács (1955), realist novels display as much as possible of a whole society at work at a particular point in time, as well as displaying tensions between the individual and this society in such a way as to expose points of prevailing ideological contradiction. Lukács, indeed, championed the cause of realism against the rival claims of modernism, rejecting the latter on the grounds of its subjective, fragmentary, and disconnected modes of representation, which he felt

---

Plate 25 The camera focuses on Arthur Seaton in his room; he loads his air-rifle
Plate 26 Seaton practises by shooting the ear from a china dog on his mantlepiece
Plate 27 Seaton picks up his rifle
Plate 28 Seaton looks out of the window
Plate 29 Match-cut to a view out of the window to reveal what Seaton can see: the woman he dislikes talking on the corner
Plate 30 Cut back to Seaton aiming his rifle
Plate 31 Cut to a front view of the woman talking to a friend
Plate 32 The woman is shot in the backside
Plate 33 Close-up of the woman in pain
Plate 34 Cut to Seaton at the window grinning
Plate 35 Seaton moves away from the window so as not to be seen

amounted to a retreat from society into pathological individualism. Bertolt Brecht, however, saw realist novels as a form of anaesthesia; readers become hypnotized by realist narrative and become uncritical of the system. Instead, he proposed a new form of art which would deny the reader the comforts of realist narrative and would encourage her or him to act on the contradictions in capitalism. Lukács is thus closer to the traditional view, and Brecht closer to the structuralist view.

ACTIVITY

The aim of this activity is to analyse two pieces of visual narrative and to identify the markers of realism and non-realism.

1 Choose two pieces of visual narrative, one which you would identify as an example of realism and the other an example of non-realism. Your two pieces must be from the same medium (e.g. from television, film, video, comic strip, photo-reportage, etc.). You will need to look closely and repeatedly at the text, so if you choose a moving image you will probably need to have it on videotape.

2 Here is a reminder of various characteristics which have been identified as typical of realist texts (for more detail see the unit):

  subject matter: domestic;
  there are characters; these are ordinary people presented as complex;
  moralistic;
  language does not draw attention to itself;
  events are arranged in chronological order;
  the narrative reaches a clear resolution;
  the narrator does not draw attention to herself or himself;
  detailed description;
  realist operators (the inclusion of arbitrary detail);
  appeal to the cultural code (views which we are all supposed to share).

3 Examine the 'realist' text, and check whether each of these characteristics is present. Add any general characteristics of realism which occur to you as you examine the text.

4 Now examine the 'non-realist' text and check whether each of these characteristics is absent. Cross off the list any characteristics which this examination suggests might be characteristic of all texts (not just realist ones).

5 For the two texts you have chosen, what are the reasons you might suggest for each text being constructed with or without the characteristics of realism.

READING

Auerbach (1953) *Mimesis: the Representation of Reality in Western Literature.*
Barthes (1986) *The Rustle of Language,* pp. 141–8.
*Leech and Short (1981) *Style in Fiction,* pp. 150–70.
*Lodge (1977) *The Modes of Modern Writing,* Ch. 3.
Lukács, Georg (1955) 'The ideology of modernism', in Lodge (ed.) (1972) *Twentieth Century Literary Criticism,* pp. 474–87.
MacCabe, Colin (1981) 'Realism and the cinema: notes on some Brechtian theses', in Bennet *et al.* (eds) *Popular TV and Film,* pp. 216–35.
Mills *et al.* (1989) *Feminist Readings/Feminists Reading,* Ch. 2, pp. 51–82.
*Williams, Raymond (1961) 'Realism and the contemporary novel', in Lodge (ed.) (1972) *Twentieth Century Literary Criticism,* pp. 581–91.

Section 6

Beyond the text

Unit 23 Positioning the reader or spectator

Texts address their readers in a variety of ways, either by directly addressing them, or by indirectly encouraging them to agree with certain statements.

THE IMPLIED READER

It is important to distinguish between the actual, real reader of any text and its **implied reader**. The real reader is any person who reads the text, but the implied reader is an idealized figure which the text anticipates or constructs. In this sense, it is rather like a role which the real reader is being encouraged to adopt, providing a 'position' from which the real reader interprets the text. For example, in the following extract from Conrad's *Heart of Darkness* (1902), the main narrator (Marlow) states:

> It is queer how out of touch with truth women are. They live in a world of their own, and there has never been anything like it, and never can be. It is too beautiful altogether, and if they were to set it up it would go to pieces before the first sunset. Some confounded fact we men have been living contentedly with ever since the day of creation would start up and knock the whole thing over.

The role which the reader is called upon to adopt here – that of the ideal reader – is in fact a male role; this is cued for the reader by the use of 'we men,' which one assumes refers to Marlow and the other men in his company who comprise his audience, and by the reference to 'women' as 'they', which signals to the reader that the narrator is referring to a group to which 'we' do not belong. The reader here may also be drawn into agreeing with what is said about women, since the statements are not modified in any way by such items as *I think* or *maybe*, or by counter-statements from Marlow's listeners. The narrator's views about women come from a position in which it is 'common sense', a 'matter of fact', that 'women . . . are out of touch with truth', that 'they live in a world of their own' and so on. In this way, therefore, we can say that the (actual) reader of *Heart of Darkness* is drawn into a position (that of the implied reader) where the obviousness of these stereotypes about women may be taken for granted.

DIRECT ADDRESS

Most texts present themselves as ignoring the presence of a reader, but some texts do address the reader in a direct manner, for example, by calling her/him *dear reader* or *you*. Advertisements in particular often address the reader in a very direct manner; for example, in this advertisement for Neutrogena conditioner:

> NOW YOU CAN CONDITION YOUR HAIR *WITHOUT* HEAVY OILS AND WAXES!

This calls upon the reader directly by addressing her/him as 'you' and by referring to 'your hair'. Some texts also address only a small proportion of their potential audience, as in the following advert for the British Nursing Association, which appeared in *Cosmopolitan*, and began:

> ISN'T IT TIME YOU RETURNED TO NURSING?

Since the advert appeared in *Cosmopolitan*, a women's magazine, it is reasonable to suppose that it addresses 'women in general'. And yet the address of the 'you', and thus the implied reader, is restricted to those women in *Cosmopolitan*'s readership who are qualified nurses who do not at present work in nursing. Thus the real reader and the implied reader may not always match up. However, as will be argued in the next section, although the reader is relegated to the position of an 'overhearer', this still may have an effect on her or him, by encouraging them to agree with particular statements or ideas.

INDIRECT ADDRESS

Whilst some texts address their readers directly by the use of *you*, others engage the reader in more subtle ways by the use of indirect address. An important aspect of the use of indirect address is the use of background knowledge. All texts, even the most simple and explicit, assume some degree of shared knowledge between the reader and the producer of the text. Sometimes, these knowledges or ideas are presented as if the reader is bound to agree with them, or are based upon implicit assumptions which prove difficult to object to. For example, in the advertisement for Lil-lets tampons (Plate 36), it is assumed that the reader will bring to bear quite particular background assumptions about menstruation. First, it is assumed that the reader will agree with the implicit assertion that periods are imprisoning (represented by the ball and chain) and that Lil-lets are a way out of this imprisonment (represented by Lil-lets as a key to the clasp on the chain). Even those women who do not in fact see their periods in such a negative way will, in order to make sense of the text, be led to draw on this shared knowledge about menstruation.

Plate 36 Lil-lets advertisement

L'ORIGINE

Pebble grey, moss green, cedar wood, sienna brown. These are the subtle harmonies of original colour, colours drawn from Nature herself.

LANCÔME
PARIS

Plate 37 Lancôme advertisement

DOMINANT READINGS

The dominant reading of a text is the one that seems to be self-evident; it is the one which is ratified by common sense or by other dominant ideologies which are available within the society of the time. Thus, rather than simply assuming that the reader will have certain knowledges to make sense of the text, the dominant reading makes sense only through larger 'stories' circulating through society. For example, many texts have a dominant reading which accords with conventional notions of femininity. In the advertisement for Lancôme (Plate 37), the dominant reading is that women who want to look like the person depicted should use Lancôme eye makeup.

In order to make sense of this advertisement, we have to decode a range of elements: first, that the natural is good. This is signalled by the inclusion of reference to colours which are 'drawn from Nature herself' and named after natural substances. It is also signalled by the inclusion of the Lancôme trademark, which is a white stylized rose running horizontally across the image, linking the woman and the makeup. The **juxtaposition** (see Unit 15) of the woman, nature and the supposedly 'natural' makeup offers itself for interpretation in ways which suggest the following kinds of connections between elements:

the makeup is coloured in the same way as nature;
natural ingredients are good;
women have a special relationship with nature;
women are feminine;
women who would like to be feminine will buy the makeup.

These are not statements which the text makes explicitly, but in order to make coherent sense of this very fragmented text the reader has to draw on these larger discourses about femininity and its relation to the natural. In this way, therefore, ideological assumptions circulate and constitute systems of shared knowledge so that the preferred sense of a particular text comes to seem self-evident.

Whilst a text will normally proffer one particular preferred or dominant reading, there is always the potential for other, contrary readings of the same text, as will be explored later. But in order to make sense of the text as a coherent whole, the dominant reading is the one which readers generally choose.

GENDER AND POSITIONING

The space or position that a text offers to a reader from which it makes most sense may be of various kinds; but one kind of position that has received particular attention of a critical and searching kind relates to the gender of the reader.

Positioning the reader as male

Feminists such as Judith Fetterley (1981) and Elaine Showalter (1977) argue that, when women read literature, they often read as men, precisely because literature often constructs the reader as male. Thus, women readers often assent to background assumptions which are actually the shared assumptions of males, masquerading as a kind of general knowledge which 'we all know' to be true. So, for example, when women readers read the passage from Conrad cited above, they may read it without questioning the sexism contained in the text since it accords with stereotypical background assumptions.

Similarly, in film theory it has been argued (see Mulvey 1981) that women characters in many Hollywood films are posed as objects 'to-be-looked-at'. The camera focuses on women characters from the perspective of male characters, and it is often a very sexualized vision of the women which is produced. This means that women spectators watching these films have to watch them as if they were male voyeurs. This may be a pleasurable experience for women spectators, but it may also make the woman spectator complicit with assumptions about women that she may not ordinarily share.

THE RESISTING READER

At the same time, no account of the positioning of the reader would be complete without some attention to the way readers may also generate alternative readings. One influential approach to alternative readings is that developed by Judith Fetterley (1981) around the term the **resisting reader**; that is, a reader who does not accept the knowledges which the text presents in the dominant reading, but resists this to construct an oppositional reading. Both male and female readers can read critically or oppositionally, as Jonathan Culler (1983) has shown, but it is often more in a woman's interest to read in this way. Thus with the Conrad text, a resisting reader will focus on the assumptions which seem to make the text intelligible (for example, by focusing on the use and effects of *they* and *we*).

In the following extract from the poem 'Valentine', by John Fuller, it is possible to trace two distinct readings, a dominant reading and a resisting reading.

The things about you I appreciate
May seem indelicate:
I'd like to find you in the shower
And chase the soap for half an hour
I'd like to have you in my power
And see your eyes dilate
I'd like to have your back to scour
And other parts to lubricate.
Sometimes I feel it is my fate

To chase you screaming up a tower
or make you cower
By asking you to differentiate
Nietzsche from Schopenhauer.
I'd like successfully to guess your weight
And win you at a fete.
I'd like to offer you a flower.

The dominant reading constructs the reader as male, so that the reader adopts the position of 'I'; the reader here will find the poem a funny, witty and rather charming poem, which retains some of the innocence of schoolboy Valentines through its bathetic rhymes and rhythmic structure. The repetition of 'I'd like', together with excessive statements in the rest of the poem, such as 'I'd like to sail with you to Tangiers' and 'I'd let you put insecticide into my wine', supposedly signal to the reader that the narrator is passionately in love with the unnamed addressee. If this reader is to participate in the humour, s/he is placed in a position of complicity with a particular set of background assumptions about women and about romantic love. So, for example, it will seem self-evident to this reader that the woman's body can be fragmented in this way and described in loving detail. (There is a long literary tradition of men extolling the virtues of the parts of women's bodies, whereas it is far more difficult for women to write similar poems in praise of men.) Such a reader will also find it self-evident that women are passive recipients of excessive love.

A resisting reader will refuse to participate in the humour of the poem and will focus more on the power relations which it expresses, and on how the ideology of romantic love also contains within it a great deal of violence. This reader will focus on the use of phrases such as 'I'd like to have your back to scour' and 'I'd like to have you in my power'. When the narrator states 'I'd like to see your eyes dilate' the resisting reader might begin to wonder whether the beloved's eyes should dilate in excitement or in fear. In such a reading the poem as a whole begins to take on a much more sinister air.

Resisting readings may be developed for most texts, and may focus on the representation of a range of issues – race, for instance, or class, as well as sexual relations. Adopting such an approach, the reader can first trace and describe the dominant reading of the text and then refuse this particular position in order to focus on other elements of the text. In this way the reader is positively enabled and encouraged to assume power and responsibility in relation to the text and to the determination of its meaning. Instead of the traditional view of the reader as a passive recipient of information, the reader is enabled to construct meaning for herself or himself.

ACTIVITY

In the advertisement for Flora margarine (Plate 38):
1 What textual cues can you find which suggest that the advertisement is aimed at women rather than men?
2 What shared assumptions does the text presume that the reader has about men/boys and women?

Plate 37 Flora advertisement

3 Is there anything strange about this advertisement in terms of its address and the potential consumers of the product?

READING

Booth (1961) *The Rhetoric of Fiction.*
Culler (1983) 'Reading as a woman,' in *On Deconstruction*, pp. 43–64.
Fairclough (1989) *Language and Power.*
Fetterley (1981) *The Resisting Reader: a Feminist Approach to American Fiction.*
Leith and Myerson (1989) *The Power of Address.*
Mulvey, Laura (1981) 'Visual pleasure and narrative cinema', in Bennett *et al.* (eds) *Popular Television and Film*, pp. 206–16.

Unit 24 Authorship and intention

In general, a text is created by an author (or a group of authors) with a particular intention about how that text should act on a reader or be interpreted. Hence we talk about authorship and (authorial) intention.

THE AUTHOR

Views of the author's role and importance

There are different views about the author's role in creating a text, and about how the author relates to other people's texts and the ways of writing which precede and surround her or him (the **tradition**). One view is that the author is a skilful agent who draws upon the tradition, but is less important than the tradition itself; this is associated with literary criticism and attitudes in Britain from the Middle Ages up to the eighteenth century. At the end of the eighteenth century, however, Romanticism offered an alternative view, according to which authors find the material for their work within themselves. This places the author at the centre of the writing; here the concern is less with authenticity deriving from the tradition than with authenticity arising from the author and his/her feelings and experiences. This view of the author became very influential in the nineteenth century, and survives today as a popular 'common-sense' view. However, the debate is a continuing one. T.S. Eliot attacked the Romantic position in his essay 'Tradition and the individual talent' (1919), proposing that 'Honest criticism and sensitive appreciation are directed not upon the poet but upon the poetry' (in Lodge 1988: 73). He suggests that we should distinguish between the poet's personal emotion and what he calls 'significant emotion, emotion which has its life in the poem and not in the history of the poet' (ibid. 76). Nevertheless, the Romantic position is maintained in many institutionalized ways of discussing literature – when, for example, a text is included in a syllabus because of its author, or an interpretation of a text is justified with the claim that the author intended us to make such an interpretation.

It is possible to understand developments and shifts in importance of these different viewpoints in historical terms (see Foucault 1988, 'What is an author?'). For example, the aesthetic focus on the author associated with the Romantics coincided with a historical development in which questions concerning the legal ownership of texts became increasingly important (e.g. laws concerning the rights of the author, rights of reproduction, etc.). Furthermore, the Romantic interest in the author was part of a more general development of interest in the individual which still characterizes much of western thinking.

There is another way of being interested in the author, which goes beyond a concern with individual personality. For example, an attention to the relation between the author's life and works can be a way into thinking about the ways in which historical circumstances shape the creation of texts through the author. It is also possible to see an author as the representative of a particular group. Feminist literary history for example has shown that many women writers are lost to us because it used to be considered improper for women to be authors. An eighteenth-century woman novelist might have been published anonymously or under a man's name because of repressive contemporary attitudes towards women writers. The identification and study of particular authors may thus contribute to the struggle of marginalized groups (such as female, Black and working-class writers). Another feminist positon regarding the author is to investigate how the author's gender influences the way s/he writes.

Interest in the author is also part of the pleasure and value of texts. Our pleasure in a text is often associated with the author, and we seek out other texts by the same person; publishers and promoters encourage this ('by the author of . . .', 'from the people who brought you . . .'), and it is a central part of the text-production industries. Furthermore, the value of a text, both in the sense of being considered an important cultural object, and in the sense of costing money to buy, often depends on who the author is (this is more obviously the case with paintings) (see Unit 25: Judgement and value).

Can an author always be identified?

While there are debates about how central the author is to a text, there is another problem hidden behind these debates, which is that it is not always clear who the author of a text is. Most texts pass through several hands before they reach their readers, and what the author originally wrote may have been changed by an editor, publisher or printer. This may happen for many different possible reasons including censorship, economizing, improvement and error. Many such changes will be trivial, but in some cases it is very difficult to know exactly who wrote which parts of a text (this is the case for some parts of Shakespeare's work, for example, some of which was not published under his control).

A different version of this problem occurs with texts created by a group of people, such as films, where contributions to the text are made by actors, producers, camera operators, the director, the writers, etc. Often the director is assumed to be the 'author' of a film; this was a central part of the 'politique des auteurs' developed by the French Cahiers du Cinéma in the 1950s, and the related **auteur** theory of Andrew Sarris in the United States (see Caughie 1981). In this theory the auteur of a film (the director) is considered to be one who expresses her or his personal vision coherently across the corpus of films which s/he makes; thus the auteur is considered as a particularly highly valued kind of director. Alfred Hitchcock is often claimed as an example of an auteur. (For problems with this view of directors, see Unit 20: Narration in film and prose fiction.)

THE AUTHOR, THE NARRATOR AND THE IMPLIED AUTHOR

Some literary critics distinguish between a text's author (the real person who wrote it) and its narrator (the imaginary person who narrates it). When we say that a text is *written in the first person* we mean that its narrator refers to herself or himself by using first person singular pronouns (*I, me, my, mine*); these pronouns are thought of as referring to the narrator, rather than the author. For example, Herman Melville's novel *Moby Dick* (1851) begins 'Call me Ishmael', and the novel is narrated (in part) by 'Ishmael', from his **point of view** (Unit 19) (this is a first-person narrative from the point of view of Ishmael). The term **persona** is often used to describe the first-person narrator or speaker of a poem.

One reason for wanting to distinguish between author and narrator is that we may be presented with a narrator who is subject to authorial irony or **structural irony** (see Unit 14) by being shown to be unreliable at some level – perhaps in terms of her or his ability to understand events or in terms of her or his moral position. For example, Huck, the narrator of Mark Twain's novel *Huckleberry Finn*, is presented from the beginning as being unable fully to understand his situation, including the fact that he himself is a fictional character:

> You don't know about me, without you have read a book by the name of The Adventures of Tom Sawyer, but that ain't no matter. That book was made by Mr Mark Twain, and he told the truth, mainly. There was things which he stretched, but mainly he told the truth.

The novel, published in 1884, is set 'forty to fifty years previously', that is before the American Civil War led to the emancipation of all American slaves. Huck is presented as sharing the conventional view that slavery is natural, but this conflicts with his personal friendship for an escaped slave called Jim. As the narrator of the novel, Huck explicitly expresses the moral confusion which results – for example, in worrying about Jim's plan to emancipate his children from slavery. Ironically, Huck is shocked by hearing Jim

> coming right out flat-footed and saying he would steal his children –

children that belonged to a man I didn't even know; a man that hadn't ever done me no harm.

Huck subsequently recognizes that he would feel just as bad if he betrayed Jim to the authorities and so abandons his attempt to resolve what for him is a moral dilemma. But to suggest that Huck's predicament is a moral dilemma for the novel itself or for its real author would be a clumsy misreading. Huck's interior monologue is both comic and tragic in its limited viewpoint and its aping of the flawed logic and morality which helped sustain slavery. Since Huck cannot see the irony which his own reasoning reveals, there seems to be a viewpoint in the novel which is not available to him (perhaps a post-Civil War viewpoint which exposes the ironic contradictions and limitations of a pre-Civil War narrator whose love for an individual slave does not allow him to see the problem with slavery in general).

In order to capture the sense that there is a narrator hidden behind Huck who allows us to glimpse another narrative behind Huck's ironized version, we use the notion of the **implied author**. It is important to distinguish between the implied author and the real author because the implied author is an **effect of the text**, an impression which it produces (one of its meanings, reached by undoing the ironies), rather than its original cause (i.e. the real author).

There are, however, some problems with the notion of the implied author. In the first place, the implied author can only ever be a critical fiction in that it is a rationalization of the impression we have in reading a novel that we are being confided in by a human consciousness. Thus the idea of the implied author relies on an understanding of novels as a kind of intimate speech. The implied author is thus more the *product* of a way of reading than a way of reading in its own right. In addition to this, however sophisticated the interpretations which the notion of the implied author allows, in the end it works in the same way as recourse to the 'real' author does: that is, to define and stabilize the possibilities of reading by suggesting that the text has a coherent moral position and meaning controlled by an authoritative moral consciousness.

INTENTION

Does the author control the meanings of a text?

In the eighteenth century, literature was considered to be the product of conscious intention, and this assumption led to a particular way of reading. One articulation of this view is Alexander Pope's couplet from his *Essay on Criticism* (1711): 'In every work regard the writer's end / Since none can compass more than they intend' (II, 255–6). In contrast, Romantic writers claimed that authors are not always fully conscious of the implications of their literary works because they were produced in moments of 'inspiration'. Thus, the Romantic poet William Blake claims that although Milton tells us that he set out to 'justify the ways of God to men' in *Paradise Lost,* in fact the poem itself reveals that he was actually 'of the Devil's party without knowing it'. In the twentieth century a new view of (the lack of) authorial control was provided by psychoanalysis. Freud and Jung suggested that we are never fully conscious of the intentions behind what we say because the 'unconscious' mind can have an effect on what we say, and do not say, without our being aware of it: for Freud and Jung, though in different ways, the unconscious mind plays a central part in artistic creativity.

A problem which arises with the notion that the author controls the interpretation of a text comes from the fact that meaningful forms are shared property; so words are not made meaningful by what individual users want them to mean and they often mean more than what the user 'had in mind'. Hence, if I say a painting or a poem is a 'masterpiece' I cannot detach the meaning of the word 'master' from the history of slavery or from the political relations between men and women in the society in which I live. Similarly, by engaging in culturally symbolic acts we often recreate meanings which we may not intend; traditional items of the bride's dress (such as the veil and the colour white) signify virginity in our culture, while the appointment of a man (usually her father) to 'give the bride away' reveals that the modern marriage ceremony is still related to the ritualistic exchange of women. Whether or not the bride or the father intend their actions to be understood in these ways does not alter the fact that they are taking part in a social ritual which still carries the vestiges of those meanings.

A further problem relates to the fact that many texts carry non-literal meaning. As we show in the units on **irony** and **metaphor** (Units 14 and 13) many texts rely on the hearer or reader to supply meanings of their own from their own context; while the author may guide this to some extent, it cannot be completely controlled. Furthermore, even the literal aspects of language change over history, and a text may no longer have its author's intended meaning because the words of the text may have lost the meanings which the author assumed.

Do we ever need to look outside the text for the author's intentions?

An influential response to this question (answering 'no'), is expressed by Wimsatt and Beardsley in their essay 'The intentional fallacy' (1946, in Lodge 1972). Concentrating on poetry, Wimsatt justifies his answer as follows:

1   In most cases it is not possible to find out what the poet intended.
2   We are primarily interested in how a poem works, not what was intended.

3   A poem is a public rather than a private thing because it exists in language – which is by definition social rather than personal. The author does not own the text once it has been made public, and does not have eternal authority over its meaning.

4   A poem's meaning can only be discovered through its actual language, 'through our habitual knowledge of the language, through grammars, dictionaries, and all the literature which is the source of dictionaries, in general, through all that makes a language and culture' (in Lodge 1972: 339).

5   'If the poet succeeded in doing [what he intended], then the poem itself shows what he was trying to do' (ibid. 334).

This last point indicates, however, that Wimsatt remains interested in the author's intention, but rather than trying to answer questions about intention by looking in diaries etc., the author's intentions are thought to be successfully embodied in the text itself.

The rejection of the author and authorial intention

Roland Barthes, in an essay called 'The death of the author' (1968, in Barthes 1977), argues that 'To give a text an Author is to impose a limit on that text' (1977: 47). To open up reading as a productive practice in which the reader is freed from the process of discovering, or pretending to discover, what the author intended, Barthes claims that 'Classic criticism has never paid any attention to the reader; for it the writer is the only person in literature.... the birth of the reader must be at the cost of the death of the Author' (1977: 148). This **post-structuralist** argument represents a radical overturning of the authority of the author and of those institutionalized ways of reading which are centred upon it. Barthes argues that:

1   The author is, by definition, absent from writing (in contrast to speech, which generally implies the presence of the speaker).

2   A text's meaning is produced in the act of reading not of writing.

3   A text is not an utterly unique artifact emerging through a kind of immaculate conception from a writer's brain; instead, the conventions and language which make up the text (any text) are available to the writer precisely because they have been used before (see Unit 16: Intertextuality and allusion). For Barthes, then, a text 'is a tissue of quotations', 'a multidimensional space in which a variety of writings, none of them original, blend and clash' (1977: 146).

ACTIVITY

The following text was anonymously written in France in the thirteenth century; it is a motet (a musical composition for two, three or four voices, each voice singing different words). The text was translated from Old French by Carol Cosman.

> I am a young girl
> graceful and gay,
> not yet fifteen when
> my sweet breasts may
> begin to swell;
>
> Love should be my contemplation,
> I should learn its indication,
>
> But I am put in prison.
> God's curse be on my jailor!
>
> Evil, villainy and sin
> did he
> to give up a girl like me
> to a nunnery;
>
> A wicked deed, by my faith,
> the convent life will be my death
>   My God! for I am far too young.
>
> Beneath my sash I feel the sweet pain.
> God's curse on him who made me a nun.

This activity concentrates on questions about the presumed author of the poem. Evidence might come from features of the text, from the description given at the beginning of the activity, or from what you know or can guess of the historical circumstances of thirteenth-century France and of the people of the time.

1 Give any evidence which you can find or imagine for thinking that the poem's speaker is the author.

2 Give any evidence which you can find or imagine for thinking that the poem's speaker is not the author.

3 Is your response to the poem affected by the fact that it is (a) anonymous; (b) written for more than one voice; (c) written in the thirteenth century; (d) a translation?

4 Temporarily assume that the author is not the speaker, and give any evidence which you can find or imagine for thinking that the author was: (a) a woman; (b) a man.

5 Below are descriptions of two imagined authors: for each one, describe how knowing that this was the identity of the author would change how you read the poem and the effects the poem has on you.

(a) imagined author X = a twenty-five-year-old male
(b) imagined author Y = a fifteen-year-old female

READING

Abrams, M.H. (1953) 'The orientation of critical theories', in Lodge (ed.) (1972) *Twentieth Century Literary Criticism*, pp. 1–26.

——— (1988) 'Persona, tone, and voice' and 'point of view', in *Glossary of Literary Terms*.

Barthes, Roland (1968) 'The death of the author', in Lodge (ed.) (1988) *Modern Criticism and Theory*, pp. 17–72.

Belsey (1980) *Critical Practice*, pp. 1–36.

Caughie (ed.) (1981) *Theories of Authorship: a Reader.*

Eliot, T.S. (1919) 'Tradition and the individual talent', in Lodge (ed.) (1972) *Twentieth Century Literary Criticism*, pp. 71–7.

Foucault, Michel (1988) 'What is an author?', in Lodge (ed.) *Modern Criticism and Theory*, pp. 197–210.

Leech and Short (1981) *Style in Fiction*, pp. 257–87.

Moi (1985) *Sexual/Textual Politics*, pp. 21–69.

Newton-de Molina (ed.) (1976) *On Literary Intention.*

Patterson, Annabel (1990) 'Intention', in Lentricchia and McLaughlin (eds) *Critical Terms for Literary Study*, pp. 135–46.

Todd (1987) *A Dictionary of British and American Women Writers 1660–1800.*

Wimsatt, W.K. and Beardsley (1946) 'The intentional fallacy', in Lodge (ed.) (1972) *Twentieth Century Literary Criticism*, pp. 334–44.

Unit 25 Judgement and value

Many kinds of writing might broadly be designated as 'literature'; but not all literature excites critical interest and comment. Literary critics have usually assumed that the texts which repay special attention, thereby gaining the status of 'classics', do so because they are somehow intrinsically valuable. And these classic texts – by virtue of their special value and by virtue of the amount of commentary which they generate – come to comprise the canon of Great Literature and tend to form the core of syllabuses in colleges, schools and universities. Judgements of value, therefore, are seen to be at the heart of literary studies and the activity of criticism.

CHARACTERISTICS OF VALUED TEXTS

It was against this background that critics such as F.R. Leavis set out to judge which texts are valuable and which texts are not. Value, in such a view, is seen as a quality residing within texts themselves. And critics of this persuasion have generally stressed the importance of characteristics such as complexity, aesthetic unity, literary language, serious subject matter and participation within the literary tradition.

Complexity

Literary texts which are assumed to be of special value are generally charac-terized by complexity of plot, structure, language and ideas. Indeed, complexity is often used in this context as a synonym of value. But complexity can be of a number of different kinds. In novels, complexity typically involves not only a skilfully constructed main plot, but often the coexistence of this plot with subplots which mirror and highlight the events in the main plot. The structure of a specially valued poem is held to be complex in ways which repay close attention: for example, the poem may be structured as a complex sequence of parallelisms. The more the reader studies the poem, the more s/he is aware of the poet's skill in composing it in this way. The language of valued literary texts is also typically assumed to be complex: writers do not simply choose 'ordinary' words, like the words we use for conversation, but words which have resonance, historical associations, beauty or 'rightness' for the particular context. The reader is encouraged to assume that writers of valued texts laboured painstakingly to choose exactly the right word, since each word forms part of a larger complex structure. Nor can the ideas of a poem or novel be taken as haphazardly chosen: they too form complex patterns or structures, either being echoed by other ideas in the text or re-affirmed in the form of general themes. The complex interweaving of elements of language, structure, plot, ideas and so on, can be seen to constitute the **aesthetic unity** of the text. Having studied the text, the reader will consequently find that all of its elements contribute to the same overall structure, and is likely to consider the poem to have achieved value, or even greatness. Alternatively, if by applying the same criteria the reader is not able to discover a unified pattern in the text, that text will not be regarded as the highest kind of literature.

Language

Of special interest, as regards the question of value, is the attention paid to the language of valued texts. Language in valued texts is elegant, witty, patterned, controlled; in short, the author has taken care in her or his choice, and the reader takes pleasure in the skill which the author displays.

Subject matter

The subject matter of valued texts is generally serious, dealing with philosophical topics of acknowledged importance. Valued texts are supposed to give the reader an insight into fundamental questions, such as the nature of evil, the corrupting effect of money, the value of love, and so on, and to rehearse for her or him the dilemmas of moral and ethical choice. For this reason, comic texts are rarely accorded status as serious texts until they appear to discuss such supposedly universal themes. Because valued texts are held to deal with such themes, they are also thought to have qualities of durability. Shakespeare's works, for example, are deemed valuable because they are believed to have significance not only for his time but for all time. When texts discuss evidently universal questions, they are unlikely to be at the same time texts which discuss specific political questions in any detail. Political polemic (open and heated critical discussion) is generally taken to be at odds with literary worth, and is often seen to detract from the universalizing aim of Great Literature (satires are often valued for their observations about humankind in general, rather than for their more specific criticisms of particular societies).

The canon

As has been suggested above, the canon is the group of texts considered to be of most value. These are the books which are generally taught in schools, colleges and universities (though the canon is constantly changing, especially in schools). Despite changes in the canon, however, when students are asked to list members of this elite grouping, the results are generally very similar: the first writers on the list are usually Shakespeare, Chaucer and Milton; and when these have been established, a certain amount of debate generally occurs on whether to include such writers as Dryden, Lawrence, Pope, Swift, Joyce, Wordsworth, Keats, Shelley, Jonson, Dickens, Hardy, Burns, Woolf, Austen, Eliot and the Brontës. These writers share certain characteristics: first, most of them are male (indeed it is not unusual for some students' lists to include only male writers); second, they are generally from the middle or upper class, and are all white; third, they are all dead. To be included in the canon, writers must be seen to have written valuable texts; but is it a coincidence that these writers also belong to basically the same socio-economic, racial and gender group? As soon as you ask one question about the canon, others arise. Who decides whether someone is in the canon and who is not? And how is it that most students of English literature know, to a greater or lesser extent, who is included and who is not? Most traditional critics do not consider that there are any agencies involved in decisions about who is in the canon and who is not; the selected texts are simply better than others. You might like to consider, however, a range of agencies which make and enforce decisions about canonical status. Within the educational context, there are examining boards, those who design the syllabus, individual teachers and groups of teachers who choose the books to be included. In universities, there are the researchers and critics who work on canonical writers and publish learned articles or introductions for students to canonical texts. Outside education, there are the publishers who commission books from critics writing about such books, the libraries who buy such books and the individual readers who accept this version of canonicity. You might like to ask yourself some questions about your own course of study: for example, do you study Shakespeare? How many texts are there by contemporary writers, women writers, working-class or Black writers? Implicit in your course construction may be notions of value.

SOME RECENT CRITICAL PERSPECTIVES ON VALUE

Modern literary theorists have professed much less certainty about questions of literary value. While many of them have considered that certain texts do seem to be better than others, others have considered that value is simply a means of excluding certain texts. A range of differing views on questions of judgement and value now exists.

Roland Barthes (1986), for example, was innovatory in analysing not only texts which were literary, but also texts drawn from popular literature, like Ian Fleming's *Goldfinger* (1959). Barthes does consider, however, that there are differences among texts; and he is concerned in much of his writing to describe those differences. But rather than assuming that value resides within the text, he shifts attention to the 'pleasure of the text'; instead of being a scholarly enjoyment of the seeming control of the writer over her or his material, the process of reading, for Barthes, involves a more sexualized pleasure. In particular, Barthes identifies the different types of pleasure to be gained from reading **realist** (see Unit 22) texts compared with other texts. He calls realist texts **readerly** because in reading such texts the reader begins not to be aware of the fact that s/he is reading, and starts to get caught up in the pleasure of narrative. But Barthes prefers **writerly** texts, which are those texts (such as experimental and avant-garde texts) which force the reader to 'work' (and 'play') more in order to make sense of them. With writerly texts, attention is drawn to the process of writing; we are unable to sink into a process of reading in the same unthinking way as with readerly texts. Thus, although Barthes claims to be opposed to constructing hierarchies, there does seem to be a value judgement made between readerly and writerly texts; despite this, his writing on the pleasure of the text does question the traditional notion of canonical texts as somehow intrinsically more valuable than others.

Marxist critics are often much less clear about whether the notions of value and evaluation are useful. Terry Eagleton (1976, 1983), for example, attacks the concept of the canon, arguing that canonical texts are so precisely because they serve to support the ruling **ideology**. He does not want to dispense, however, with the notion of value completely, since he also thinks that there are literary texts which question or 'escape' ideology, and so force the reader to consider her or his position and perhaps lead to a form of consciousness raising. Within the Women's movement, for example, feminist novels written by Fay Weldon, Erica Jong, Margaret Atwood and Angela Carter have been very important in bringing about changes in women's thinking. These literary texts have brought about a questioning of certain ideological assumptions about the position of women, and could therefore be considered valuable for that reason.

Michel Foucault (1980) takes a more sceptical position, questioning the idea of attributing value to texts at all. He argues that literary texts are really empty texts, containing *less* rather than more than other texts. They display, as he puts it, 'enunciative poverty'. With literary texts, critics have to work hardest, in order to fill gaps which the text leaves gaping open. It is critics themselves, writing scholarly articles and books on canonical writers, who repeat over and over the message which the text itself failed to tell. Foucault also questions the notion that the writer is totally in control of what is written. He draws attention to the importance of other factors in the writing process, such as the common-sense knowledge of the time, literary traditions and the economic and literary pressures which led the writer to write within certain genres or styles and on certain subjects.

VALUE AND GENRE/MEDIA

So far, we have been considering mainly literary texts; but criteria of value are also important for the way that we view other genres and media: for example, when going to the cinema to see a film which has been made of a book (for example, *The Color Purple* or *The Company of Wolves*), people often leave the cinema dissatisfied, saying, 'It wasn't as good as the book.' Perhaps this judgement stems less from the merits of either the particular book or film, than from implicit assumptions about the relative cultural merits of films and novels in general. (See Unit 20: Narration in film and prose fiction.) Because film is a more recent medium, more popular and seemingly 'parasitic' on the novel, many people assume that it is of less value than literature. The same can be said of songs, when judged against poetry. We may memorize the lyrics of a pop song which we like, but we are unlikely to analyse those lyrics in the same way that we might analyse a poem by Shakespeare. Nor would we generally expect to analyse a popular song in an English literature class, since songs, particularly pop songs, are rarely given canonical status.

If you look back to our initial description of the canon, you will see that many of the writers who were included were poets rather than novelists or dramatists. Poetry is often seen as a more valued genre than prose.

Poetry appears to call for closer attention than prose. Within poetry itself, further distinction is often made between poetry and verse. Verse is sometimes regarded as poetry less skilfully written than 'poetry'. A recent book of poetry by a feminist group, *In the Pink,* was labelled by critics as 'verse' rather than 'poetry'; and much of the poetry written by working-class writers is also (dismissively) labelled verse.

Literary texts and popular culture

Literary texts are generally considered superior to the fictional texts which many of us read to relax in our spare time: romances, detective novels, thrillers, comics and so on. But we might like to ask why it is that the judgement is made in this way. The pleasures we gain from literary texts and popular texts may be different, because we read them in different environments and for different reasons; but it is debatable what benefit comes from saying that one type of text is therefore better than another.

JUDGEMENTS OF VALUE MARGINALIZE TEXTS

Rather than considering the valuing process as something which simply focuses on what is good, we might instead say that evaluation functions to prevent books from being read. The fact that we study mainly canonical texts in school and higher education, for example, may mean that we do not give the same analytic or critical attention to the texts we read at home. This has the more general effect that the critical skills of literary analysis which we learn at school and university tend not to be used once we leave those institutions.

Women's writing

Feminist critics such as Elaine Showalter (1977) and Dale Spender (1986) have shown that women have conventionally been discouraged from writing literary texts. First, women were not given, historically, the education needed to write extensively, especially literary texts; so it was generally only women of the upper classes, such as the Duchess of Newcastle, who wrote before the eighteenth and nineteenth centuries (when women began to write in large numbers). Second, writing was seen by society at large as a form of self-display, generating sexual innuendo; 'decent' women did not write. Writing in the seventeenth century, for example, Katherine Phillips was horrified when she found that some friends had published her poetry, since she was worried that her reputation would be ruined. Many women writing even during the nineteenth and twentieth centuries have done so under the cover of a male pseudonym (such as George Eliot, Georges Sand, Currer Bell) or else have given their name in a way which does not expose the author's gender (P.D. James, A.S. Byatt). As well as avoiding being accused of indecent behaviour, such writers are responding to the problem that their texts are likely to be judged as inferior simply on the basis of their sex. Some critics even go so far as to argue that women cannot produce literature because their creative energies should be reserved for child-bearing (see Battersby 1989). Women have been encouraged to see certain styles or less-valued genres of writing as their domain (such as autobiography, religious and sentimental verse, letter writing and so on); and through a process of circular logic, their writing has been viewed as inferior because they have written within these genres. Women's poetry dealing with emotional responses to situations such as enforced partings, tragic death of loved ones and so on has been labelled 'sentimental' by many critics. Because many women poets of earlier centuries have written poems concerned with certain types of subject matter, their work is considered less important – a contrast which is particularly clear between the work and reputations of Elizabeth Barrett Browning and Robert Browning, for example.

Black writing

There has been a great deal of writing by Black people in English. Some of this writing is by Black British people, such as Caryl Phillips, Barbara Burford and Jackie Kay; some is by writers from countries which were colonized by Britain, such as Chinua Achebe, Ngugi wa Thiong'o and Buchi Emecheta, who have English as one of the languages available for literary writing. Little of this writing is considered within schools or institutions of

higher education. This may be because of the fact that university departments of literature concentrate on canonical literature and therefore have
little time for other writing; on the other hand, it may be that traditional
value judgements about what literature should be like exclude Black writing,
in much the same way as they often exclude women's writing.

Working-class writing

So few working-class writers make their way onto the syllabus of literature
departments that it would be possible to believe that working-class people
do not produce literature. If you were asked to name a working-class writer,
you might cite D.H. Lawrence or Robert Burns; but there are very many
other working-class novelists and poets, such as Margaret Harkness, Lewis
Jones, Harold Heslop, Ethel Mannin, Ellen Wilkinson, James Hanley and
Robert Tressell. Writings by these authors seem to meet all the criteria of
complexity, seriousness and so on; and within the traditional value system,
they should be considered alongside canonical literature. Alternatively, it is
possible not to argue for their inclusion on the syllabus simply on the basis
of their conforming to the models of what might be thought of as bourgeois
literature; instead, it can be argued that in schools and universities students
should study a full range of writing and not simply the writing of one particular class grouping.

ALTERNATIVES TO THE CANON

For many critics, it is difficult to imagine doing without the notion of a
canon. It is for this reason that, when the canon has been challenged, critics
have often attempted to set up a new one. Thus, Elaine Showalter, because
of the exclusion of women writers from the mainstream canon, felt it necessary to set up a canon exclusively for women writers. For many teachers, it
also appears unthinkable that a syllabus could be constructed without some
kind of canon. But since canons inevitably exclude writers as well as include
them, we should now consider alternatives to the canon.

One alternative is to refuse to take part in the valuing process at all, and
simply to give descriptive accounts of texts. Much structuralist criticism is
based on the principle that it is possible to analyse the structure of a work
without necessarily referring to the skill of the author, or suggesting that the
work is therefore better than any other work. Another approach is, instead
of studying canonical literature, to analyse a wider body of work, 'writing'.
From such a perspective, literary texts are still studied, but only within the
context of other texts such as advertising, scientific texts, film, television,
popular literature and so on. In this way similarities across genres and
media can be analysed (in much the same way that we have adopted in this
book). A third approach is, instead of analysing any given work as the
product of an isolated genius, to analyse the socio-political and literary

pressures on the writer to write in particular ways. While not reducing the writer to an automaton, this process recognizes that there are many factors which determine the way that the book is written which lie beyond the control of the writer or her conscious intentions. Finally, some critics have turned from the studying of literature to an analysis of the valuing process itself; they examine, as we have done here, why it is that certain texts are studied rather than others.

ACTIVITY

Read the two extracts below. Passage A is from a Mills and Boon novel, *Stolen Summer* by Anne Mather; passage B is from *Women in Love* by D.H. Lawrence.

1 Which text do you think would generally be seen as of more value?
2 Make a note of differences between the two texts which might lead to their being considered of different value. (Pay special attention to the language of the texts, what you imagine to be their intended audience, critical reception, subject matter and so on.)
3 Make a note of similarities between the extracts which might lead you to question the notion that one of the texts is of more value.

Passage A

They were silent, enjoying the feel of the sun warming their bodies.
'Angharad ...?' She heard him gently speak her name.
'Yes?' She turned to him and gave a little gasp, freezing quite still.
His face was only inches from hers, his blue eyes gleaming as they gazed at her mouth. Instinctively, her lips parted for his kiss, responding to it when it came as she had always responded; transmitting all the love in her heart. It was a gentle, almost lazy kiss, and all too soon it was over, and Saul was pulling her into the crook of his shoulder and settling down to sleep. Angharad could not sleep herself. She was far too aware of his near-naked body touching hers. She could feel his warmth burning through the thin cotton of her dress, and his heartbeat was close to her ear. Her head was filled with the musky scent of his aftershave as she lay still, tense and aware, aching with the need to reach out and touch him, to have him respond to her caresses.

(Anne Mather: *Stolen Summer*)

Passage B

'Is it you Ursula?' came Gudrun's frightened voice. He heard her sitting up in bed. In another moment she would scream.
'No, it's me,' he said, feeling his way towards her. 'It is I, Gerald.'

She lay motionless in her bed in sheer astonishment, too much taken by surprise, even to be afraid.

'Gerald!' she echoed in blank amazement. He had found his way to the bed, and his outstretched hand touched her warm breast blindly. She shrank away. . . .

He had come for vindication. She let him hold her in his arms, clasp her close against him. He found in her infinite relief. Into her he poured all his pent-up darkness and corrosive death, and he was whole again. It was wonderful, marvellous. It was a miracle. This was the ever-recurrent miracle of his life, at the knowledge of which he was lost in an ecstasy of relief and wonder. And she, subject, received him as a vessel filled with his bitter potion of death. She had no power at this crisis to resist.

(D.H. Lawrence: Women in Love)

READING

Barthes (1986) *The Rustle of Language.*
Battersby (1989) *Gender and Genius.*
*Culler (1975) *Structuralist Poetics,* esp. Ch. 11, pp. 255–65.
Eagleton (1976) *Criticism and Ideology,* esp. Ch. 5, pp. 162–87.
*—— (1983) *Literary Theory: an Introduction,* esp. Ch. 1, pp. 10–16.
Foucault, Michel (1980) 'What is an author?', in *Language, Countermemory, Practice.*
Showalter (1977) *A Literature of Their Own.*

Appendix: notes on activities

UNIT 1 ASKING QUESTIONS

The author, Ee Tiang Hong, is a Malaysian writer, who was born in Malacca in 1933 and educated at Tranquerah English School and High School, Malacca. He now lives in Australia.

Tranquerah Road: the road is an extension of Heeren Street, in Malacca.
Kampong Serani: 'Portuguese Village', in the suburb of Ujong Pasir.
Limbongan: a suburb adjacent to Tranquerah. The Dutch used to moor their vessels off the coast here.
Kimigayo: the Japanese national anthem.
Nihon Seishin: 'Japanese Soul'.
Greater East Asia Co-Prosperity Sphere: the Japanese scheme to unify Asia, during the Second World War.
Meliora hic sequamur: the motto of the Malacca High School ('Here let us do better things').
Merdeka: 'Independence'.
Negara-ku: 'My Country', the Malayan, and then Malaysian, national anthem.
pontianak: succubus (female demon supposed to have sexual intercourse with sleeping men).
jinn: genie; evil spirit.
Omitohood: a Buddhist benediction (*Om Mane Pudmi Hum*), in the Hokkien Chinese dialect.

UNIT 3 ANALYSING UNITS OF STRUCTURE

The first sentence should read:
   Following Nancy's death Sikes tries to escape the hue and cry.
The order of the sentences given in the published companion is:
   15, 11, 3, 8, 9, 2, 6, 12, 4, 7, 1, 14, 5, 10, 13

References

Abrams, M.H. (1988) *A Glossary of Literary Terms*, 5th edn, New York: Holt, Reinhart & Winston.

Aitchison, J. (1972) *Teach Yourself Linguistics*, London: Hodder.

Aristotle, Horace, Longinus (1965) *Classical Literary Criticism*, Harmondsworth: Penguin.

Attridge, D. (1982) *The Rhythms of English Poetry*, Harlow: Longman.

Auerbach, E. (1953) *Mimesis: the Representation of Reality in Western Literature*, Princeton: Princeton University Press.

Baker, N.L. (1989) *A Research Guide for Undergraduate Students (English and American Literature)* 3rd edn, New York: MLA Publications.

Bal, Mieke (1985) *Narratology: an Introduction*, Toronto: Toronto University Press.

Barber, C. (1976) *Early Modern English*, London: Andre Deutsch.

Barthes, R. (1977) *Image–Music–Text*, Glasgow: Fontana.

—— (1982) *Selected Writings*, London: Fontana.

—— (1986) *The Rustle of Language*, Oxford: Blackwell.

Bate, J. (1970) *The Burden of the Past and the English Poet*, London: Chatto & Windus.

Battersby, C. (1989) *Gender and Genius: Towards a Feminist Aesthetics*, London: Women's Press.

Belsey, C. (1980) *Critical Practice*, London: Methuen.

Bennet, T., S. Boyd-Bowman, C. Mercer and J. Woollacott (eds) (1981) *Popular Television and Film*, London: Open University Press and BFI.

Bloom, H. (1973) *The Anxiety of Influence: a Theory of Poetry*, Oxford: Oxford University Press.

Booth, W. (1961) *Rhetoric of Fiction*, Chicago: University of Chicago Press.

Bordwell, D. (1985) *Narration in the Fiction Film*, London: Methuen.

Bordwell, D. and K. Thompson (1979) *Film Art: an Introduction*, Reading, Ma: Addison-Wesley.

Branigan, E. (1984) *Point of View in the Cinema*, New York: Mouton.

Brewer, E.C. (1978) *The Dictionary of Phrase and Fable* (facsimile of 1894 edn), New York: Avenel Books.

Brown, G. and G. Yule (1983) *Discourse Analysis*, Cambridge: Cambridge University Press.

Burton, D. (1982) 'Through glass darkly: through dark glasses', in R. Carter (ed.) *Language and Literature: on Introductory Reader in Stylistics*, London: Allen & Unwin, 195–214.

Cameron, D. (1985) *Feminism and Linguistic Theory*, London: Macmillan.

—— (ed.) (1990) *The Feminist Critique of Language*, London: Routledge.

Cameron, D. and J. Coates (eds) (1989) *Women in their Speech Communities*, Harlow: Longman.

Carter, R. (ed.) (1982) *Language and Literature*, London: Unwin.

Caughie, J. (ed.) (1981) *Theories of Authorship: a Reader*, London: Routledge & Kegan Paul and BFI.

Chatman, S. (1978) *Story and Discourse: Narrative Structure in Film and Prose Fiction*, Ithaca and London: Cornell University Press.

Cook, P. (ed.) (1985) *The Cinema Book*, London: BFI.

Coward, R. and M. Black, (1981/1990) 'Linguistic, social and sexual relations – a review of Dale Spender's *Man Made Language*', *Screen Education* 39; reprinted in D. Cameron (ed.) (1990) *The Feminist Critique of Language*, London: Routledge, 111–33.

Cruse, D.A. (1986) *Lexical Semantics*, Cambridge: Cambridge University Press.

Culler, J. (1975) *Structuralist Poetics*, London: Routledge & Kegan Paul.

—— (1983) *On Deconstruction*, London: Routledge & Kegan Paul.

Daly, M. (1978) *Gynecology*, London: Women's Press.

Davies, C. (ed.) (1934) *English Pronunciation from the Fifteenth to the Eighteenth Century*, London: Dent.

Durant, A. and N. Fabb (1990) *Literary Studies in Action*, London: Routledge.

Eagleton, T. (1976) *Criticism and Ideology*, London: Verso.

—— (1983) *Literary Theory*, Oxford: Basil Blackwell.

Eliot, T.S. (1953) *Selected Prose*, Harmondsworth: Penguin.

Ellis, J. (1982) *Visible Fictions: Cinema, Television, Video*, London: Routledge & Kegan Paul.

Erlich, V. (1969) *Russian Formalism: History–Doctrine*, The Hague: Mouton.

Fairclough, N. (1989) *Language and Power*, London: Longman.

Fawcett, R. (1980) *Cognitive Linguistics and Social Interaction*, Heidelberg: Julius Groos.

Fetterley, J. (1981) *The Resisting Reader: a Feminist Approach to American Fiction*, Bloomington: Indiana University Press.

Fiske, J. and J. Hartley (1978) *Reading Television*, London: Methuen.

Foster, H. (ed.) (1985) *Postmodern Culture*, London: Pluto Press.

Foucault, M. (1980) *Language, Counter-memory, Practice*, London: Blackwell.

—— (1981) *The History of Sexuality*, Vol. 1, Harmondsworth: Penguin.

Fowler, R. (1986) *Linguistic Criticism*, Oxford: Oxford University Press.

Fraser, D. (1988) *Dictionary of Quotations*, Glasgow: Collins.

Frye, N. (1957) *Anatomy of Criticism*, Princeton: Princeton University Press.

Garvin, P. (ed. and trans.) (1964) *A Prague School Reader in Aesthetics, Literary Structure and Style*, Washington DC: Georgetown University Press.

Giddings, R., K. Selby and C. Wensley (1990) *Screening the Novel: the Theory and Practice of Literary Dramatization*, London: Macmillan.

Gilbert, S. and S. Gubar (1979) *The Madwoman in the Attic*, New Haven: Yale University Press.

Gregory, M. and S. Caroll (1978) *Language and Situation*, London: Routledge & Kegan Paul.

Hackman, S. and B. Marshall (1990) *Re-reading Literature*, London: Hodder & Stoughton.

Halliday, M.A.K. (1978) *Language as Social Semiotic: the Social Interpretation of Language and Meaning*, London: Edward Arnold.

—— (1985) *Functional Grammar*, London: Edward Arnold.

Halliday, M.A.K. and R. Hasan (1976) *Cohesion in English*, London: Longman.

Halliday, M.A.K., A. McIntosh and P. Strevins (1964) *The Linguistic Sciences and Language Teaching*, London: Longman.

Handel, S. (1989) *Listening: an Introduction to the Perception of Auditory Events*, Cambridge MA: MIT Press.

Harari, J.V. (ed.) (1980) *Textual Strategies: Perspectives in Post-structuralist Criticism*, London: Methuen.

Hawkes, T. (1972) *Metaphor*, London: Methuen.

Hutchinson, P. (1983) *Games Authors Play*, London: Methuen.

Jakobson, R. and M. Halle (1956) *Fundamentals of Language*, The Hague: Mouton.

Jameson, F. (1981) *The Political Unconscious: Narrative as a Socially Symbolic Act*, London: Methuen.

Jeffers, R. and I. Lehiste (1979) *Principles and Methods for Historical Linguistics*, Cambridge, MA: MIT Press.

Johnson-Laird, P.N. and P.C. Wason (1977) *Thinking*, Cambridge: Cambridge University Press.

Kachru, B. (ed.) (1982) *The Other Tongue: English across Cultures*, Oxford: Pergamon.

Kidd, V. (1971) 'A study of the images produced through the use of the male pronoun as generic', in *Moments in Contemporary Rhetoric and Communication* 1: 25–30.

Kiparsky, P. and G. Youmans (eds) (1989) *Rhythm and Meter*, San Diego: Academic Press.

Kramarae, Cheris and Paula Treichler (1985) *A Feminist Dictionary*, London: Pandora Press.

Lakoff, G. and M. Johnson (1980) *Metaphors We Live By*, Chicago, Il: Chicago University Press.

Lakoff, R. (1975) *Language and Woman's Place*, New York: Harper Colophon.

Leech, G. (1969) *A Linguistic Guide to English Poetry*, London: Longman.

Leech, G. and M. Short (1981) *Style in Fiction*, London: Longman.

Leech, G. and J. Svartvik (1975) *A Communicative Grammar of English*, Harlow: Longman.

Leith, D. (1983) *A Social History of English*, London: Routledge.

Leith, D. and G. Myerson (1989) *The Power of Address*, London: Routledge.

Lemon, L.T. and M.J. Reis (eds) (1965) *Russian Formalist Criticism*, Lincoln: University of Nebraska Press.

Lentricchia, F. and T. McLaughlin (eds) (1990) *Critical Terms for Literary Study*, Chicago: University of Chicago Press.

Lodge, D. (ed.) (1972) *Twentieth Century Literary Criticism: a Reader*, London: Longman.

—— (1977) *The Modes of Modern Writing: Metaphor, Metonymy and the Typology of Modern Literature*, London: Edward Arnold.

—— (ed.) (1988) *Modern Criticism and Theory: a Reader*, Harlow: Longman.

MacCabe, C. (1979) *James Joyce and the Revolution of the Word*, London: Macmillan.

—— (1981) 'Realism and the cinema: notes on some Brechtian theses', in T. Bennett, S. Boyd-Bowman, C. Mercer and J. Woollacott (eds) *Popular Television and Film*, London: Open University Press and BFI, 216–35.

McConnell-Ginet, S. (ed.) (1982) *Women and Language in Literature and Society*, New York: Praeger.

McCrum, R., W. Cran and R. McNeil (1986) *The Story of English*, London: Faber & Faber and BBC Publications.

Mast, G. and M. Cohen (eds) (1979) *Film Theory and Criticism*, New York and Oxford: Oxford University Press.

Miller, C. and K. Swift (1979) *Words and Women*, Harmondsworth: Penguin.

Mills, J. (1989) *Womanwords*, London: Longman.

Mills, S., L. Pearce, S. Spaull and E. Millard (1989) *Feminist Readings/Feminists Reading*, London: Harvester.

Moi, T. (1985) *Sexual/Textual Politics*, London: Methuen.

Montgomery, M. (1986) *Introduction to Language and Society*, London: Methuen.

Muecke, D.C. (1970) *Irony and the Ironic*, London: Methuen.

Mulvey, Laura (1975) 'Visual pleasure and narrative cinema', *Screen* 16, 3: 6–10; reprinted in T. Bennett, S. Boyd-Bowman, C. Mercer and J. Woollacott (eds)

(1989) *Popular Television and Film*, London: Open University Press and BFI.

Newton-de Molina, D. (ed.) (1976) *On Literary Intention*, Edinburgh: Edinburgh University Press.

Ngugi wa Thiong'o (1986) *Decolonising the Mind: the Politics of Language in African Literature*, London: Currey.

Ong, W.J. (1982) *Orality and Literacy*, London: Methuen.

Propp, V. (1968) *Morphology of the Folktale*, Austin: University of Texas Press.

Quirk, R. and S. Greenbaum (1973) *A University Grammar of English*, Harlow: Longman.

Richards, I.A. (1936) *Philosophy of Rhetoric*, Oxford: Oxford University Press.

Rimmon-Kenan, Shlomith (1983) *Narrative Fiction: Contemporary Poetics*, London: Methuen.

Scholes, Robert (1982) *Semiotics and Interpretation*, New Haven, CT, and London: Yale University Press.

Sebeok, T. (ed.) (1960) *Style in Language*, Cambridge MA: MIT Press.

Showalter, E. (1977) *A Literature of Their Own*, Princeton: Princeton University Press.

Spender, D. (1979) *Man Made Language*, London: Routledge & Kegan Paul.

—— (1986) *Mothers of the Novel*, London: Pandora.

Spender, D. and J. Todd (eds) (1989) *Anthology of British Women Writers*, London: Pandora.

Sperber, D. and D. Wilson (1986) *Relevance: Communication and Cognition*, Oxford: Basil Blackwell.

Steedman, Carolyn (1982) *The Tidy House*, London: Virago.

Strang, B. (1970) *A History of English*, London: Methuen.

Thompson, J. (1971) *English Studies: a Guide for Librarians to the Sources and their Organisation*, London: Bingley.

Todd, A. and C. Loder (1990) *Finding Facts Fast; How to Find Out What You Want and Need to Know*, Harmondsworth: Penguin.

Todd, J. (1987) *A Dictionary of British and American Women Writers 1660–1800*, London: Methuen.

Toolan, M. (1989) *Narrative: a Critical Linguistic Introduction*, London: Routledge.

Tripp, E. (1970) *Dictionary of Classical Mythology*, London and Glasgow: Collins.

Uspensky, Boris (1973) *A Poetics of Composition*, Berkeley: University of California Press.

Watt, I. (1972) *The Rise of the Novel*, Harmondsworth: Penguin.

Williams, R. (1966) *Modern Tragedy*, London: Chatto & Windus.

—— (1976) *Keywords: a Vocabulary of Culture and Society*, London: Fontana.

Woolf, V. (1965) *Contemporary Writers*, London: Hogarth.

—— (1979) *Women and Writing*, ed. Michele Barrett, London: Women's Press.

Young, R. (ed.) (1981) *Untying the Text: a Post-Structuralist Reader*, London: Routledge & Kegan Paul.

General index

Index of texts discussed